THE SHAAR PRESS

THE JUDAICA IMPRINT
FOR THOUGHTFUL PEOPLE

Ask

A
SHAAR
PRESS
PUBLICATION

REBBETZIN FEIGE TWERSKI

Rebbetzin Feige

A popular and insightful counselor deals with real-life situations

Published by **SHAAR PRESS**
Distributed by MESORAH PUBLICATIONS, LTD.
4401 Second Avenue / Brooklyn, N.Y 11232 / (718) 921-9000 / www.artscroll.com

Distributed in Israel by SIFRIATI / A. GITLER
6 Hayarkon Street / Bnei Brak 51127

Distributed in Europe by LEHMANNS
Unit E, Viking Business Park, Rolling Mill Road / Jarrow, Tyne and Wear, NE32 3DP/ England

Distributed in Australia and New Zealand by GOLDS WORLD OF JUDAICA
3-13 William Street / Balaclava, Melbourne 3183 / Victoria Australia

Distributed in South Africa by KOLLEL BOOKSHOP
Shop 8A Norwood Hypermarket / Norwood 2196, Johannesburg, South Africa

ISBN: 1-4226-0049-1 Hard Cover
    1-4226-0050-5 Paperback

Printed in the United States of America by Noble Book Press
Custom bound by Sefercraft, Inc. / 4401 Second Avenue / Brooklyn N.Y. 11232

Dedicated to my parents

Rabbi Israel Abraham Stein

הרה"ג רב ישראל אברהם
בן הרה"ג רב אפרים אהרן זצ"ל

and

Rebbetzin Sarah Stein

הרבנית שרה בת הרה"ג רב אלעזר ע"ה

*of blessed memory, whose example, teaching,
and enduring love inform and inspire
every moment of my existence.*

Table of Contents

Foreword

I remember hearing that Rabbi Israel Rosenberg, of blessed memory, head of the Union of Orthodox Synagogues, when presented with conflicting opinions regarding a projected course of action, would cut to the chase by asking, "Un vos vill G-t?" ("And what does G-d want?")

I reference this criteria in explaining the appearance of my essays in the form of this current book. I had been urged over the years by the readers of my essays to gather them for publication and distribution as a book. Flattered by the suggestion, I was concomitantly aware that indulging one's ego is a poor justification for such a project, and suggested as much to my enthusiastic readers. Their counterargument that my reticence was denying the broader public important and enriching information, persuaded me to finally seek objective "Daas Torah." "What does G-d want?" This book represents what I have been advised is the Torah response to that question.

My list of thank-you's for this endeavor is quite extensive. First and foremost, I owe a debt of gratitude to Rabbi Nechemiah Coopersmith of Aish HaTorah, Jerusalem. It was he who insisted that I overcome my "writing anxiety" to launch the "Ask the Rebbetzin" column from which, for the most part, these essays emerged. Though I had lectured, counseled, and taught for many years, I felt uncomfortable and graceless putting my thoughts into words. Rabbi Coopersmith's encouragement, positive criticism, and devotion on so many levels warmed my heart and gave me the fortitude to continue. May he and his wonderful family have nachas and continued success in all their efforts.

My friend, Rechie Frankfurter, came on the scene more recently and encouraged me to write for "Hamodia." This, too, has been a very rewarding experience and I thank Rechie for her friendship and trust.

On the home front, almost everyone has been supportive and encouraging. Among a community of truly exceptional people it is virtually impossible to single out anyone. Nevertheless, there are some debts that cannot go unacknowledged, especially because these individuals stepped in to compensate for my technological ineptitude. Respectful of the fact that computers and word processing programs have been known to break out in unabashed hysterical laughter at the mere suggestion of my approach, my articles have been crafted in a multitiered process requiring the charity and indulgence of many. Ordinarily, I write a piece longhand, dictate it, have it printed out, re-write it, edit it, and finally have it e-mailed to one or another of the sites which re-edit it for my final re-editing. The saints, who have painfully suffered through this ordeal, deserve something more than I can put into words. Our very remarkable and wonderful shul-administrator, Cheryl Armstrong, has most kindly and generously provided much of this service. Others who have intrepidly ventured onto this minefield are Shira Speiser, a colleague and very busy woman, Mechie Nebenzahl of Lakewood, New Jersey, whose "hachnasas orchim" (hospitality) includes literary and secretarial services, and Ro Tatum, the capable secretary of Attorney Jim Hiller, who magnanimously put Ro at my disposal in times of need. At the very outset, it was Jim's wife, Lisa, a longtime devoted friend, who eased me into the process with her considerable editing skills and suggestions.

There is much to be said about the eager support of family. There is, however, another group of unsung heroes whose contribution to these essays in particular, and my personal growth in general, is of inestimable significance. These heroes are the members of my Milwaukee community and the many readers worldwide, whose friendships and quest for knowledge have been the ongoing source of my creativity and inspiration. The context of their yearning to grow and their aspirations for spiritual integrity have drawn me into partnering their passion for serving Hakadosh Baruch Hu (G-d) in ever more insightful and informed ways. To paraphrase Rabbi Akiva's acknowledgment of his debt to his wife, Rachel, "Everything I have created I owe to them." May Hashem Yisbarach reward them all with the realization of their hopes and dreams and together may we continue to try scale the heights of Sinai.

"Acharon acharon chaviv," last but by no means least, I thank the Almighty constantly for the blessing of my husband, Rebbe, mentor, and role model of singular stature, Rabbi Michel Twerski (shlita). Above and beyond unfailing support, he has given me of his most precious commodity — his time — to edit, guide, and critique my work. May Hashem bless him with good health and the wherewithal to continue his unparalleled contributions to all of us—his family, his community and to the entirety of Klal Yisrael, the Jewish people.

Without "siyata d'shmaya," Heavenly assistance, nothing would be possible. I hope and pray that the "Ribono Shel Olam" (Master of the Universe) will derive great nachas from all of us, His beloved children.

Challenges

Challenges
A Scratch in the Diamond

*I*t's an age-old question: Why do the righteous suffer and the wicked prosper? Thinkers and philosophers of every generation, as well as every person afflicted by the vicissitudes of existence, have struggled to find clarity on the subject.

Moses, the greatest prophet known to man, asked the Almighty, "Show me Your face," rendered as "Let me see up front why things happen as they do." G-d's response was, "No human being in this lifetime can see or comprehend the meaning of My ways." G-d did however show Moses His back, intimating that it is only hindsight that will provide meaning, coherence, and perspective.

There are moments in everyone's life when we feel as though we are hovering over the abyss — a vertigo of sorts — when the world seems to be moving uncontrollably, serving up waves of events that threaten to overwhelm and crush us. King David in the Book of Psalms cries out to G-d and says, "When You hide Your face, I am thrown into this state of vertigo, of losing my bearings." Elsewhere he exclaims, "It is only when You shed Your light that we glean enlightenment, that our plight is illuminated."

PAIN AND DEFERMENT ·

I rushed to the hospital where my dear friend Debbie had just given birth to a Down syndrome baby. Entering her room, I was greeted by what appeared to be a reaction of contradictions — tears streaming down her cheeks, coupled with a big smile that illuminated her beautiful face.

"I never would have chosen or asked for this challenge," she admitted candidly, "but if God was looking for a kind, loving home for this little soul, He has found the right place."

Debbie's response to suddenly finding herself confronted by adversity captures the classic, courageous faith-based attitude. It admits to the pain and sorrow, and simultaneously acknowledges and defers to the will of the Almighty, the Omniscient, All-Knowing Being Whose unfathomable wisdom drives and orchestrates all the circumstances of our life.

Sir Bertrand Russell, philosopher and well-known agnostic, in a conversation with a cleric, asserted that he could not believe in a G-d in Whose world a child cried out in pain. The cleric responded that as for him, he could not believe in a world in which a child cried out in pain and there was no G-d to justify it. Pain is the inevitable lot of the human condition. Faith does not eliminate suffering, but it does provide a perspective of meaning and purpose. It allows for the comforting knowledge that although the Almighty's ways are often inscrutable and beyond our comprehension, they are not arbitrary or capricious. They follow His plan for the ultimate destiny of humankind that takes into account past, present, and future.

Only a Being Who is not circumscribed and limited in time can see the whole picture. We all exist in a small slice of time, out of context, and we have access only to a tiny segment of the huge puzzle that will make sense only when all the pieces have been set into place.

· · · · · · · · · · · · · FINDING MEANING IN SUFFERING

My father-in-law, of blessed memory, was fond of relating the story of a man who, in the time of the Czar in Russia, was wrongfully imprisoned for many years. Before beginning his incarceration, he pleaded with the guard to give him something constructive to do during his long solitary confinement behind bars. The guard pointed to a wheel on the wall of the starkly bare cell. He advised the poor fellow to keep turning the wheel, which, according to the guard, would activate an irrigation system that would bring trees and vegetation into bloom.

For 20 years the prisoner tirelessly turned the wheel, picturing in his mind magnificent gardens resulting from his hard work. At long last, old and spent, he was set free. His first request was to be led to the gardens, the product of his many years of tirelessly turning the wheel. The guards laughed scornfully at his gullibility and informed him that the wheel he had been turning all those years was connected to nothing at all.

Upon hearing this terrible news, the prisoner instantly collapsed and died. Dungeons and confinement of many years did not destroy his spirit, but he could not survive the knowledge that all those years had served no purpose. Indeed, if suffering has no meaning, life is reduced to nothing more than a cruel joke, and hardly worth the effort required to make it through the day. As Nietzsche once said, "He who has a why can endure any how."

There are instances when events at the outset appear tragic or less than desirable, and down the road prove to have been an impetus for growth and development, indeed a blessing in disguise.

Miriam, a young, beautiful woman struck in her prime by a debilitating and terminal illness, expressed gratitude at the conclusion of her long struggle. She shared that left to her own devices and her life in the fast lane prior to her illness, she had been marching headfirst into oblivion. Jolted by the turn of events, she was forced to dig deep into her being and find a path of constructive living and meaningful existence.

The Sfas Emes, a Chassidic commentator, explains the concept of G-d in search of man. He sees it expressed in the consequences suffered by Adam and Eve following their fateful mistake of eating from the Tree of Knowledge. The apparent difficulty in the narrative is why the snake, which was responsible for luring man into the act, was simply condemned to a life of crawling on his belly and eating dust, whereas human destiny would thereafter be one of hard work and endless toil. "By the sweat of your brow will you eat bread" and "in pain shall you give birth" would be their fate. Is it fair that the perpetrator, the snake, should be set for life, since dust is ubiquitous while the descendants of Adam and Eve have to struggle in every aspect of existence, i.e., livelihood, raising children, etc.?

The Sfas Emes suggests that the snake did indeed suffer the ultimate punishment. He would eat the ever-present dust and thus his needs would forever be accounted for. He would never have to raise his head heavenward to ask G-d for anything. In effect, G-d rejected him and never wanted to hear from him again.

In contrast, Adam and Eve and their progeny would inevitably encounter the challenges of sustenance and parenting. Their struggles would ultimately motivate them to seek and importune the Almighty, Who longs for a loving relationship with each and every one of us. There is no worse fate than estrangement from G-d. Adversity can often be a powerful catalyst for connection.

Miriam understood that her illness, though painful and challenging, was an invitation, a wake-up call from her loving Creator. It forced her to stop, think, and take stock of her life run awry. It ultimately gave her the opportunity, after much soul-searching, to forge a gratifying bond with the Source of her being.

· · · · · · · · · · · · · · · · · · ·MY SON-IN-LAW'S ACCIDENT

My son-in-law, Rabbi Elimelech Eliezer ben Henna Fraydel, a Rosh Yeshivah (dean of an academy of higher learning), was in Israel, on his way to Tzfat to conduct a Shabbos of inspiration for his alumni. He was on a chartered bus with 60 of his rabbinical students when the driver fell asleep, crashed into a disabled army vehicle that was jutting out into the road, and he was thrown through the windshield. He suffered a massive brain injury, and four months later is still unconscious. He is the father of 12 children.

My daughter, Baila, hadn't accompanied him on this trip because she was at the beginning of a pregnancy. Rabbi Elimelech Eliezer is a mentor to thousands. His yeshivah, bearing his unique imprint, is a model of learning and living every aspect of life with passion. He is an imposing 6'2" figure, whose presence and brilliance brought a remarkable energy and joy wherever he went. "Gevaldig" (awesome), was his ready and consistent response to every inquiry about how things were going.

Ultimately he did not know where he was going when he left on his trip. No human being, no matter how great and powerful, can predict the circumstances of their life. G-d Alone knows and is in charge. What we can control, however, is our response to those events. Response-ability — the ability to choose our response — is always our prerogative.

Victor Frankl, in his work on logotherapy, maintains that even in the concentration camps, where death was inevitable, there remained a choice of how one would die — whether with dignity and compassion for others, or railing against G-d and behaving inhumanely to others. Life presents us daily with many challenges and the measure of a person is in the responses we choose. Someone aptly observed that everyone's life is circumscribed in one way or another, in a prison of limitations. The challenge is: Do we focus on the bars that confine us or do we look through and beyond them?

TRANSFORMING THE GASHES · · · · · · · · · · · · · · · ·

A king in ancient times owned a precious gem of unparalleled beauty. It was his most prized treasure. In times of celebration or when he hosted foreign dignitaries, he would proudly display it. On one of these occasions, as he lifted it out of the case, it fell to the ground and suffered an ugly gash that severely marred its extraordinary beauty. The heartbroken king announced that whoever would repair his valued possession would be granted any request. But should one undertake the task and fail, he would be summarily executed.

Artisans and craftsmen came from near and far, but upon viewing the extent of the damage, declined the attempt. Finally, a craftsman agreed to undertake the risky task. He was provided with a room and the requisite tools and after a long time emerged and presented the diamond to the king. The king gasped. The diamond still had the massive gash, but the artisan had turned it into a stem, around which he had engraved petals that formed a magnificent flower. As striking as the gem had been before, it was now many times more exquisite.

There are those among us who are capable of taking the 'gashes' of life and by drawing on inner resources, transforming them into strengths that make of them human beings of far-greater depth, understanding, and compassion than they could have been otherwise.

A cautionary note is in order. It must be noted that taking the high road does not mean that we deny the pain, or that we look at those afflicted and expect them, with self-righteous piety, to be stoic and to rise to the occasion. Our role is to do everything we can to mitigate the suffering and misfortune of others.

When another person is in crisis, it is not the appropriate time to preach faith. Rather one should alleviate the situation, by offering one's emotional, material, and spiritual resources.

Some pointers for survival in times of crisis (G-d should spare us all) are in order.

1. *Beware of the "why" question.* I.e., why did G-d do this to me? Why must I go through this? These questions get us nowhere. Perhaps a more constructive approach is to change the "why" question to a "what" question. Given the circumstances, what is my role? What does G-d want me to do? What should be my response? What goals do I need to set for myself to both survive and make this a growth experience?

2. *The basis of all 12-step programs is to turn over your problem to the Almighty.* Relinquishing the illusion of control can be very liberating. The caveat, a psychologist noted, is that in many instances

when people "turn it over to G-d," they have a set of expectations of how things should turn out. If these expectations are not met, they quickly cease trusting that Power's capacity and grab their personal steering wheel back. Their attitude seems to be "I'll turn it over to G-d, so long as G-d does things my way." Although "turning it over" may sound easy, it is actually a profound act of trust through which one relinquishes control to the unseen and, for many, the uncertain. Sometimes, the result is not a convenient, painless or clear path toward problem resolution, but rather a proverbial long and winding road. Many of us simply don't have the faith and courage to take a leap into what feels like very thin psychological air.

3. *Faith is a learned response.* It is not an innate conferral or revelation. One must work hard to develop a faith position. It is an inner discipline. The Hebrew word for faith is "emunah," which shares a root with the root, "emun," which means be trained or be taught. The soul must train itself to achieve a meaningful response. This is done by surrounding oneself with people who model this faith, support groups, experiences, reading materials, tapes, and appropriate guidance. Introspection and meditation can be very helpful.

4. *The power of prayer.* Prayer and the recital of Psalms are powerful tools toward cultivating the most significant of all relationships — our connection with G-d. Only that bond will give us the strength to navigate the trials and tribulations of life. Every person can begin where they find themselves, and build day by day and bit by bit.

The sages of the Talmud teach us that the verse in the Book of Zechariah, "On that day the Almighty will be One and His Name will be One," refers to the time when all the puzzle pieces will fall into place, and the Almighty's elucidating light will illuminate the darkness. Currently, in our times, we recite two separate blessings. When events occur that in our estimation are "good," we recite, "Blessed are You, G-d, Who is good and does good." However, if the nature of the event is death or misfortune (Heaven forbid), we state, "Blessed are You, the true Judge."

In our world of illusion, this is the best we can do in the midst of pain, suffering, loss, bereavement, and tragedy. But in the time to come, when we will be the beneficiaries of that ultimate clarity, there will be only one blessing for everything, thanking G-d for everything that is ultimately the "good." We will understand then why all things had to be as they were and as they are, and that all along they were ultimately for our good.

May that day come speedily in our time.

Challenges
Body and Soul

*E*ating disorders of all kinds have become an all-too-common and familiar phenomenon in our society. Moreover, this problem appears to be on the increase and seems to hit closer and closer to home.

Many have suggested that it is a phenomenon, if not born of, then at least exacerbated by our culture's obsession with the human body. Physicality and external beauty are the major preoccupations and focus of the popular media.

Psychologists have observed that the person most prone to succumb to certain types of eating disorders is one with a perfectionist nature, who is under stress (sometimes self-generated), who feels a loss of control over life and a commensurate desperate desire to regain it.

The dysfunction manifests itself in overeating and then regurgitating — so-called "binging and purging" — as a means of achieving illusory control over one segment of life. Anorexia is another manifestation. A noted psychotherapist observes, "Food is the symptom for everything. Using food or weight to solve problems gives one a feeling of control and empowerment."

THE JEWISH VIEW ·

How does Judaism see the body, beauty, and physicality?

Judaism in contrast to most other religions does not negate the physical world. Nor does it dichotomize the spiritual and the material. The Torah approach is that we should bring G-dliness to every aspect of our life. G-d is no less present and accessible in the boardroom and bedroom than He is in our places of worship. Moreover, tradition teaches us that it is a result of G-d's Omnipotent will and His deliberate plan that we find ourselves not in a spiritual setting but indeed in physical surroundings.

A number of weeks ago, my husband and I celebrated our 40th wedding anniversary with a trip to Switzerland. It was at my urging (I don't want to say nudging) that we took this trip. One of what I thought was my most cogent arguments was that the Talmud advises that after 120 years of life on earth, when we come before the Divine tribunal for judgment, the Almighty will ask us if we fully enjoyed this world. I reminded my husband that we will be asked, "Did you see and appreciate My magnificent Alps?" (It's very helpful to have a religious argument when you want a vacation.)

There is a Torah imperative to notice, appreciate, and relish the beauty of our surroundings in our world. They are G-d's gift to us and an expression of His love for us. As a means of heightening our sensitivity, we are in fact instructed to recite blessings when we encounter fragrant trees, awesome storms — thunder, lightning, majestic mountains, beautiful people, etc. The Almighty's mandate for us is to bridge heaven and earth — the spiritual and the physical — though they might appear to us as diverse and even conflicting dimensions of our existence.

·············THE TENSION OF BODY AND SOUL

The human being reflects this tension. On one hand, there is the body with its needs, demands, impulses, urges, etc. On the other hand, there is the spiritual aspect, the Divine soul, our essence, our very link to eternity. The requirements and needs of the soul are not as readily discernable and tangible as the needs of the body, but are, in fact, much more critical. The well-being of the body has to be maintained as the vessel, the repository of our

G-d-invested essence. This vessel has to last a lifetime — 70 or 80 or 90 years or, as the expression goes, "may you live to be 120 years old." That seems to be the maximum in life expectancy on earth. In contrast, the soul is of eternal substance, which means that we have to nurture it so that our achievements can endure forever and ever.

Hillel, one of the great sages of Israel, was greeted on a Friday afternoon by a number of his disciples. He had what was the equivalent of a towel swung over his shoulders which piqued the curiosity of his students who questioned him about his destination. "I am going to the bathhouse, to take care of my host," he answered. Upon further inquiry, he explained that his body was the host for his soul for the duration of his journey on earth and that there is a Torah obligation to treat one's host with respect, care, and concern.

The Torah recognizes that if one's body is neglected and in disrepair the soul will suffer.

Reb Avrohom — known as the malach, "the angel" because of his enormously pious and spiritually focused nature — was a young man whose service to G-d was so intense that he tended to disregard his basic physical needs such as eating and sleeping. When his father, Rabbi Dov Ber, the Maggid of Mezeritch, was about to depart from this world, he called in his son. His parting words were "Avremele, Avremele, be very careful, give great care to your health and physical well-being, because a small hole in one's body will create an even greater hole in one's soul."

THE CHALLENGE····································

The challenge of our existence here on earth is to successfully negotiate the tension between body and soul. While we must give our body its due, it should not become the exclusive or even primary focus. After all is said and done, the body is only the outside shell — the packaging that after it exhausts its usefulness will die and be buried. But the spirit of the human being — which is dependent on a lifetime of spiritual awareness and investment and commensurate good deeds — joins other souls in a world of eternal duration.

How can we fathom eternity? Someone once explained that if we filled Madison Square Garden with sunflower seeds and a bird would come once in a thousand years to remove a single seed, the time it would take for all the seeds to be cleared out would not even begin to capture a definition of eternity.

Yes, the body is very important. Our physical configuration, — the brains, heart, kidneys, intestines, etc. — are inspiring in their harmony and synchrony and serve as testimony to the presence of a purposeful creator. The Torah commandment "only be observant for yourself and greatly concerned for your soul" (Deuteronomy 4:9) enjoins us to be very careful not to do anything that would be in any way injurious to our bodies. We must eat well, sleep, exercise, seek medical attention, whatever will promote our health and well-being.

In addition, the Torah places value on pleasing appearance. Since the body is the garment of the soul its presentation is a commentary on its bearer. The Talmud states that a Torah scholar dare not appear in soiled clothing. We understand that to mean that a person who represents a Torah standard must take care that his outer appearance is in sync with the values he personifies.

Moreover, traditional sources are replete with exhortations to a husband and wife to groom, maintain, and dress so that their spouses will find them pleasant and appealing. This is especially relevant in an open society where men and women interact and interface freely on a daily basis. Opportunities and temptations are a consistent challenge to every marriage. It seems that today's reality is to make every effort to be presentable and appealing to our spouses ("attractive but not attracting others," the saying goes).

At the same time, we must maintain a balanced approach, aware and cognizant that there is more to the human being than meets the eye.

EATING DISORDERS····························

Eating disorders are one of the many manifestations of the vulnerability and ensuing dysfunction in a society that excessively focuses on externalities.

The question of one of our readers was what to do if one suspects a friend, acquaintance, or family member of being anorexic. I would advise this person to immediately bring it to the attention of whoever would be in a position to get this individual professional help. It would not be productive to confront the person because undoubtedly they are in denial. The person with such a problem — and some eating disorders are actually life threatening — is not tuned in to their bodily needs.

When the crisis is over, ongoing therapy with a specialist in this specific field of eating disorders would be indicated. At the same time exposure to our rich Torah heritage would provide a critical anchor to a healthy, wholesome, and holistic approach and understanding to the balance between the physical and the spiritual.

Challenges
Dealing With Loss

I am having a very hard time dealing with the loss of one of our beloved community members at a young age. She was the same age as I am and my very first friend here in the Dallas community.

She has been gone for five months, but I can't seem to move past my feelings of loss, sadness, and guilt for not spending more time with her when she was so sick.

What can I do to overcome this sense of sadness and loss? Watching her children grow and mature makes me smile, but at night, I can't seem to stop crying ... I miss her so.

Any thoughts or suggestions would be greatly appreciated as I try to get past this depression.

My heart goes out to you on the loss of your friend.

Your feelings of guilt can alleviated by:

1. Considering an ongoing act of charity, lovingkindness, learning, or desisting from some less than desirable behavior and dedicating the effort to your friend's memory. Examples of this might be visiting a nursing home, volunteering at a school, refraining from gossip, replacing negative expressions with positive ones, etc. This will not only benefit her soul but will keep your deceased friend "alive" and present in your daily life. At the same time, the

merit of the spiritual growth you attain will serve you in this world and your friend in the eternal world.

2. Keeping an eye on your friend's children. There might come a time now or in the future when you can be helpful to them in some capacity and that would be a kindness their mother, in her heavenly repose, would certainly appreciate.

As to your sense of loss, your grieving and your feelings of depression, I will share with you what has worked for me.

The blessing we recite in response to hearing of a loss is "Baruch Dayan haemes"— Blessed is the true Judge. The segment we all say in unison in Kaddish, the mourner's prayer, is "yehei shemei rabba mevorach" – May His (G-d's) exalted Name be blessed forever and ever. Even as we are struck by tragic news, we seek to make it intelligible. We proclaim the Almighty as being the only Force Who is eternal and hence the only one who qualifies as the true Judge. He has the vantage point of seeing the entire picture — past, present, and future — before Him as a coherent whole.

Our perspective as mortals is confined to a tiny slice of life. It is like trying to envision the finished picture of a fully constructed massive puzzle when we have only a few tiny pieces in place. Hence, our perspective and vision is myopic and limited.

The repetition of "yehei shemei rabba mevorach" — May His (G-d's) exalted Name be blessed forever and ever — throughout the prayer services, serves not only to express our prayer that His Sovereignty be acknowledged, but also as an anthem that embraces us, reminding us over and over again that our Heavenly Omniscient Parent knows what He is doing and that, for the ultimate destiny of creation, painful as it is at this moment, it must be so. Without faith in the true Judge, there can be no solace.

I would encourage you, my dear reader, to let the words of "yehei shemei rabba mevorach" wash over you again and again, with particular emphasis on the words forever and ever. It will help bridge the gap, the big divide, between what we know and what we can't know; this life and other lives; this world and other worlds, and bring it all closer together as one congruent tapestry.

The second instructive tool on coping in adverse circumstances comes from an insight of a cousin of mine who is a dean of a yeshivah. He had just buried (may no one ever know of such tragedy) his third child. The first had died of leukemia. The second, some years later, was an infant lost to a crib death. The third loss, just recently, was his daughter, the mother of two children who was killed in a tragic car accident.

After shivah, the requisite week of mourning, he returned to the yeshivah and presented his students with an analogy, alluding to his recent tragedy. He said that navigating through life is like driving a car. You have to have a destination and in order to effectively negotiate the journey, you have to drive looking at the road ahead, with only an occasional glance in the rearview mirror. If one attempts to drive while focusing totally on the rearview mirror, he will most certainly crash and never reach his destination.

As long as we are blessed with life, our focus has to be on the road ahead.

A tragic loss makes us more conscious of our own mortality and the fleeting quality of life. It impresses upon us the urgency of maximizing every moment to make our individual contribution, and to do what we have to do to reach our goals and destinations. We must move forward. Every moment is precious and we have no time to lose. We will be joining our departed loved ones soon enough. But as long as we are blessed with life, our focus has to be on the road ahead. The occasional glance in the rearview mirror is for a reality check. It instructs us as to what really matters, what survives and makes a difference when all is said and done.

With the lesson gleaned from the deceased's life, we must quickly shift our view back to the road ahead and engage the precarious but precious gift of life that is still ours.

May G-d bless you with occasions of joy from this day on.

Challenges
Soul Mate

I have a question about bashert — one's soul mate. I always assumed that the person I am looking for should have many things in common with me, with a few opposite areas in which I could use strengthening.

However, I have heard recently that one's bashert is opposite of you in every way so you constantly struggle with each other. What do you think on the matter? Is there a point in which there is too much opposition?

I am asking in the context of someone I have known for years. I have recently felt a strange intuition that perhaps we are destined for each other, for indeed we connect on a very deep level in many ways.

However, in almost everything on the surface, we are exactly the opposite. The way we think, our strengths and weaknesses, our talents. I approach the world more from the perspective of fearing G-d, whereas he focuses on loving G-d.

We share a deep love for wisdom, communication, and Torah, but I wonder if there would be too much conflict, or if it's supposed to be this way.

The identity of the "bashert"— perhaps best translated as "soul mate" — is not as clearly defined as we might like. "Bashert" is understood to be the principle that all that occurs in every aspect of our lives is orchestrated by the Divine hand. Relating to marriage specifically, the saying "a match made in heaven" is consistent with the Talmudic dictum that 40 days before a child is born, a heavenly proclamation declares, "the daughter of so-and-so is destined for this person." It would seem from this statement that whomever we marry is our predestined mate.

This, however, begs the question. Can it be that no matter how poorly we choose that we will still marry our preordained partner? The conclusion of necessity must be that if we choose with integrity — selecting a spouse for the right reasons — we are assured that we will access our destined counterpart.

Likewise, misguided choices that cater to the frivolous and lesser part of ourselves remain just that, and do not plug into the "bashert" opportunity.

"Bashert" does not effortlessly deliver everlasting bliss. Marriage, if it is to be fulfilling, requires consistent attention and hard work. Invariably, you get out of it what you put into it.

Compelling arguments can be made for either finding a spouse who is similar or for one who is different. It is somewhat reminiscent of the humorous anecdote attributed to the great philosopher Socrates. It was common knowledge that Socrates had a shrew for a wife and that she made his life miserable. On one occasion, a disciple of Socrates inquired of his master whether he would recommend that he get married.

Socrates reflected for a minute and said, "I think it's a good thing." By way of explanation, he commented, "If you find a good match you will be very happy, and that's a good thing. If not," he concluded, "you can always become a philosopher, and that's a good thing, too." A basic premise that one must recognize is that every marriage requires accommodations. After all, marriage is a union between two people born and raised in different families of origin and background. In addition, as the popular book suggests, men are from Mars and women from Venus.

Some contend that the merger is not only one of two parties coming from two different planets, but from totally disparate solar systems. Add to that the inevitable stresses of day-to-day living, the crunch and grind of pushing through the day, i.e., the socks left on the floor instead of tossed into the hamper, the toothpaste left uncovered, dishes in the sink, books not replaced on the shelf, the thermostat up, the thermostat down, etc. These may appear to be of no great consequence, but in reality they can be very stressful to the relationship. At the very minimum they demand adjustments and compromises on each partner's part.

It would stand to reason that given the above-stated realities, one should at least seek a mate of similar temperament, thinking, and perspective that would mitigate against the need for changes that might totally overwhelm the relationship.

On the other hand, it is argued that the "opposites attract" dictum is based on the quest for balance. If one partner is more uptight, rigid and exacting, an embracing, more laid-back effect would make for a good synthesis, generating a state of equilibrium. If one partner, for instance, is spacey or off into lofty spiritual realms, a grounded practical orientation in the other would be a welcome counterbalance.

Appreciating differences and making them work in harmony requires great effort and willingness to compromise and/or concede. Someone remarked that "the objective of marriage is not compatibility but how to deal with incompatibility." Many valuable lessons can be learned in the process — to defer, to set aside one's ego, to be less self-absorbed, to focus on another. The challenges of the marriage relationship can and should be the most fertile ground for personal growth.

While the merits of similarities or dissimilarities as a possible mate can be debated, there must be, in any case, a firm foundation of two nonnegotiable components. The first is best expressed by the comment that "it's not the gazing into each other's eyes that counts, but the two gazing in the same direction."

Sharing transcendent goals and objectives and striving toward a common purpose are the essential requirements for building a life together. This creates a common bond that reaches above and beyond the couple's individual pursuits for personal happiness and fulfillment. This common striving gives them the energy and strength to ride out the stresses, pressures, trials, and tribulations in the more challenging seasons of their relationship.

The second, equally essential component is the capacity of reciprocal giving. A couple must have the wherewithal to create a joint "emotional bank account" with daily deposits of acts of caring, gentleness, mutual affirmation, support, and nurturance. No couple can endure the wear and tear of daily existence without investing in each other's well-being.

You, my dear reader, have a true dilemma. Intuition and chemistry weigh in favorably in your situation, as does a mutual abiding love and interest in Torah. Yet, you and the fellow you are seeing differ in the manner in which you think and process emotion. Since there are no generic answers to the "bashert" question and no "one size fits all" approach, I would recommend that you seek out a third party (therapist, rabbi, or wise friend):

1. Who knows both parties well, their strengths, weaknesses, and needs,
2. Who shares their value system,
3. Who has a working knowledge of the dynamics of marriage.

Present your case with its pros and cons that will:

• Clarify your own thinking.
• Give you the benefit of the third party's objective reading of the situation.

I would also advise that you pray daily for clarity, insight, and Heavenly assistance. King David says, "Please, God, lead me in paths that will be right for me" (Psalms).

In conclusion, I see the concept of "bashert" as similar to the partnership of man and G-d at the time of Creation. The Almighty said, "Let us make man." The commentaries on the Torah all struggle with the question of whom G-d was addressing with the word "us." No one existed as yet at that time. The most cogent explanation is that G-d was speaking to man himself, the human being about to be created, advising him that this was to be a joint effort. G-d would provide the raw materials, the potential, but it was up to man to bring them to fruition, to actualize them.

Similarly, it seems to me, "bashert" invokes the same partnership. Heaven provides the opportunities, the challenges, and the circumstances, but it remains our responsibility here on earth to see it through and to make it work.

Challenges
Embracing Challenges

On our recent trip to Israel we visited the tomb of Rachel. I joined with Jewish women of all different backgrounds and locations: Sefardi, Ashkenazi, secular, observant, etc. We came together, a seamless tapestry, bound by our relationship to our Matriarch, Rachel, whose voice on behalf of her children reverberates throughout the ages.

The verse, in bold letters above her tomb reads, "A voice on high is heard ... Rachel is weeping (in the present tense) for her children and refuses to be consoled ..." (Jeremiah 31:14). Scripture concludes that G-d Himself promises that there is hope for the future and her offspring will return to their boundaries.

As we clustered around her tomb, each one of us with our own "pekel tzoris," individual set of problems, we prepared to beseech "Mama Rochel" to intervene on our behalf. We knew she would understand our pain, our trials, and tribulations because Rachel herself was no stranger to adversity. She was the victim of her father's treachery when he gave her sister in marriage to the man destined for Rachel. Despite the knowledge that this act of self-sacrifice might forever separate her from a union of love and destiny, Rachel initiated the plan to spare her sister the pain of shame and rejection. When she was finally united with Jacob, she struggled with childlessness. At long last, she bore a son, only to die in childbirth with her second child, going to the grave with the knowledge that she would not see her children grow to manhood.

Indeed, Mama Rochel was no stranger to pain. Our sages tell us that she was deliberately buried alone, apart from the other Matriarchs and Patriarchs so that her tomb would be accessible to her descendants, so that they might pray there on their way to exile. This is the site where we have come in our hour of need to implore Rachel's advocacy in bringing our supplications before the Divine throne. Crying our hearts out and praying at the tomb of Rachel is cathartic, healing, and enlightening.

Unquestionably, a good part of what comforts us is the sanctity of the space as it coalesces with the historic significance of the tomb. These variables comprise the mystery of our visit. But on the more accessible level, what is so healing and inspiring is the knowledge that the human being is capable, regardless of how daunting the challenge, of acting with transcendent selflessness and courage; that pulsating in our veins is the blood of a woman who transformed the values of Torah into living tissue, real deeds in a real world.

The tomb of Rachel reminds us that we are endowed with the ability to overcome adversity and change our world, not with our dreams and good intentions but with our actions.

· · · · · · · · · · · · · · LIVING IN THE WORLD OF ACTION

Our sages teach that "a person is born to struggle." As the Talmud states, "The reward is commensurate with the pain." Nothing worthwhile in life, even birth itself, can be achieved without pain or toil.

An admirer of the great violinist Jascha Heifetz pursued him after one of his magnificent performances and breathlessly asked him, "How does one get to be such a virtuoso?" To which the maestro replied, "With great difficulty and hard work."

Whatever is precious in life demands high premium, whether it is the athlete training for the Olympics, the ballet dancer, the accomplished scholar, the devoted spouse, the dedicated parent, etc. Whatever the pursuit, there are no shortcuts, no easy answers, no automatic conferrals of success — only hard work and perseverance. And even to those whom we love with our whole heart and soul, we cannot bequeath a finished product. The best we can do is leave a legacy of the value of the process, the struggle and the sweat.

Historically, the name "Israel" conferred upon the Jewish people, after the epic battle between Jacob and the Heavenly representative of the evil forces of Esau, derives from the word "sarisa" (you struggled). The verse reads, "You struggled with G-d and with man, and you were victorious." It is noteworthy that the exalted designation in the name "Israel" is not derived from the word denoting victory but from the root that connotes struggle. It is the struggle that G-d values.

It is precisely the exertion, the anguish, and the living experience that transforms us. Thoughts and feelings alone, as important as they are, do not suffice. We live in what our sages refer to as the "world of action." Behavior and deeds are what modify and define us. It is in the doing that we draw on resources deep within us to actualize what heretofore was mere potential.

Ann, a prominent journalist, had just apprised her superior that she had become a Sabbath-observant Jew, and would no longer be available to cover stories from sundown Friday to sunset on Saturday. The following week on a Friday afternoon, a plane went down in Ann's city. It was a major news-breaking story and it was specifically assigned to her.

Ann's resolve was put to the test and it was only engaging in the struggle and drawing on the resources within herself that Ann defined herself as a true Sabbath observer.

Remember that most difficult "first day," when, with palpitations, we gently coax our youngster out the door to a waiting school bus. "Necessary losses" is the term used to describe the heavy heart that accompanies both mother and child as they negotiate the figurative big steps of life's bus that, of necessity, wrests them from the warm, the comfortable, and the familiar, and forces them to confront the inevitable unfeeling challenge that lies ahead.

Rationally, we recognize it cannot be otherwise. If a child is to be healthy, we cannot arrest his growth by keeping him attached to us forever. We must give him the wherewithal to be an independent and self-reliant individual. As much as we would like, we cannot spare him the bumps in the road ahead. He must experience his own triumphs and failures. We must, if we are to be good parents, provide him with the wings to fly on his own and to set him free.

Analogously, we are all children of the Almighty. He, too (so to speak), hates to part with us. He invests us with a magnificent soul that is hewn of His very essence. He then endows us with free choice, the ability to become and to define ourselves on our own, and sends us into a world fraught with challenges. His Divine Presence accompanies us and never leaves us throughout our journey over the hills and valleys of life. He roots for our success, but it is only in giving us the freedom to make our own decisions, whatever they may be, that define us and give us our personal dignity.

There will be a time, hopefully in the near future, when the need to struggle will be over. It will be an era when the destiny of mankind, as we know it, will be concluded. The promise to "Mama Rochel" will be fulfilled. Her children will be gathered in from all their exiles. The Kabbalists assure us that not a single tear from the ocean of tears that have been shed throughout Israel's painful journey in history will be lost. Every tear is quintessentially precious to the Master of the universe. And He stores these tears in a special place. The new millennium will finally see the fulfillment of the prophecy, "and God will wipe the tear from every face."

Challenges
Loss Before Life

My precious daughter carried a perfect little "angel" for exactly nine months. Two days after her due date, she suddenly did not feel life and, upon rushing to the hospital, was told that the baby had died.

Why oh why, does my child have to suffer this immeasurable pain? I understand the "mystical" aspect and that they were chosen to carry this soul, but my pain — as a mother, watching my precious daughter give birth, knowing that this "angel" was no longer alive — is so indescribably painful that for months I thought I could never wake up again.

My daughter did everything so perfectly throughout her pregnancy. Never for one moment did we imagine that anything like this would happen. During her entire pregnancy, I prayed for this baby to be born healthy and well. What good were all my fervent prayers?

Since there is no funeral, no shivah and no Kaddish, how does one actually "mourn" for this loss? I felt that there was no conclusion to the grief — it just went on and on with nothing to console me. To any woman who has carried a child for nine months with all the trials and discomfort, to suddenly be "empty" with nothing — how much more painful can anything be in this world?

*Y*our pain is palpable, real, and totally understandable, especially to those of us who have shared the agonizing experience of losing a baby at or prior to birth.

Intellectual, religious, and Kabbalistic insight do not assuage the pain or speak directly to the bleeding heart. The Mishnah so wisely advises: "Do not try to comfort the mourner as long as the deceased is still before him." There are no arguments, rationales, or theories that can address suffering and pain that are emotional expressions of the heart. The heart and mind deal in totally different currencies.

Nonetheless, borrowing from the verse in the Shema: "these words shall be placed upon your heart," a commentary suggests that it would have been better articulated if we were charged to "place the words within your heart." There are times, such as a grievous loss, that our hearts are not open or ready to absorb words of reason. The wound is too fresh and too raw. This thought is captured by the wise Yiddish adage: "What mind and reason cannot do, time will eventually accomplish." And when time has exercised its healing effect, the words that we were unable to relate to — that we had placed "upon" our hearts — will then penetrate, be heard, and support the healing process.

· REALMS OF ETERNITY

For the duration of the nine months of pregnancy, a woman has the unparalleled privilege of carrying and nurturing new life within her. She feels alive and creative. The death of the newborn, whether prior to or at the time of birth, is a heartbreaking and grotesque betrayal of the primal maternal instinct. Death and sadness are the very antithesis of the life and joy she legitimately anticipated bringing into the world.

The Jewish mystical tradition informs that every soul enters this world with a mission. The context and challenges of a person's life provide the necessary tools to discharge the raison d'etre of this individual. Our definition of what is "good" or "bad" in life conforms to our finite vision and limited experience in the here and now. The Kabbalistic view, in contrast, encompasses past, present, and future — both our temporal world and the supernal realms of eternity. The "full picture" is not within our human grasp. In the framework of ultimate reality, this little soul has completed its journey, its mission in its brief nine months' sojourn in utero.

Your daughter, perhaps paradoxically, precisely because she was not blessed with the joys of raising this child, provided a totally loving and selfless environment for this soul to finish its work and achieve its eternal peace. In this vein, the definition of "life" is expanded. Providing the eternal peace and serenity to a soul whose life's objective has thus been completed can certainly, from a spiritual prospective, be seen as a conferral of "life" of the highest order.

G-d's ways are inscrutable, beyond our comprehension. But it is a fundamental principle of our faith that He knows what He is doing. There is consolation in the certainty that this was not a meaningless fate — nor that it was an arbitrary occurrence. There is purpose and meaning to everything that happens.

This brings to mind the classic exchange between Sir Bertrand Russell and a cleric. Russell commented, "I cannot believe in a G-d in Whose world a child cries out in pain." To which the cleric responded, "As for me, I cannot believe in a world in which a child cries out in pain and there is no G-d to justify it."

You describe so beautifully your children's excited anticipation and attendant religious ceremonies, juxtaposed by the subsequent poignant pain of loss and deprivation. Your description resounds with that age-old and ever-prevalent question of "why them?" Why do the righteous have to suffer?

The Talmud tells us that this very question was asked by Moses, whose prophetic powers are unrivaled in history. The text relates that the Almighty answered Moses with the words, "No man can look upon My face and live," meaning that no mortal can comprehend G-d's just but unfathomable governance of the world. Ultimately, only G-d, Who has the master plan for the destiny of humankind, can answer that question.

As for us, we have to do our thing: choose to celebrate the good in life, attempting day by day to get a longer glimpse of the sun shining, and closer bonding with spouse, parents, family, and friends.

······························ **MOURNING RITUALS**

There are many questions about the provisions in Jewish law — halachah — and Jewish practice attending the loss of a baby prior, during, or following birth.

The rituals of shivah — the 7-day mourning period — eulogy, public burial, Kaddish, Yizkor, and gravestone unveiling are not observed for a baby who did not reach the age of 30 days. Two explanatory points are in order:

1. The soul that has not survived for 30 days in this world is certainly of no less significance. However, that soul is not seen as having had a presence in the social and communal parameters of conventional existence. The above rituals are seen as public manifestations directly related to the impact on the community and society, and since this child did not have an existence, presence, or role within these parameters, rituals such as these would be superfluous and inappropriate.

2. One must not see this as a reflection on the preciousness of this soul. This soul, as mentioned before, completed its mission, and while its existence is not acknowledged in a public modality, it is celebrated in the place it will forever occupy — in the hearts and minds of the parents of whom it was an integral part, and by the Almighty from Whose essence it was hewn.

We must remember that our culture gives undue attention and importance to what is public, but for Jews the private and the personal has always been the domain venerated and respected as being the more authentic. I have known parents who, in lieu of public ceremonies and in a desire to benefit this little soul, have dedicated learning, acts of charity, and the assumption of self-improvement modalities.

One rabbi and teacher, upon the loss of his own baby, painstakingly developed a comprehensive, Torah-based curriculum for grieving parents. He has presented this to hundreds of families who have received this desperately needed guidance and comfort based on wisdom and expertise. Perhaps, he suggested, this was the contribution, the gift that his child's loss had brought to the world. Without the loss, he said, none of this would have happened.

It must be noted that the absence of a public ritual may leave friends and family at a loss as how to respond. It does not however, relieve them from extending an appropriate expression of sympathy and caring — a card, a call, an offer of assistance, etc. We dare not allow the bereaved to feel shunned and abandoned in their time of grief.

DEALING WITH DEATH ·························

There is the cultural and generational gap between grieving practices of today and yesteryear. In both Europe and America, death was always very much an everyday, hands-on part of life. Because of the high infant mortality rate and in an effort to encourage moving on with their lives, members of the burial society would unceremoniously remove the miscarried and stillborn from the home and bring them to proper burial. Since they had a healthy way of dealing with death, rituals and ceremonies did not seem to be necessary.

In our culture, there is an illusion perpetrated that if we are lucky, death does not have to be a part of life. Hence we have a tangible discomfort with the concept of death. We seek to keep it at a distance. It is kept sterile and anesthetized, and perhaps it is this discomfort that necessitates rituals for psychological closure.

Common practice recommended by grief counselors in hospitals everywhere suggests seeing and holding the deceased baby. Though picture-taking provides a sterile image of the soul that was, some may find it therapeutic. For some, these practices lend reality and confirm at an emotional level that the nine months of gestation did indeed produce a real baby. Other rituals, seen as acts of possible closure, if deemed helpful, are not objectionable. It would, however, be advisable to seek the guidance of a rabbi.

There are many customs regarding naming the baby before burial. A fetus born with a recognizable human form should be given a name before being buried. Some suggest choosing a name that one would not use in the future for other children. Others suggest names that are expressive of the themes of consolation (Nechamah) or mercy (Rachamim). Yet others use a name they hope to give in the future, but paired at that time by an additional name, usually of someone who enjoyed longevity.

·················· LESSONS OF THE SAGES

My friend Judy, who lost a baby at birth, sought the advice of a renowned sage. He inquired about her family and asked her how many children she had. She responded that she had two sons, ages 3 and 6, but that she had also had a daughter, Esther, who would have now been 8 years old. The sage gently but very sternly and empathetically corrected her. "No," he said, "Esther would never have been 8 years old. She wasn't meant to live or have a presence in this world."

As hard as we try, it is difficult for us to disabuse ourselves of the illusion, the mistaken notion that these, our babies, were unrealized and unactualized potential. Coming to terms with the certainty that they were not meant to be spares us the torturous self-blaming trips to which we subject ourselves. The "if-only" trips: if only I'd had a more competent doctor, if only I hadn't exerted myself, if only I had prayed more, if only I had been a better person, etc.

While positive steps toward self-improvement are always beneficial, blaming yourself and others is counterproductive and totally out of line.

Rabbi Moses Feinstein, of blessed memory, a revered halachic authority of the past half-century, unequivocally states in his responsa that all that issues from the union between husband and wife, while unviable in this world, will be united with their mother in the future, with the coming of the Messiah and the resurrection of the dead.

Rabbi Yaakov Weinberg, of blessed memory, in consoling one of his students who had just buried his oldest child, told him that the merit of his family, in being the crucible through which this soul found its peace, would make possible blessings for the entire family that were heretofore obstructed and could not have been possible. The student reports that indeed the child born thereafter was very special and that many other unexplainable and remarkable benefits ensued in his extended family shortly thereafter. The merit of being the vehicle for enabling the rectification of a soul, painful though it was, was rewarded. It opened doors of joy for many.

My daughter Yocheved lives in Manchester, England. Over the years, I was privileged to hear about and on one occasion to meet the saintly Rosh Yeshivah, Rabbi Yehudah Zev Segal. He was that enviable combination of extraordinary Torah knowledge and a magnificent human being. His humility was legendary. He was accessible to all, and people flocked from everywhere to seek his wise counsel. He was lucid up to the last moments of his life, and upon his passing, they found that he had left instructions declining burial in Israel or in other significant family plots. He requested to be buried in the lot reserved for and among the miscarried, stillborn, and very young departed children.

It seemed that his purpose was twofold. The first was that these were the purest and most exalted of souls and he sought the privilege of making his eternal rest among them. The second was that Rabbi Segal wanted to assure the mothers who had not had the opportunity or the joy to care for these children that he would care for them until they would be reunited with their families at the time to come.

Some practical notes are in order. The postpartum condition of weight gain and hormone fluctuation can be challenging even in the best of times, but certainly without a baby to love and care for. There is no compensatory factor, only the negative effects of pregnancy. In recognition of this, the family needs to be especially sensitive, understanding, and patient with the process of recovery.

Your daughter needs to help herself by actively seeking ways to promote her own well-being; a vacation with her husband, a change of scenery, exercise, a class she has been meaning to attend, reading, writing, meditation. Constructive pursuits will give her something of a growth mode that will have been born and nurtured in a time that has been punctuated by death and loss. She needs to know that her roller-coaster emotions are normal and will abate with time and eventual healing.

Finally, while no one deliberately seeks adversity, there is a profound well of sensitivity, creativity, and wisdom that only deep pain can excavate from the recesses of our being. We are never quite the same. What we have endured and overcome makes us bigger, stronger, and wiser. A secular writer echoes this very sentiment when he asks: "Is not the cup that holds your wine the very cup that was burned in the potter's oven? And is not the lute that soothes your spirit the very wood that was hollowed with knives?"

Though there were times when we thought we would not survive the pain, we find out that situations such as these can bring us closer to G-d and closer to our loved ones. And we realize that we are resilient and equal to life despite — or perhaps even because of — its challenges.

Challenges
Coping With What's Eating You

When dealing with pain, there's no time to wait: addressing problems at their inception averts much heartache.

~~~

Some years ago, I took my father, of blessed memory, to a physician in Milwaukee for a consultation. After the examination, the doctor shared his conclusions with us, and we prepared to leave. Just as my father was about to walk out of the office, he turned to the doctor and said, "Doctor, you're the first medical professional who didn't hassle me about my weight. How come?" The doctor's wise response was memorable and I have quoted it often since. He said, "Rabbi, it's not what you eat, it's what eats away at you that really matters."

I thought about that this morning when a young woman came to see me to discuss her troubled marriage. She unloaded 15 years' worth of pain, anguish, and emotional deprivation. My heart sank as the picture grew darker and more hopeless. When I could bear it no longer, I erupted, "Why did you wait so long to get help? What have you been doing for the last 15 years, while all of this was eating away at you?"

PRIDEFUL RELUCTANCE ·····························

Indeed, one of the greatest frustrations I have experienced in more than 30 years of counseling is the prideful reluctance of individuals and/or couples to seek intervention when a problem first arises, or at the very least, when it becomes clear that the problem is not going away.

Invariably, by the time the situation comes to our door there is so much accumulated anger, bitterness, and resentment that a veritable wall, impenetrable to scale, has been erected; by then an almost superhuman effort is needed to break through.

Negativity of this magnitude ravages not only its object, but its bearer as well. Resentment, someone explained, is like drinking poison and hoping that the other person will die. The fact is that, as my father's doctor observed, "it eats away at us." We become the victims.

·APPROPRIATE ASSISTANCE

King Solomon exhorts us that if there is worry or concern in one's heart, one should speak about it to those who can be of assistance:

> If there is anxiety in a man's mind let him quash it, and turn it into joy with a good word — a righteous man gives his friend direction ... (Proverbs 12:25).

In modern day we have many choices available to us — rabbis, therapists, counselors, and other professionals that a particular situation might call for.

Articulating one's problems and issues in the presence of an objective party gives one access, at the very least, to greater clarity and insight. Dealing with a problem at its inception can avert much heartache and many tragedies — divorce, alienation, destroyed relationships, etc.

Many hesitate to get help, because they see it as a sign of weakness. Others believe that they deserve to suffer. Still others mistakenly think time will cure everything. All are misguided rationalizations.

A woman at a seminar once asked me how we can teach our children to deal effectively with the stresses and challenges of life.

I responded that our children watch us very carefully. Our behavior is the example we set for them to follow. Our message to them needs to be that when life gets tough, we don't crumble or run away, we don't give up the ship. We don't avoid facing our issues such that we become frustrated, bitter, angry, and resentful.

ALL ONE'S STRENGTH ··································

The story is told about a little boy who, while playing in the backyard, tries to move a big rock from its place. He pushes and pushes but to no avail. The rock doesn't budge. Frustrated, he turns to his father who, instead of being sympathetic, admonishes his son, "You are not using all your strength." The boy turns once again to push the stone, huffing and puffing, pushing and pulling, but once again with no success. Much to his surprise, he hears his father, chiding him, "But, son, you are still not using all your strength." Spent and fatigued, the young lad cries to his father, "How can you say that? I have tried my best!" "No you haven't," responded his father, "you didn't ask me to help you."

Meeting the challenges of life effectively belongs to those who have the foresight and the courage to seek out, in a timely fashion, those who can enable them to use all their strength.

And it also most definitely belongs to those who turn to the Source of all strength — to G-d. Prayer gives strength. Faith gives strength. Recognition that we were placed on earth for a purpose and that the One Who put us here gives us reservoirs of strength to cope with the challenges of life — that, too, gives strength and perspective. And with proper perspective, even mountains become molehills.

Challenges
Filling the Void

I am 37 years old and have battled a weight problem since I was a teenager. I have received all kinds of assistance and nothing works. I feel I am at a dead end with my relationship to food. I have prayed to G-d to help me combat this "evil inclination." I would appreciate any guidance.

O besity is one of the ubiquitous issues of our time. Being over-weight in a society whose motto is "you can never be too thin or too rich" can be a heart-wrenching experience. There are those who have seriously expressed an "if only" wish that they might have lived in previous eras where it was desirable to be full bodied. They point to the paintings of the masters of that day (e.g., Rembrandt) whose female figures were certainly not of the emaciated variety that are nowadays considered attractive. The fuller figures of yesteryear represented a status of plenty, whereas today's idealized specimen would have raised concerns of poverty, or worse yet, of illness.

We live in a time, as reflected in the voice of the reader, where the problem of being overweight is of paramount concern and has been labeled a "deadly epidemic," "plague," or at the very least a "crisis." Health issues such as high blood pressure, cholesterol, diabetes, and heart disease, etc., all seem to be exacerbated, if not caused by, obesity.

The psychological fallout is equally devastating. Obesity in a culture that worships "thin" must perforce lead to painful issues of low self-esteem.

In addition, it often gives rise to depression defined by psychologists as anger turned inward. Obese people often find themselves isolated, a self-imposed isolation brought about by a perception of what others think of them, or by lethargy, despair, etc. This in turn leads to more overeating and initiates a vicious cycle.

Kate is a person of keen mind and great accomplishments. She is a wife and mother and has advanced degrees in law, architecture, business, and a myriad of other talents. Her husband used to jokingly comment that he could never predict which hat she would be wearing when he came home from work.

Despite all her achievements, Kate found no peace or pleasure in life, because she could not master what, in her mind, was her greatest challenge — controlling her weight. Ultimately, when health issues surfaced, both her doctors and her rabbi supported her decision to have gastric bypass surgery. The change was dramatic. It was as though she got a new lease on life. She was no longer driven feverishly to find new horizons to conquer. She had finally found a sense of peace and tranquility.

This solution may not be viable for everyone, but there is a solution for everyone. It may entail time and effort but each individual can find something that works for him. Similarly, Rachel has battled weight all her life. The extent to which she is tormented by it was revealed in conversation one day, when she shared that the challenge of raising her seriously compromised special needs child did not come close to the agonizing challenge of dealing with her obesity.

SEDENTARY LIFESTYLE

To treat the syndrome of overeating as the inability to eat in a disciplined fashion is perhaps an oversimplification of what is often a multilayered and complex issue.

It goes without saying that the first order of treatment for the overweight person is to have a thorough medical evaluation to rule out metabolic issues. Genetics often play a role, but the overwhelming thinking is that one is not hopelessly doomed by genes.

A major contributing factor to this raging problem has been identified as today's sedentary lifestyle. An innovative primary school in Chicago introduced the "walking school bus" concept, where children are encouraged to walk the mile or so to school. They begin the day with 60 minutes of yoga or body movements. Their lunch program consists of only healthy choices. This, parenthetically, is a public school, not a school for privileged children. Both students and parents are delighted. It has been indisputably demonstrated that children who eat healthy and are active perform better in school and have higher self-esteem.

Another nemesis to healthy eating is that many, if not most, families today often have two working parents, where "take-out food" is frequently the comfortable solution. Furthermore, hours of sedentary leisure promotes, among other noxious results, eating with no recourse to burning off calories.

EIGHT PRACTICAL STEPS

It is imperative to get to the root of the problem and, perhaps with the help of outside intervention, ascertain what triggers the overeating response. If seriously addressed, one can begin to recognize patterns that will help uncover why or when overeating takes place. There are weight-control programs that focus primarily on how and for what reason one eats.

Here are eight basic guidelines to prevent overeating that can be incorporated into one's daily habits.

1. If you are not really hungry, but just want to "cozy up" with a piece of chocolate cake to assuage a concern or a worry, try seeking comfort elsewhere — i.e., call a friend, take a walk, clean a closet, etc.

2. Eat consistently. Don't fall prey to feast or famine by starving yourself and then stuffing yourself at dinner. Small meals throughout the day when you are hungry work better. In many cultures the main heavy meal is consumed at lunchtime, rather than in the evening. This enables one to more readily burn off the calories.

3. Exercise regularly, not only for weight control, but for both physical and mental health, such as mood enhancement. Exercise has also been shown to diminish the craving for sweets and junk food.

4. Eat smaller portions — one cookie instead of a batch. Total denial gives food more seductive power. Everything is acceptable within limits.

5. Keep sweets and other problematic foods out of reach and out of sight. Studies have demonstrated that those who keep candies on their desk or easily accessible, have a five-times greater propensity to eat candy than those who have to get up to reach them.

6. Preplate your food. Remove a designated portion from the bag, can, pot, or whatever container the food came in — and put the rest away.

7. Use smaller bowls, plates, and spoons. This fool-the-eye trick will also make for eating less.

8. Eat lots of fruits and vegetables. Unlike calorie-dense foods such as cake, candies, and other sweets, fruits and vegetables have a high-fiber content that helps you feel full. Some of my friends keep prepared platters with bite-size snacks of fruits and vegetables, so that when they and their children walk into the house famished, they will grab a healthy snack instead of junk food.

Next, I would like to address how the reader refers to his "relationship with food" as his "evil inclination." I think it is a rather harsh assessment. "Challenge," in my estimation, would be a better term.

Gary has been struggling with a weight problem for years. In past conversations, he attributed his overeating to simply opting for pleasure over pain — the pain of denying himself and the unwillingness to incur the discomfort of postponing gratification. Lately, he has been looking slim and healthy, and he shared that he'd made a chart of gains and losses to analyze whether to eat sensibly or to overindulge. He categorized them in the following way:

Gary's Gains of Sensible Eating:

a. *The way I feel about myself — i.e., improved self-esteem.*

b. *The willingness to take risks, and the resulting empowerment of other areas of life.*

c. *The sense of pride that others would take in my accomplishment.*

d. *Success in managing my weight allows me to be a role model and mentor in this and other areas.*

Gary's Losses from Overeating:

a. *Settling for defeat, and hence the inability to accomplish other goals.*

b. *The thought that if prayer had not been successful in this area, it raises questions about other things for which I would pray.*

c. *How people looked at me, and how opportunities are missed because of my physical appearance.*

I asked Gary about the role of prayer in achieving his success. He explained that his request of G-d was very specific. He prayed that G-d assist him by strengthening and reinforcing his resolve and determination.

Gary spoke of his uphill battle to disabuse himself of his addictive behavior, and to opt for the best and most self-respecting part of himself. He admitted that, consciously or subconsciously, he had been sabotaged by self-defeating behavior, which kept him stuck in mediocrity. His full potential and creativity were constantly being stifled by his posture of least resistance. Now, his new dynamic of control over food had empowered him to consider possibilities of growth and achievement in other areas of his life that he had never previously entertained.

TRANSFORMING THE ORDINARY·················

There is a story told of a simple Jew in the time of pogroms in Europe who used to gorge himself obsessively with whatever food came his way. Though reluctant to respond when questioned about his strange behavior, he finally broke his silence, and with tears streaming down his face, spoke of his father, a pious Jew, who, because of his slight physical stature, was an easy target for his treacherous attackers. When his father was murdered, he vowed that he would eat and eat so that his huge body could put up greater resistance when the time would come for him to defend his Judaism.

The dedication of this pure, simple soul — misguided though it might have been — is touching but far beyond our scope.

What is relevant for us, however, is that every behavior — no matter how physical its expression — is an opportunity for a spiritual connection by means of mindfulness and sublimation. Blessings of gratitude and thanksgiving — recited with intent, before and after ingesting food — move us into a G-dly realm.

Our typical day provides countless opportunities to make formal or informal appeals to the Master of the universe — to help us use the energy derived from the delights of this world, to do His Will, and to be better people. This attitude transforms ordinary acts — eating, sleeping, vacationing, etc. — into one seamless tapestry of spiritual service. If we would integrate this approach into daily living, slowly but surely we would plug into the image of Jacob's ladder — with feet firmly planted on the ground, and head reaching the heavens.

Chassidic writings discuss how many of our daily activities are actually tools to access a higher reality. Love of children, spouse, friends, and pleasures can be a medium through which to achieve love of G-d. Likewise, the experience of fear — thunder and lightning, dark, vulnerability, etc. — can be converted it into awe of the Infinite One.

EMPTINESS INSIDE

My 3-year-old grandson, Yitzl, was having a rough day, nudging his mother that he was bored. After rejecting suggestion after suggestion, my daughter, Chadshie, in exasperation, told him to just go out into the backyard and find someone with whom to play. Two minutes later, he was back, saying to Chadshie, "Mommy, there's no one out there. No boys, no girls, no one at all. It is just full of empty."

"It is just full of empty" is an apt description what many of us feel at one time or another as we move through life. But there are those whose "feeling empty" is a more constant and desperate existential state. And this may compel one to try to fill that emotional or spiritual void with binging on food, or whatever they think might fill the emptiness inside of them.

The prophet Isaiah states that there will come a time of great hunger and great thirst, "Not a hunger for bread or a thirst for water, but rather to hear the word of G-d." I have a strong feeling that if we would carefully examine the underpinnings of hunger and thirst gone awry in our time, we would discover that these sensations are in fact a spiritual hunger for the word of G-d.

It is conceivable that this phenomenon is an expression of "G-d in search of Man," an invitation from the Master of the universe to His Table. Food for the soul is the currency. Increasing our commitment to Torah study, prayer-meditation, and transcendent acts of kindness would be a meaningful and potent response to the insatiable hunger we feel.

Twice in Deuteronomy the Torah assures us: "You will eat and you will be satisfied." The second identical verse seems repetitive but, in fact, it comes to tell us that when we are spiritually aligned with the Almighty, blessing will be inherent in the morsel of food that we ingest, such that the minimum amount will satisfy us.

Indeed, there is a holistic congruence, a correspondence between the physical and spiritual spheres of existence. When all is well in one realm, it resonates with the other. Like the reader, each one of us has battles to fight, challenges to overcome, and issues to rectify. Let us hope that our dedicated efforts to do so will hasten the long-awaited redemption when all the pieces will finally fall into place, and mankind will hunger solely for the word of G-d.

Challenges
What Price Equality?[1]

*I*t is difficult to dispute that women have made significant inroads in the workplace. Although management analysts maintain that a "glass ceiling" still prevents women's access to the highest rungs of the corporate ladder, the gap between compensation and benefits levels for women vis-a-vis their male counterparts has been considerably narrowed.

Furthermore, harassment litigation brought to national exposure within the last ten years has secured a safer, more respectful work environment for women.

For the most part, I think we have successfully proven that, given the chance, we can "do a man's job" or "fill a man's shoes."

We have become empowered and influential. Power, in our society, translates into money, and the ability to "make a living" is our most vaunted value. In the contemporary secular world, we define and judge ourselves by the material possessions our "purchasing power" affords us.

From a time-honored and time-tested traditional Jewish perspective, however, the view is very different and cause for great concern. In the traditional landscape, a woman's primary place is not upon the public stage or out in the marketplace. In the words of the psalmist King David, "the beauty, the dignity of the daughter of a king is her inwardness" (Psalms 45:14).

---

1. This article was originally published in *The Wisconsin Jewish Chronicle*, and is reprinted with permission.

HOME AN OASIS·····································

Throughout the ages, in history's glorious seasons and in times of persecution, trials, and travails, Jewish homes have served as an oasis, resistant and free of the raging storms, the corrosive values plaguing civilization.

As the Midrash in Genesis Rabbah asserts, "everything is determined by the woman." It has been women, throughout history, who have been the vigilant guardians of the Jewish home and thereby Jewish values, mores, and ethics. "The wise among women builds her home; and the foolish one destroys it with her own hands" (Proverbs 14:1).

Unlike the contemporary feminist whose vision is fixed solely upon success in the marketplace, the Jewish feminist places her home as her primary, though not exclusive, priority.

The "woman of valor" of Proverbs 31 excels in her entrepreneurial endeavors, but her home stands as the primary axis around which her life revolves.

As a result, she is the truly powerful woman. They rise and they praise her in the gates, they call her blessed (see Proverbs 31:28 and 31).

A Jewish feminist, as equated with the "woman of valor," is able to transcend the egoism required for success in the marketplace since success in the Jewish home is based on the ability to give and reach beyond oneself.

Abraham Maslow, one of the fathers of modern psychology, purports "self-transcendence" as the ultimate achievement in human development. The Jewish perspective invokes the paradox that it is only in looking away from ourselves that we begin to find ourselves.

In reaching beyond the narrow confines of self, we access an energy that lifts us into a new and infinite realm. In so doing, we are able to maintain nurturing, noncompetitive relationships with our husbands and children.

Our society has authenticated Thomas Wolfe's well-known book title "You Can't Go Home Again" by devaluing the home and by offering little or no support for the courageous woman who chooses being a wife and mother as her primary career. Her rewards, even the revitalizing nachas (contentment) she may experience from time to time, are inconsistent and elusive.

Nevertheless, I believe these women to be the unheralded heroes of our time. They are the ones who impact our lives in far deeper realms than do publicly renowned women.

These are the mothers, grandmothers, aunts, and teachers who notice us and go beyond themselves to show us care and concern. It is the memories of these women that fill us with warmth and solace in the cold winters and fragile moments of our lives.

· MANY FEEL BETRAYED

For Jewish women, therefore, the question is not are we able to be successful "out there," but should being successful "out there" be our major goal in life. Are we being true to the legacy left to us as a sacred trust throughout the ages?

And perhaps an even more important question within the framework of our times is: Are we being true to ourselves as women? Anthropologist Ashley Montagu in his book "The Natural Superiority of Women" refers to our gender's "genius of humanity."

Throughout my travels on the lecture circuit, I have run across accomplished businesswomen who have felt betrayed by contemporary feminism. Being successful in the workplace has necessitated the repression of their natural feminine responses, intuition, empathy, and other natural emotional resources.

They have had to adopt a more masculine posture in order to be accepted by the male-dominated marketplace. In the end, they are left empty, questioning the long-lasting benefits of "equality."

I am not suggesting that all women throw away successful careers and stay home exclusively. For one thing, economic necessities may preclude that possibility.

Secondly, there is room within the traditional perspective for personal fulfillment. The Zohar, the foremost kabbalistic (Jewish mystical) work of our tradition, defines the commandment to "be fruitful and multiply" in Genesis 1:28 to include a wide spectrum of human creativity.

I do think, however, that before we applaud contemporary feminism and hop on its bandwagon, we must become aware of its pitfalls. We must be mindful of our priorities.

We must remember at all times that strange winds have blown in the past, shifting values throughout history; the pendulum has swung back and forth.

Through it all, the Jewish people have survived because the women among them refused to compromise their values and roles in the face of the superficial and capricious fads of the societies in which they lived.

While contemporary feminism strives for equality on our behalf, we have to be ever wary that "our gains not be outweighed by our losses" (Avos 2:1).

Challenges

National Pain and Personal Joy

I recently gave birth to a baby boy. I have been feeling pangs of guilt, in that I did not fast on Tishah B'Av, due to some recovery complications from the birth and breastfeeding full time. So while I did the right thing according to Jewish law, I feel detached from the pain that the Jewish people are going through. I was unable to attend any of the large prayer rallies in connection with the Gaza disengagement.

So while I am elated and ecstatic over my newborn, I wonder: How can a Jew allow herself to experience personal joy instead of feeling and participating in national pain? I am feeling guilty. Please advise.

*Y*our question reflects truly admirable sensitivity, and at its core addresses the dialectic of Jewish existence: the ability and the necessity to cry and laugh at the same time. King David, the great psalmist, captures this when he exclaims: "We sat by the rivers of Babylon (when we were taken into exile), and we cried when we remembered Zion ... Our captors demanded that we sing," but our hearts recoiled, "How can we sing the song of G-d on foreign soil?" (Psalms 137).

Collectively, since our inception as a people, whether on our own soil, or dispersed among the nations, we question whether we can sing, as long as our brethren, or members of our community, are in a state of suffering. Certainly, on a personal level, we wonder whether we can legitimately rejoice when a part of us is gripped in the unrelenting sorrow and grief of loss and tragedy.

Nonetheless, the Torah exhorts us, under all circumstances, "and you shall rejoice in your holiday." Similarly, we are obligated to celebrate a wedding, even as we temper that joy with the shattering of a glass under the chuppah, to remind us that as long as Jerusalem is not fully rebuilt, our joy is not fully complete.

King Solomon, the wisest of all men, offers his immortal sage counsel, "There is a time to cry, and there is a time to laugh." We are called upon to juggle our emotions, to walk that fine line throughout life in an effort to achieve the appropriate balance. While on the one hand, we cannot ignore the pain, at the same time, we must be grateful for the blessings of the good. And we must sustain hope, born of the knowledge that it is the Almighty Who is the Choreographer of all events.

SONG IN THE CATTLE CAR ·

A digression of a personal nature comes to mind. My father, of blessed memory, was a rabbi in Falteceni, a small town in Romania before the war. It was on a fateful Friday morning that the Nazis invaded the town and ordered all the men to report to the train station that afternoon. The men, to the horror of their grief-stricken wives, mothers, sisters, and friends, were loaded into cattle cars with no indication where they were being taken.

My mother, of blessed memory, pregnant with me, and clutching my 18-month-old brother in her arms, accompanied my father. As they tearfully parted, my father instructed my mother to hurry home to light the Shabbos candles. As the train, packed beyond human capacity, began to pull away from the station, my father looked out and realized that since the sun was setting, Shabbos was approaching. As the cries of the women and children echoed and pierced the air, my father, in the characteristic tradition of prayer, clapped his hands and began to sing the verse that precedes the Shabbos service.

A young secular Jew, standing next to my father, witnessed this incongruous scene, and with great dismay, nudged the fellow next to him for an explanation. He was told that the man singing was the rabbi of the city, and that the verse he invoked was a tribute to G-d that explained, "Let us give thanks to G-d, for His kindness is forever."

The train was taken to a labor camp, where they were required to do backbreaking work, day after day, from dawn until late at night, for months on end. Most of the inmates perished from disease and exposure, but fortunately my father was one of the survivors. The Russians, who were as feared as the Nazis, liberated my father.

Upon his return to Falteceni, my father was informed that the official appointed to govern the town was a young Jewish man, a doctrinal Communist. My father was also advised that this young governor had had a son born to him that very day.

My father moved quickly into his rabbinic mode and insisted that he had to go and apprise the new father of his obligations as a Jew to circumcise his baby. The traumatized surviving members of the Jewish community pleaded with him "not to rock the boat," and to abandon this most preposterous plan. They pointed out that Communists have no use for G-d and religion, and that my father would be needlessly endangering his welfare and that of the entire community.

My father would not be deterred, insisting that he would jeopardize no one but himself. In the end, his attendant refused to let him go alone, so together they appeared before the governor at the appointed time. They were greeted and asked to sit down, and the official inquired as to the nature of their business. My father replied that it had come to his attention that a baby boy had been born, and as leader of the Jewish community, he had come to wish him 'mazel tov,' and at the same time, inform him that, as a Jew, the governor was obligated to have a bris for his child on the eighth day.

The official was silent, staring at my father. After a long moment, he said, "Okay, Rabbi. I will do as you say. But let me tell you why I will concede to your request. You don't remember me, Rabbi, but I remember you. I was standing next to you in that cattle car on that terrible Friday afternoon. I was there when, despite the captivity and the wailing of women and children still echoing in our ears, you clapped your hands and began to sing your prayers, praising G-d for His kindness. For such a man as yourself, who demonstrates such awesome faith in the face of terrible adversity, I would do anything you would ask."

UNIQUE CONTRIBUTION ·······················

The story of my father is the story of every Jew. Adversity will not claim us. There are myriad accounts of heroism, of Simchas Torah dancing and singing in the bunkers and even the gas chambers. Despite our blood-drenched history, our song has never and will never be silenced, our celebrations never compromised, and our spirit never diminished. This is the strength of the Jew: we persevere, we laugh, we sing, and we celebrate through our tears.

The dear reader feels guilty at experiencing exhilarating joy at the birth of her baby, while concurrently Jews everywhere are mourning the loss of the Temple of old and the current painful dismantling of Jewish homes. I would suggest that there are many ways to express and register hurt, pain, and prayerful appeals heavenward. Undoubtedly, when you look at the innocent, trusting face of your newborn, your heart is bursting with love, and in that boundless overwhelming emotion, there is, unquestionably, an ache and a prayer that pleads that this precious child be privileged to grow up in a safer and better world.

Be assured that there is no prayer more powerful than that of a mother beseeching on behalf of her children, and when you importune the Almighty for a future free of hatred and strife, filled with lovingkindness and peace among men, not only your child, but all of us are the beneficiaries of that prayer.

Clearly, the Almighty created a world in which all of us contribute in our own unique way. Consider the analogy of what it takes to negotiate a successful battle of war. It requires the input of many divisions: generals, frontline soldiers, strategists, those in charge of morale, supplies, etc. Each unit plays a critical role in an effective war effort and the ensuing victory.

Similarly, each one of us can effect the changes we so desperately need in the context of our individual circumstances. The dear reader has countered and protested the destruction of both the past and present in the most meaningful way possible. She has brought a new soul into the world, and thus has committed herself to banishing the bitter darkness around us with the gift of new life, new energy, and new hope.

Understandably, it is for this reason that you were not only exempt, but also enjoined from fasting on Tishah B'Av. Your marching orders were different from those of others because your role in the battle for a sane world is unique and specific to the priority of the moment. You have to conserve and build your strength for the crucial role you have to play. You are the soldier entrusted with the future, and that needs to be your exclusive focus.

The beauty of halachah, Jewish law, is that it helps direct our attention to where we need to be, and what we must do, at the different seasons and given times of our life. Trust that process. Go with its flow and you will find there is no contradiction between joining in the pain of your people, while taking joy and delight in your new addition. G-d willing, he will grow up to join the ranks of the Almighty's soldiers, and hopefully help bring us to the long-awaited millennium of peace and blessing.

Family

A Parent's Remarriage *Family*

After battling lung cancer my beloved mother passed away at the age of 57 (I was 38). My parents met each other when they were very young, married and were happily together for nearly 40 years. They lived a simple life, never buying much or doing much because my father never wanted to and my mother never pushed him to do what she really wanted.

My father was heartbroken when she passed away, but five months after her death, he began dating Bonnie. At that time I was expecting with my third son. I had gone through many years of infertility problems, and now I had another difficult pregnancy during my mother's illness.

My father began urging his friend on me and my siblings. I didn't want to meet her. I was grieving for my mother and I couldn't do it. Finally, he prevailed upon me to meet her. It was so uncomfortable as he laughed and joked with her in front of me.

I began to think of the life my mother had with him and I resented him for living it up with Bonnie in a way he wouldn't have with my mother. If my mother wanted something, she couldn't just buy it. When Mom was sick, crying in pain, he said to wait for the cheap drugstore to get her medication (which took five days). I would not let her suffer one second. I went to the hospital pharmacy, with my young son when I should have been in bed, as she would have done for me!

I stayed at their house from 9 a.m. to 9 p.m. every day and night, shopping for them, cleaning, and taking care of her. It was my honor to do so. I am grateful to have spent this time with her. I took her to the hospital five days a week for five weeks for her radiation treatments, because she needed help and support and someone to speak to doctors and nurses regarding day-to-day problems. My father went a few times, and when he did, he sat and made small talk with the other families.

He eventually married Bonnie. They bought a beautiful new house, a new car, and have traveled extensively. They eat out in the best restaurants and go to the theater. My mother had two insurance policies totaling over $60,000. She would turn over in her grave knowing the money was spent on his second wife.

I know it's not fair to resent him "living" when my mother is gone, but to "live it up" is unacceptable to me. I've heard him tell people that Bonnie is "the joy of my life."

The bottom line is: I no longer talk to him. I did not attend his wedding and I've never seen his new house. I never want to go there and see my mother's personal things used by her.

I have chosen to go on with my life and spend my time with my wonderful husband and three beautiful boys. I've heard people say that "life is short" and that I should mend my fences and get along with my father. But I feel, especially after losing my mother so young, that because "life is short," I shouldn't waste time on him.

My question is this: Based on the commandment "honor your mother and father," am I wrong not to forgive him and not to talk to him?

*Y*our pain and torment is gripping. It is always devastating to lose a mother. Your mother's untimely passing so prematurely in your own life exacerbates this situation. Most poignant of all are your feelings that your mother could have had a better life.

You do not indicate whether you have sought grief counseling. Even though several years have passed, I would think that someone professionally trained to walk a person through the many stages of grieving could still help you gain insight, perspective, and take the edge off your massive sorrow.

Here are some points to consider as they relate to your father:

1. My experience, supported by many studies, shows that men are at a far-greater loss and less able to cope when they lose their spouses than women. They don't seem to have the same resilience, the same capacity to pull themselves together and carry on with their lives in a reasonable fashion.

Often, finding himself at a loss and unable to cope on his own, a man will marry shortly after his wife's passing. This may seem callous to his children, but is actually an affirmation of his positive attitude toward marriage.

Surprisingly, men often let go of the very preconceived notions that previously held them hostage and limited their ability to fully enjoy life.

A case in point would be my friend Dr. Larry, a noted physician, who was a workaholic. His wife Judy was a beautiful and brilliant women who was obsessed with the well-being of her husband and three children. She was a hypercompulsive individual who worried about her family all the time. She became ill and battled cancer valiantly for seven years.

Dr. Larry was devoted and caring, but throughout all the years of her illness, he never missed a day's work. Judy understood and would have it no other way. Predictably, not too long after her death at age 52, Dr. Larry married a woman with two children. Lo and behold, he immediately took early retirement, moved to a quiet country estate with his new family, and took up gardening, reading, and a laid-back mode of living. I was incredulous.

I called him on some pretext, hoping for an explanation for this bizarre change in behavior that to me felt like a total betrayal of his wife.

He did explain. He told me of his terrible loneliness following Judy's death. He affirmed emphatically that he had loved Judy totally and completely. Then he met Ann. She was the complete antithesis of Judy. She was fun loving where Judy was intense. She was optimistic where Judy lived in constant fear of something awful happening to her family. Judy had an air of heaviness and Ann was light hearted and a ray of sunshine.

He told me that he made a conscious decision that having lived with the imminence of his wife's death for so long, he wanted the remaining years of his life to be as joyous as they could be. In a sense, the combination of confronting mortality with Ann's life-affirming personality liberated him, allowing him to make the most of his present situation.

Then he added a concluding statement that really touched me and gave me a window of insight that might benefit you as well. He said that despite the much-needed consolation and his new lease on life that he found with his present wife, without question he still wished he could have lived out his remaining years with his first wife Judy had he had the option.

Often the startling accommodations that are made in the second marriage, that, in retrospect, appear to have been impossible the first time around, are in fact more a product of "necessity is the mother of invention" and also born of insecurity. In a first marriage, the shared years of having and raising children, with all the good and the bad, forge a relationship of such oneness that the couple take each other for granted and take liberties they wouldn't dare risk in the more fragile second marriage.

The second time around, instinct dictates that they must open themselves up to a new way of thinking if the marriage is to survive. In the end, the concessions made of necessity may in fact result in a better life as one sheds old confining and limiting habits.

The point for you to consider is that your father's new life is not necessarily a value judgment, a condemnation, or even an improvement over his life with your mother. More constructively, you might view it as a different season in his life, one that requires changes and accommodations.

2. You state that your parents lived happily for nearly 40 years. Then you follow it up with the injustices, i.e., the miserliness and the lack of sensitivity on your father's part. If what you state is indeed the truth, no one can condone this behavior. But I think it might be instructive to recognize that in a marriage of many years' duration, both spouses must bear the responsibility for the nature and quality of that relationship. "Nobody can do to you what you won't allow them to do" goes the saying. Implicit in that statement is that somehow their life together worked for both of them. It was a product of who they were and what they needed from each other.

Projecting onto your mother a life of deprivation and the lack of the full joy she might have had, based on the life your father has today, is simply subjecting yourself to unjustifiable and unnecessary punishment and heartache.

3. You mention your father's insensitivity in the hospital, manifested in his infrequent visits and his passing the time by chatting with the other families. Here, as well, I would urge you, my dear reader, to assume a more charitable approach. People react to crisis and misfortune in different ways. Some fall apart, others withdraw. Your father may have been in denial, conducting business as usual in an effort to convince himself that life was normal. Remember that, by your own description, your father was heart broken after your mother died.

4. Another issue for you to confront is that in large measure your pain is due to the fact that your mother's passing came at a difficult time in your own life, when you needed her nurturing and support. You probably wished that your father would have stepped in to somewhat fill the terrible void in your life. Instead, he found "the joy of his life," leaving you feeling totally abandoned.

Most certainly, if he hadn't been so focused on himself and breaking out of his own grief and pain, he might have been more sensitive to your and your family's needs.

5. I also want you to consider the flip side of your situation. Over the years, I have seen situations where the grief-stricken father did not embrace life, and in addition to everything else the children had to contend with, they were saddled with the burden of a non-functioning, depressed parent. There is that silver lining in your cloud. Your father has a life and you don't have to worry about his well-being.

6. Your heartwarming account of what you did for your mother is inspiring. Be sure that every bit of it will always be a source of comfort to you. Nobody will ever take that away from you, and G-d will bless you for it.

7. Finally, your specific questions. I would advise you to work very hard to find within yourself the ability to establish a relationship with your father. It will require a great deal of strength. You will need to let go; to set aside your formidable resentments, and, based on the above-mentioned points, make a decision to think charitably and interpret events in the most positive way possible.

Ultimately, if you can do this, you will be the greatest beneficiary. You will be liberated from the necessity of constantly seeking negative justification to validate your denying the relationship. And make no mistake in thinking that you are taking up your mother's cause. Your mother, of blessed memory, is now residing in the world of truth, and most certainly does not take pleasure in this fractured relationship. Her soul will enjoy greater peace on high if there is peace in her family here below.

Moreover, you will grant your children the privilege of having a grandfather. And, perhaps most significantly, when your children grow up, you will have given them the greatest gift of all, a precious legacy — a lesson in life — namely, that through thick or thin, in gladness or great disappointment, as difficult as it may be, we do our utmost to accord honor to our parents. It may be the hardest work you will ever have to do, but "commensurate with the difficulty is the reward." All the best.

Family
Parenting Fundamentals

It seems that most of my friends and I grew up in dysfunctional homes. I am now married with four children ages 4 months to 6 years old, who all end up screaming at me if I don't do what they want right away. I think they learned the screaming from me. This is how they communicate because this was how I was communicated to as a child. I would like to have a healthy relationship with my children and want to stop this cycle of screaming. I would appreciate receiving some pointers from you on how to deal properly with my children. I tell myself not to get angry and in the meantime a bubble of anger and impatience slowly boils inside until I blow up. I know I'm doing something wrong and would love some advice.

Dysfunction has been defined as the state of affairs when there is a group of more than one person.

For starters, it is important to note that we are not doomed to perpetuate dysfunction or negative ways of interacting. We can, decisively, with the requisite effort, choose to break the cycle.

There is a wonderful comment by Rabbi Samson Raphael Hirsch regarding the Almighty's marching orders to Abraham upon his initiation as the first Patriarch of the Jewish people. He was commanded to "go, leave your land, your birthplace, and your father's home." Rabbi Hirsch posits that in order to build a Jewish world, it was necessary for Abraham to:

1. Leave his land, his country, his society, and its decadent culture.

2. Leave his birthplace, its cultural assumption of being locked into genetics and heredity.

The Jewish view is that while we may have predispositions, we also have the wherewithal and the free choice to get beyond them and make our own decisions.

And finally,

3. His father's home refers to the way he was raised in his family of origin. Abraham was instructed that it was imperative to abandon the destructive approaches of his own upbringing and to cultivate in their stead constructive modalities to raise his own offspring. The Torah records this road map as a guide for all of us, the descendants of Abraham.

Dealing with four little ones under the age of 6 can be a daunting task under the best of circumstances. I would recommend that you, my dear reader, not be so quick to judge yourself harshly. If you and your family can make it through the day intact, you're doing great.

As for bruised egos and the concern of scarring children for life, my rule of thumb (perhaps it was rationalization for survival's sake) was balance. Simultaneous with the goal to constantly upgrade my coping skills, I deliberately tried to offset any negative outbursts and overreactions by compensating for them with equally passionate and sincere expressions of love and positive effects such as compliments and boundless hugs and kisses. The good news is, thank G-d, despite my many mistakes, my children, for the most part, turned out great.

A helpful tool is to imagine a higher power dispatching an angel to videotape our response to the given situation. This tool can shape our attitude and moderate our reaction. Whether it's sliding on the kitchen floor courtesy of the spilled juice, the scattered Cheerios or the many little hands tugging at us all at once, a major shift takes place when we become aware and conscious that we are not alone and are being observed. Instead of "blowing it," we can, with a bit [maybe a lot!] of self-control, turn it into a moment of "profiles in courage."

Another tool is to disengage oneself (perhaps with just the infant in hand) and spend a brief few moments alone in another room. This might help to gain perspective, compose oneself, and avoid a major eruption (variations of the counting to 10 approach).

While there are many wonderful books on the subject of parenting, I believe every parent needs to keep the following four fundamentals in mind:

1. We are always the models for our children. They are constantly watching and observing us very carefully. They register our every behavior and response — especially when we are under stress. The Mishnah teaches that there are three ways to really know the truth about a person's character:

a. How does one act when he is angry?

b. How does one relate to spending money?

c. How does one behave when under the influence of alcohol, or what, in fact, intoxicates and thrills a person?

We transmit values to our children by what registers high on our emotional Richter scale. Is it a bad mark on the report card or being mean to another child? Is it crayon marks on the wall or beating up a sibling?

What intoxicates and exhilarates us? Is it the joy of a friend or a beautiful dress? For what are we willing to dish out money? Charity to the poor or redecorating the house? A new car? Designer clothes? Something to enhance the Shabbos table?

At a lecture a woman once asked me how she could transmit the skills to cope with the inevitable challenges in life to her children. The obvious response was that by the way we handle our own life's issues when we are stressed and overwhelmed conveys the message loud and clear.

2. Don't underestimate the value of staying home and doing your own parenting, regardless of the times you fall short of the excellence you would like to bring to this sacred trust. My most precious memories of childhood centered on the knowledge that my mother could always be found in the kitchen. It made us feel that there was nothing more important in my mother's life than caring for us.

Parenthetically, my mother didn't sit on the floor and play games with us or give us endless undivided attention, but she was there if we needed her and we knew where we could find her.

Of course in today's world not every woman can be a-stay-at-home mother. I have advised women who go to work to be very vigilant about the excitement they exhibit when coming home to their children. The message needs to be that they work in order to come home and not that they need to discharge their responsibilities at home in order to go to work. Implicitly and explicitly, home has to resound as the clear and unchallenged priority.

3. We need to be on a constant lookout to catch our children doing something right. The tendency is to take appropriate behavior for granted and comment only on the negative. Training ourselves to notice the positive and to give positive feedback on those occasions can be a behavior-altering experience for them. We can go a step further and not only compliment them but let them hear us tell a friend about it.

To this day, I recall overhearing my father, of blessed memory, talking late at night to his best friend. He extolled my virtues and spoke about how special I was to him. That moment gave me a wonderful, positive sense of self and strength that I have drawn on until this very day. There is no motivation more powerful than being treasured, respected, and held in high esteem. We are loath to disappoint the good opinion others have of us, most especially those of our parents who know us best.

4. Finally, a great rabbi once said that the key factors in raising good children are 50 percent prayers for strength and Heavenly assis-

tance and 50 percent "shalom bayis"— peace in the home between husband and wife. A psychologist recently noted that in his practice, teenagers are commonly brought into his office by their parents to deal with their acting out, chutzpah, and lack of respect toward their parents, siblings, and others. Invariably, he commented, that teenagers say to him, "Ask our parents how they interact with each other."

He concluded that in his experience, lack of respect of the children is most often a mirror image of what is happening in the home. Too many of the couples I counsel are so consumed by the demands of their children that the need to work on the spousal relationship is all but forgotten. Jewish tradition teaches that the focal point of the home must be the husband and wife — Mommy and Daddy. Children should be taught from the very start, that as important as they are, attention to one's spouse comes first. Knowing that Mommy and Daddy are there for each other, first and foremost, with respect, love, and caring infuses the children with a wonderful sense of well-being and confidence, as well as setting the example for the entire family.

I would encourage you, my dear reader, to network with friends who are experiencing this stage in life. There is no "one size fits all" solution but shared insights and tidbits can, at times, be helpful.

From my vantage point, looking back, my urging to you is that even as you struggle to do your best, don't miss out on the beauty. Even though you may not believe it, this stage goes by real fast and is no more than a memory all too soon. Sneak into your children's room at night when they are asleep and angelic looking, and thank G-d for the blessing even as you pray for the strength to do right by them.

Cookie and Baila, our oldest daughters, were born 14 months apart. I remember tiptoeing into their room one night, turning to my husband and saying, "Can you imagine that someday they will talk to each other and be good friends?" We blinked twice and today both are grandmothers!

Hang in there — the best is yet to come.

Sibling Rivalry

My husband does not get along with his older brother; they have huge problems, and money and ambition have driven them apart. My in-laws have never taught them how to avoid confrontation and how to respect each other.

I have three boys, ages 14, 10, and 4, and I worry a lot about their relationship with one another. I'm fearful of making the same mistakes as my in-laws. Whenever the boys fight over something I remind them that I don't want them to become like their father and uncle. I pray that they respect and love one another forever. Please give me any advice on how I can achieve this.

Your fervent desire to create an intact, loving family is admirable and an effort well placed. The family unit has been integral and essential to society as a whole and most certainly to the Jewish people. At the very beginning, even before our formal consecration as a people, we were instructed as a family to slaughter the deified paschal lamb before leaving Egypt. This courageous act required the nation, family by family, to observe what would henceforth be known as the Passover Seder.

To this day, no matter how estranged a Jew may be, this annual celebration still resonates, in great measure, because it is a family-centered holiday.

The concept of 'family' correctly conjures up images of caring, concern, brotherhood, acceptance, support — people who are there for us in the best and the worst of times. The sad reality is that the existential state of man is a very lonely one. This is especially true in our narcissistic and self-centered society where everyone is out for themselves. The fear of finding oneself alone, abandoned, and rejected is greater than ever before. The extended family of the past served as a refuge, a protective oasis against this existential terror.

Today, all that remains of this glorious institution is the immediate nuclear family, a mere vestige of what once was. We must be very cautious not to burn our bridges, but rather to preserve what remains of the family.

Our family recently suffered a tragedy. Our son-in-law was critically injured in a bus accident in Israel. The family mobilized instantly. Vigils around the clock were immediately organized. Offers of help came from everywhere. Unquestionably, only the Almighty can send our son-in-law a recovery. But we were able to survive and deal with the trauma because immediate family and all of our wonderful friends, who are our extended family, were there with us and for us, offering material, emotional, and spiritual support. Indeed our hearts are still broken, but thankfully we do not feel alone or abandoned.

Your worries are legitimate. The past can impact the future unless something interferes to break the pattern. Your impassioned expressions of concern to your children and your exhortations that they behave differently than the previous generation, while not useless, are of limited value and are only a very small piece of what needs to be done.

Robert Frost wryly remarked that the reason why worry kills more people than work is because more people worry than work. Changing a pattern requires a lot of hard work. Problems of sibling rivalry and hatred between brothers do not suddenly appear out of nowhere in adulthood. It does not happen in a vacuum. Parents like yourself, who are wise enough to want to avoid issues down the road, need to take action in the formative years of the children's lives when they are developing their sense of self.

For starters, each child must be appreciated for his own uniqueness, his individual assets. This, of course, is easier said than done because, invariably, the particular disposition of a given child may not as readily click with our own as that of another sibling who is more easily likable or more in sync with our expectations of them.

To favor one child over the other or to invoke comparisons between children, i.e., why can't you be as smart, kind, tidy, good etc., as your brother, is an almost sure guarantee of trouble, if not immediately, then certainly down the road.

Children must each be seen as diamonds in the rough. Some need a bit more polishing than others, but the objective is to uncover the particular facets of their individual, inherent brilliance. The ideal would be that every child should emerge from their home of origin convinced that they were their parents' favorite. A prominent psychologist noted that in an interview, when his teenage sons were asked what impacted them most in their childhood, they recalled their bedtime routine. When they were in pajamas, ready for sleep, their dad would come into the room to wish them good night. He would tickle them and remark lovingly, "How is it that of all the adorable and cute children in the world, I got the cutest and the most adorable?"

That special comment still warmed them so many years later. If a positive posture of secure standing and self-esteem can be fostered and achieved in this primary setting, children are unlikely to feel competitive and threatened by the good fortune of their siblings.

·JOSEPH AS A PARADIGM

Consider the Biblical example of Joseph and his brothers. The Patriarch Jacob had favored Joseph with a "coat of many colors." While there are many layers of deeper meanings not accessible in the literal interpretation, nonetheless, this did not bode well for the family dynamics and culminated in the brothers feeling sufficiently threatened that they sold their favored brother into slavery. The narrative relates how Joseph, after a painful odyssey, rose to power and became viceroy in Egypt. A famine in the land of Israel (Canaan at the time) brought the brothers to Egypt to seek food. The person holding the key to their survival was none other than the brother whom they had sold into bondage, who now recognized them, but whom they did not recognize. Joseph put his brothers to the test. He orchestrated events so that it appeared that their youngest brother, Benjamin (his only sibling from the same mother), had stolen a silver cup and would have to be detained and incarcerated in Egypt. The brothers made it clear to the viceroy (Joseph) that under no circumstances would they abandon or leave their brother Benjamin behind, even if they had to wage war and forfeit their lives.

It was at this moment that Joseph realized they had come full circle. Apparently, their deep remorse for the grievous mistake they had made 22 years earlier informed their present uncompromising stand. Repentance had taken place and Joseph knew the time had come to reveal his identity to them. Our Sages comment that as a result of his own suffering, Joseph's sensitivity to sibling issues was so strong that it configured his own parenting mode. The test of his success came when he brought his two sons, Menashe, the eldest, and Ephraim, the younger, to be blessed by his dying father, the Patriarch Jacob. Jacob prophetically intuited that Ephraim, the younger, would be the greater of the two boys, and hence when he placed his hands on their heads to bless them, he crossed them, so that his primary right hand would be positioned on the younger lad's head. Joseph objected, thinking his father had inadvertently made a mistake, but Jacob insisted that he knew exactly what he was doing.

Our Sages note that Menashe, the older son, could have perceived this as a terrible slight, a blow to his ego, but to his credit, it turned out to be a total nonissue. The two brothers were happy for each other. Joseph had raised two intact sons who were secure in their relationship, both with themselves and with each other and did not feel threatened by a sibling's good fortune.

MONETARY VALUES

The second issue implicit in your question is one of values. You write that "money and ambition have driven them apart." Unfortunately, this is a very familiar refrain. Consider the many "good" families that are convulsed and torn apart by issues of inheritance. The matriarch of a nationally prominent family confessed recently "money had destroyed her family."

Indisputably, money and material resources are important. Clearly, families have to be supported; food, clothing, shelter, leisure enjoyment, etc., have to be provided. But money must not become the be-all and end-all of human existence. It dare not become the shrine on which we bring our best offerings. It must not consume the best of our time, energy, and thoughts.

There is a very delicate balance in life between the pursuits of material resources and that of values. We must be careful not to cross this very precarious line. When life is tested to the ultimate, the bottom line is that it is the significant relationships in our life that matter, not money.

Someone aptly said: "Things that count can't always be counted. And things that are counted, don't always count."

When money becomes the priority in one's life, then wealth becomes the identity of the person and, consequently, a diminution in material resources comprises a lesser sense of self. Thus, sharing or parting with money becomes virtually impossible for this individual. Indeed it is tantamount to an amputation, an excision of a piece of his self, his very identity. He will stop at nothing to guard and protect his territory, even at the cost of the sibling relationship. If we don't want money issues to tear our family apart, then money cannot be the supreme value in our homes. The values of caring, feeling, giving, kindness, charity, relationships, learning, and growing need to be nurtured and celebrated.

In summary, our lines of defense must include the following:

1. Affirming and validating the personality of each child with love and affection.

2. Filling the family's life with values and worthwhile pursuits. For example: quality time together, classes on ethics and personal growth, charitable activities like visiting hospitals, homes for the elderly, hospices, volunteering, modeling the value of family cohesion by allowing the children to observe the homage and respect accorded to family members including and especially your own siblings.

3. Be mindful of family dynamics. If there is a healthy energy between parents, children's affection and fidelity will not be polarized; they will not have to take opposing and conflicting sides. Speak respectfully to each other. Disagree respectfully, appreciating that differing ideas are okay and should be heard, that everyone is entitled to his opinion.

4. Read books on constructive problem-solving. You might also feel better if you occasionally touch base with a professional to make sure you are covering all your bases.

5. Pay attention to the words you use in speaking of others, especially family members. Observe carefully to see if you find the good and positive in people. Do you give them the benefit of the doubt? Or do you jump to negative conclusions? It is crucial to create an atmosphere of approval and trust in order to avoid or counteract the cynicism and suspicion that is at the root of sibling rivalry. Toward this end, some families have incorporated a dinnertime routine where each family member shares something nice about the others at the table. Mom and Dad can begin the activity to break the ice. This can be an effective medium to train the minds of the family to think positive and engage in the kinds of behaviors that will be worthy of noting.

6. Notice and applaud the nice things that others and especially that your children do for one another. My son, Reb Ephraim, recently related that he had taken his 7-year-old son, Yidele, to the local Jewish library where each family was permitted to reserve two books. On the way out he asked his son which two books he had reserved. His son replied that he had reserved only one. When questioned as to why not the two allotted to each family, Yidele replied that perhaps his sister would want one in the future, so he did not want to use up the quota. Not a big deal perhaps, but for me it was reminiscent of Yidele's father, my son, who, as a young child, would never accept a gift of candy for himself if one was not forthcoming for his sister who was 13 months younger. (I have to admit this was not necessarily ubiquitous behavior among all my children.)

These are the attributes to talk about, celebrate, and make a big deal over, thereby demonstrating to our children that these behaviors are greater accomplishments in our eyes than good marks or scholastic achievements. We will thereby establish them firmly as cherished and essential values in our home.

Here, a note of comforting qualification is in order. Quibbling and occasional spats among siblings, such as the older besting and pulling rank over the younger, and the younger crying wolf over the injustice of it all, while not pleasant or desirable, is for the most part within the range of normalcy. It comes with the territory of raising children. My family came to American after World War II. We were five siblings at the time. We were temporarily housed in a hotel for refugees in Manhattan. We were objects of interest — we were Yiddish-speaking tots, delighted with life, and everyone thought that we were absolutely the cutest. On one occasion, my older 8-year-old brother (I am second in line) had just finished giving me a punch in the back (of course, for no reason at all, I was such an angel). An unsuspecting, admiring stranger approached us just at that moment and commented, "You're such darling, well-behaved children. I bet you never fight." My brother looked up and with angelic innocence replied, "Oh, no. We never fight. The Torah prohibits it." As soon as the fellow turned his back, he hit me with another punch, the second installment. Nonetheless, even at that moment, had a stranger or an outsider threatened to hurt me, my brother would have punched his lights out. Gratefully, in our adult life, all my siblings, with my oldest brother at the helm, are very devoted and protective of one another.

7. Finally, pray for Heavenly assistance and wisdom and may the Almighty grant you success.

Family
Age-Old Tension

A year and a half ago, I lost my only sibling, an older brother. This loss occurred at a particular difficult time in our life. I had difficulty in conceiving and when I did, I suffered multiple miscarriages. My mother has suffered terribly through this difficult time, and we have tried very hard to be there for her, but lately that has become more difficult.

You see, after a complicated pregnancy, I am finally about to give birth to what appears to be a healthy son. My parents are over the moon and my husband and I are also thrilled that we can help the whole family affirm life again after a period of so much loss. As the months have ticked by, a new problem arose. My mother seems to have become more and more confused about whose baby this is. I know it's not deliberate. I even understand that boundary issues are inevitable with a first child who is also a first grandchild. But I'm so emotional lately, and we've all been through so much, that even though I try to set limits in the kindest and most loving manner, I come away from each discussion wracked with guilt.

Most of my mother's suggestions have some merit, but sometimes she takes them to an extreme level. For example, during my first trimester, she said she wanted to keep a crib in her house so that the baby would have a place to nap when we visit. This seemed reasonable, so of course we said thank you and offered to pay for a portable crib that would stay in her house. We didn't feel comfortable with the part of her plan that involved buying a used crib at a garage sale. We gently explained that we had read that used equipment didn't always meet today's safety standards, and though we knew she wouldn't pick anything obviously dangerous, it would be difficult to assess wear and tear, etc. She seemed to understand.

As time went on, the simple crib has evolved into a fully equipped nursery with all the trimmings that she refers to as "Aaron's room." (That will be his name, after my husband's grandfather.) We find the phrasing a little unnerving, and though we certainly plan to visit my parents with the baby, there's no need to set him up to live in her house. We haven't confronted her about this, because we simply can't think of a compassionate way of saying that we're sorry she lost her son, but she can't replace him with ours.

Meanwhile, every time we see her or speak to her, Mom talks about more and more equipment she can get for "her nursery" at a good price at flea markets and garage sales. Every time we answer that buying books, toys, or clothes at these places is fine, but when it comes to cribs, high chairs, and car seats, we would rather bring our own on visits. Then she says yes, yes, sure, only to bring up the idea again the next time we speak.

Finally, a few days ago, she cheerfully told me that she had just bought a stroller at a garage sale. I told her I didn't feel comfortable with that, and instead of acknowledging that she had just stepped over a line I had long since established, she pretended we had never had a discussion about this. So after repeating my concerns, I explained that I was beginning to wonder whether we could trust her to respect our wishes when we left the baby alone with her if she couldn't even respect them in our presence.

I didn't yell; I tried to phrase things as gently as possible, but I felt I had to say something. Mom has made it clear that she not only expects frequent visits with the three of us, she *also expects us to leave the baby with her overnight on a fairly regular basis. And as much as I want to grant her wish, especially after all of her hardships, I can't believe that Jewish law would require me to ignore my own maternal instincts, and allow my feelings to be trampled just to please my mother, no matter how much grief she has endured.*

She hasn't heard what I've been saying for months; but she heard me a few days ago, and now she's not speaking to me. I feel terrible for having hurt her, but also angry that she's hurt me, and unsure of what to do now. My whole life I've tried to be a good daughter, balancing caring for my parents with tending to my own needs. But I've never been a mother before. Suddenly I'm about to have a whole new awesome priority, the care of a helpless child. And I feel that his well-being has to outweigh everything, even my mother's feelings.

I try to live my life guided by Jewish values, and I wasn't sure who else I could share this with who would take the mitzvah to honor parents seriously. Is there some way I can help my mother hear me? Is there some way I can help myself let go of the guilt I feel for causing her pain?

Thank heaven for the blessing of your forthcoming child (with G-d's help). As you intimated, the intensity of your responses to your mother are colored by the enormous tensions produced not only by the loss of an only sibling but also by the emotional drain of your efforts to have a child. It is a tribute to your sensitivity that you recognize this and a measure of your character that you seek the clarity of a balanced perspective.

Interacting appropriately, effectively, and responsibly with parents is a challenge even in the best of times. There is a delicate and precarious juggling mode that has to be invoked and constantly refined. We owe our parents a great deal, if for nothing else than for the gift of life itself. It is also undeniable, that in most cases, as seems to be the case with your own mother, that they have the benefit of the wisdom born of experience. They can potentially be an invaluable resource and it would be foolish not to take advantage of it. Concurrently, parents don't always negotiate the tension between enhancing their children's lives with the legitimate expertise, while also giving them wings to chart their own course, even if it involves making mistakes.

Similarly children struggle with, on the one hand, honoring their parents, while attempting to define themselves as a distinct identity of their own. In either case, it is a very delicate and often painful balancing act. One of the essential points to remember is to choose your battles very carefully, to be certain, as someone put it, that this is "the hill we want to die on." There are times when we attribute too much importance and even malevolent intent in a given interaction where none exists. In our mind, conceding is tantamount to capitulation that in our estimation will result in total loss of control. There are times when this might be well founded, but more often than not, we are best advised to deal with the immediate situation at hand and not to "awfulize" — to take it to the worst possible conclusion of what might be, could be, or will be. Our sages advise "suffice or limit a troubling situation to its hour of conflict." Obviously, limits and boundaries must be respected and violations of such addressed. Often, as appears to be the case here, when the waters are made too murky with misunderstanding and miscommunication, and vision is clouded, the input of a third party, a mediator, might be advisable.

You do not indicate whether your family sought counseling in the aftermath of your terrible loss. Therapeutic intervention would be advisable in dealing with the complicated issues that surface in situations such as these. It must be remembered that if they are not confronted, they will invariably spill over and taint other areas of life.

You are anticipating a blessed event, the realization of a long-awaited personal dream. A child thrives in an environment of extended family. "It takes a village to raise a child" is not an exaggerated statement. While parents are the primary source of influence, grandparents for those who are fortunate to have them can be a very close second. Husband and wife need to nurture their own relationship, and that can be done much more easily when there are grandparents who can fill in for an evening or a weekend. They are not mere babysitters. They can be a uniquely loving and beneficial influence in a child's life. They are also a critical link in the generational history of a people and help a child understand the concept of being part of a whole — with a past, present, and future.

An apocryphal anecdote is related of a three-generational family living together: Grandpa who was getting on in years, Mom and Dad who went to work daily, and 5-year-old Davey. Grandpa's health began to deteriorate, his gait become unsteady, and his hands began to shake. On occasion, he would drop a glass or plate at mealtimes. Mom decided that to avoid the aggravation, the cost, and the hassle, she would henceforth provide Grandpa's meals in a wooden dish and a wooden cup. And so it was, the family ate on bone china and Grandpa had his wooden plate.

Mom came home from work one day and found Davey making an awful racket, with play hammer in hand, chopping away with great intensity. Exasperated by the noise, she asked Davey what in the world he was building. Davey responded, "I am getting your wooden plate ready for you for when you get older and your hands begin to shake."

We all need to be aware that even as we move toward motherhood, the status of the grandparent awaits us around the corner. By the grace of G-d, you will, inevitably, be in that role and in a sense, as life takes its toll, you will be at the behest of your children's charitable understanding. There is no teacher more powerful than a model of behavior. If you can be charitable, especially in difficult situations, your children will learn charity. They will understand that circumstances are not always ideal and there are times when painful choices have to be made. Though such concessions might appear to be to our own detriment, ultimately they define us as better human beings.

I would recommend that you do the following:

1. Focus on taking care of yourself physically and emotionally.

2. Don't obsess about worrisome eventualities, i.e., your mother's taking over and claiming the baby as her own. The baby is yours and you alone will determine the parameters and extent of your mother's involvement when the time comes.

3. Relax and appreciate the value of an interested, experienced, and caring grandparent in the awesome responsibility of raising a child. There are few things in life that I envy. I do remember, however, many years ago on my many trips to the park with my young children, that I would observe a kindly grandfather lovingly overseeing the well-being of my neighbor's children. I lived at a great distance from my parents and for me this privilege was never an option.

4. The way you interact with your mother, your sensitivity and deference will ultimately serve as a guide as to how you will be treated by your own children.

5. I would suggest that you call your mother and apologize for any hurt you might have caused her. Tell her that you appreciate her caring and her desire to be involved — and that certainly you will draw on her wisdom and experience. In an effort not to overreact, try to steer clear of elaborations and discussions of "Aaron's room." You might tell her that you are more comfortable minimizing extensive discussion of such before the actual fact of his birth at which time it will be more relevant and appropriate. (This, parenthetically, is the traditional approach. In most communities, practical and concrete preparations are made only after the birth of a child.)

Furthermore, you might gently say that since you both are presently stressed to the limit, further plans about visitation, etc., should be postponed and dealt with when it becomes relevant. At that time, you will be able to evaluate it on a situation-by-situation basis and decide what you feel comfortable committing to.

Remember that nothing is written in stone — no lifetime contracts have been signed. Relax. Cherish every moment. And may G-d bless you with a healthy baby and him with a healthy mom.

Family
Broken Home, Shattered Family

My husband's 14-year-old daughter is constantly in a rage. This is acceptable behavior at her mother's house, but I cannot tolerate it when she visits us. We have a 12-year-old plus three younger children, and I am concerned about them emulating her behavior.

On one occasion I asked her to clear away the breakfast dishes. When she refused, I punished her by taking away her phone. Her father was not at home when this happened and she repeatedly screamed at me, "You can't punish me, you're not my mother." Since then, she has not been back.

I believe she owes me an apology, but I've been assured that there is no hope of one in my future. How do I handle this? We attended a funeral for a family member, and she used the opportunity to tell the other mourners how much she hated me. She says I have taken away her father. Please help.

THE TEEN CHALLENGE ·

A stepmother's role is difficult at best, especially if the natural parents fail to realize that they are harming their child if they fail to maintain a cordial, if not friendly relationship. Much too often, these parents use their children as pawns to hurt the ex-spouse, and when they do the children are the innocent victims. Nevertheless, stepmothers can succeed even in such situations.

Teenagers, like your 14-year-old, can indeed be a handful, either because they are groping for self-identity and/or because they are struggling with hormonal changes.

Part of this is manifested in their reluctance to readily accept adult authority — that is, they resist being told what to think, do, or how to behave. Even biological parents, who represent the primary authority figure in their children's lives, don't win popularity contests in this season of the teenager's life.

It helps to keep in mind that this is one of the most conflicted times in their lives albeit a necessary passage. We have to work hard not to take the flack too personally. We have to try to go with the flow. On one hand, we must maintain boundaries, and on the other, not overreact.

The Rabbi of Kotsk gave a very powerful interpretation of this commandment from the Torah;

"You shall not oppress any widow or orphan. If you oppress him so that he cries out to me, then I shall surely listen to his cry" (Exodus 22:21-22).

In this verse, in the Hebrew, three verbs are used consecutively: "oppress," "cry out," and "listen." The Rebbe of Kotsk explained that when a person has experienced a traumatic blow in life such as losing a spouse or a parent, and is dealt yet a new blow, not only does the current pain hurt and shake his system, but it rips open the gaping wound of the original trauma. Any offense to these victims is a double offense, one for the current pain and one for the original pain.

· **PROFOUND PAIN**

Children of divorced parents are vulnerable. Their sense of loss is close to the surface and always with them. If we add a divorce situation to the teenage scenario described above, the reader's description of her situation is fairly predictable. Outbursts, lashing out, and "hating" a stepmother are expressions at some basic level of the profound pain a child of divorce feels.

But these children are true victims. Their world has fallen apart. They have lost the feeling of being safe; a feeling that is essential to every child's healthy growth and development. They live in constant fear of abandonment always thinking, *Who is going to walk out on me next?* They consciously or unconsciously yearn, no matter how unrealistically, for their natural parents to remarry, and thus to be reinstated into a "real" family once again.

I would advise the stepmother not to take the situation personally. Instead, she needs to reach out and try to alleviate the child's feeling of loneliness and possible depression.

Engaging the intervention of a third party, such as a counselor or therapist, would certainly be advisable, but sensitive consideration should be given before suggesting therapeutic intervention. I would recommend presenting the therapeutic option as a means of building a constructive relationship by addressing deeper issues that are getting in the way. The natural parents would be ideal candidates for initiating the discussion.

The choice of a therapist is also critical. He or she must have expertise both in dealing with children of divorce and with teenagers.

Concurrently, as part of the process, the therapist would help the stepchild understand his or her boundaries, such as acceptable language, tone of voice, content of discussion, etc.

The great Chassidic master, the Baal Shem Tov, once counseled a parent distraught over his son's wayward behavior with the ever-powerful advice, "You must love him more than ever."

Blended families are an enormous challenge and require an immense investment of time, sweat, and tears before desirable results are achieved. But, take heart: it has been done before, and with perseverance your family will be successful as well.

Family
Childhood Jealousy

I have two children — one is 22 months old and the second is 7 months. At first my older daughter hardly noticed my younger daughter, but now she sometimes displays acts of jealousy. For example, sometimes while she is playing with the baby and making her laugh, she will suddenly hit the baby. I'm not sure how to react to this, and I would appreciate some advice. Thank you.

our concern is quite understandable. Fortunately, there is no need to agonize over the scenario you described. Early-childhood sibling rivalry is very common and developmentally appropriate for the ages of your children. Your eldest daughter being your first child enjoyed an almost idolized place in your mind. And to see her respond to her sister in a less than desirable way is disconcerting.

To best appreciate where she is coming from you need to understand her perception of reality. Until the arrival of her sister, her status was one of exclusivity. She was the one and only, with all the attention of her parents lavished on her alone. Now along comes this interloper who doesn't go away and, what's more, gets cuter and invites more attention away from her every day.

The Talmud comments that no two people can wear one crown. Your eldest is feeling that her crown is being threatened. She is at risk of not reigning supreme. Understandably, this is not a good feeling and her attempt to defend her territory is inevitable and completely normal. Rest assured that this situation does not imply in any which way that you are deficient in your mothering skills or that your love when extended to both children is lacking. It is merely a necessary passage.

A compelling interpretation of your child's perception of reality with the new arrival on the scene is what to women would be comparable to a husband bringing home a new wife with the expectation that this new darling creature would be enthusiastically welcomed and embraced as the new beneficiary of shared love and attention. Needless to say, even a seasoned adult would be less than thrilled at the prospect.

The transition for your child, while painful, is one of those "necessary losses." My brother-in-law, a psychiatrist, once noted that the valuable but painful lessons in life are most effectively and best learned in the loving and supportive context of the family. It is inevitable that when your child comes out into the world, she will have to share center stage in life with many others. Much as we might like, life does not allow us, nor would it be in our ultimate best interest, to exclusively occupy the center of the universe. There is no better place to adjust to what might appear as this harsh, existential reality than within the home, where the care and affection of parents, in a sense, eases the blow by lovingly teaching the values that make it all the more palatable.

Some practical suggestions offered by expert mothers I consulted are:

- A child under the age of 2 must always be watched and not allowed to be in the company of the baby alone and unsupervised. A child of 2 cannot be expected to exercise self-control. Since the response to the new baby will invariably be, as you described it, a love tinged by resentment, it may well be the resentment will be expressed in injurious ways, such as biting and hitting, etc.

- A protected area, out of bounds for the baby and, laden with the older child's favorite toys, i.e. puzzles, building blocks, etc. and perhaps even covered with her favorite sheet, might work as her "kingdom" — as her special place to play while Mommy is attending to the baby.

- Supply the older child with a doll or stuffed animal, with attending crib, changing pad, and stroller to care for simultaneously as Mom nurses and feeds the baby. Get as much mileage out of it, by making it a venue for instruction. If the child handles the doll or stuffed animal too roughly, shaking or throwing it vigorously, etc., very calmly point out that this is not the way we do it. We care for a baby by holding it gently, patting it on the back, making nice, and kissing it.

- When feeding and attending to the baby, sing a song with the older child, read or tell her a story, play a game, or whatever is age appropriate. Take every opportunity to point out that she is "the one," the one who is old enough to do all these wonderful things, and when baby grows up perhaps she will also be able to do them.

- You might allow your child to sit down and with your assistance briefly hold the baby and make nice, etc., but when you see her beginning to get a bit rough, take the baby and assure her that tomorrow we will do it again.

- Give your older child as much personal attention as you can and be sure to express your love for her. Remind her that the baby loves her so much and is lucky to have such a wonderful big sister.

A calm, watchful response is the desirable approach. Try not to let your disappointments evoke anger. In anger you are almost certain to overreact and your daughter will learn to engage in negative behavior to provoke you in order to get your attention, which in turn will make you angrier, and you will have started the cycle spinning.

Stay calm. Remember that this is all part of the agony and ecstasy of raising children. One of my daughters claims that commensurate with the sibling rivalry of their youth is the great love and admiration they have for each other as adults. In her opinion it is still a combination of love and resentment — love for the remarkable people their siblings are, and resentment of herself for coming up short. She insists that among the families she has observed, those who had little discernable rivalry as youngsters ultimately had an apathetic attitude toward one another as adults (This has not been, to the best of my knowledge, confirmed by official studies.)

As conscientious and devoted mothers, all we can do is try our best. Our children are our most sacred trust — diamonds in the rough — to be polished in order to uncover their own personal and individual brilliance, each one unique and special in his own right. May G-d bless you with the requisite patience, strength, and insight. And may your children give you great joy.

Family

Celebrating Differences:
Tips for Effective Parenting

Some of our readers have requested insights and tips on child-rearing. I, like parents everywhere, have researched, soul-searched, agonized, and prayed a lot for guidance in raising children. Thank G-d, I have 11 truly wonderful children, who have provided me with a lot of instructive experience. There is a Hebrew expression that translates into "what wisdom does not confer, time will."

In Genesis, Jacob at the end of his life blesses his 12 sons. Each blessing is distinct, more a description of a given son's particular strength and concomitant responsibility than an overall wish for his well-being. The individuality of each son emerges clearly, indicating a unique role for each in shaping the totality of the Jewish people.

From our inception, Judaism celebrates and applauds differences and diversity.

· · · · RESPECT THE INDIVIDUALITY OF EACH CHILD

As a mother of 11, I have often been approached by mothers and fathers for advice and have heard them verbalize some frustrations at the lack of generic tools for parenting. What works with one child fails miserably with another.

Most recently, I was struck with a perfect example of this while being escorted to a speaking engagement by a mother and her six children. During the drive from the airport, I was surprised by how well mannered and respectful the children's interactions were with one another, as well as with their mother. Yet, I could glean from the various conversations that the children had very different personalities.

When I remarked on this, the mother, Nancy, told me that she had a rude awakening when her second child was born. Her first child had been what you'd describe as a "perfect" baby — calm, serene, a real pleasure. The second child was easily agitated, temperamental, sensitive, and generally difficult. Those very effective parenting techniques she employed with her first child became totally ineffective with her second. Then came child number three, four, five, and six.

After reading many books and seeking out networking and professional support groups, Nancy figured out that she'd be a more successful parent by celebrating her children's differences rather than imposing upon them identical preconceived notions and expectations. Her newfound openness allowed her to identify each child's personality traits — strengths and weaknesses — thereby enabling her to formulate realistic expectations for each child.

Nancy realized that comparisons among her children were irrelevant. She committed her energy to the development of each child's individual potential. She sought out extracurricular activities and encouraged avocations that suited each child's temperament — art and music for the creative one, supplementary learning for the scholastically inclined, and social opportunities for the "people person." In short, she worked hard to provide opportunities for each one of her children to shine, and in so doing helped each develop a healthy self-esteem.

INSTILL POSITIVE SELF-IMAGE·················

Every human being yearns for a positive self-image. If a child senses he is a disappointment to those who should love him unconditionally, in desperation, he might seek approval elsewhere, often with negative and destructive peer groups.

Parents are powerful influences in their children's lives. They need to be conscious that children see themselves as reflected in their parents' eyes.

Jamie, a bright, good-looking young man, tearfully described to me how his father's approval had eluded him throughout his 20 years. His father's steady stream of criticism and infrequent kind words had bruised and battered his psyche until there was little left to his self-esteem. He is depressed, unmotivated, and without any direction. He has already been in therapy for a long time and the road to achieving emotional health seems long and arduous.

On the other hand, I was blessed with a father who contributed in every way possible to developing my positive self-worth. Memories of overhearing my father speak glowingly of me to his friends during late-night chats still warm me. Positive feedback offered to a child, either directly or indirectly, is essential to raising emotionally healthy children.

············CRITICIZE BUT ALSO COMPLIMENT

For those who are undertaking the journey to effective parenting, the following points might be considered:

1. Heed King Solomon's exhortation to "raise each child according to his or her individual path."

2. Criticize sparingly and at the appropriate time. Wait until criticism can be heard effectively.

3. Offer criticism with love. My father-in-law rebuked his sons with "this behavior doesn't become you." Twenty-five years after his passing, his sons still strive to live up to his high opinion of them.

4. Counter every piece of criticism with five positive comments. Always be on the lookout to catch your children in the act of doing something right for which they can receive praise.

5. Hug and kiss your children for no particular reason. This might compensate for those times you might inadvertently hurt their feelings.

6. As the saying goes, "Our children will do as we do not as we preach," and therefore it is important that we model the behaviors we expect from our children.

7. Our mental health impacts immeasurably on our parenting. Children pick up on the slightest nuances in emotional balance. It is therefore imperative that along with our efforts to be good parents, we pursue avenues of personal growth be it through therapy, learning, support groups, creative outlets, etc.

8. Finally, pray, pray, and pray some more. Pray that your efforts will be met with success and that you'll see much nachas, pleasure, from your children.

Family
Retirement Blues

Retirement often makes people feel useless and worthless, but a change of perspective can turn that around.

> *My husband and I are together 24/7. He is retired and does not have a lot of interests. I try to stay busy, yet want to include him in my life and to meet his needs. Please give me your wisdom.*

Retirement is a difficult passage to negotiate. For one, we live in a capitalistic society where "productivity" is the primary value, and to that end "making money" is the measure of a person's success. Given this perspective, as long as one is hustling in the marketplace, there is an illusion of a sense of purpose.

My father-in-law, of blessed memory, a very wise rabbinic counselor, advised his aging constituents to slow down, but never to retire. He maintained that for most people giving up what was their only source of gratification could send them into a downward spiral of ultimately feeling useless and depressed.

Consider Sherri whose father had been a prominent physician. He suffered a debilitating heart attack. The practice of medicine was no longer an option for him. But medicine was all he knew. He had never cultivated any other interest in life and when the context of his single focus was no longer viable, his life fell apart and he lost his desire to live.

PERSPECTIVE ON MORTALITY

One of the basic underlying currents of our society's obsession and frenzied preoccupation with "work" is the lack of perspective on death and mortality.

A comedian once commented that in our society death appears to be optional, or put another way, "he doesn't mind dying as long as he doesn't have to be there when it happens."

Since we don't have a handle on our mortality, we deal with it by distracting ourselves. Work, careers, making money, and being "successful" are all convenient and often desperate ways of deluding ourselves into thinking that we can escape the inevitable.

This may appear to work as long as we are marketable, in our prime years, and still have the requisite physical stamina. However, when the retirement years set in, and we are bereft of our busy routine, the exits are closed; facing our mortality becomes inescapable. We find ourselves staring at a massive bridge to be crossed with no tools or mechanism in place.

THE JEWISH VIEW

In contrast to the current youth-oriented society, Judaism has always venerated its elders. It was understood that age brought with it wisdom and valuable experience. The Torah states:

> *Remember the days of old, consider the years of many generations; ask your father, and he will relate it to you; your elders, and they will tell you (Deuteronomy 32:7).*

Jews were enjoined to rise in respect before their elders, and the older the sage, the greater was the honor accorded to him. Deference to age was mandatory.

My parents, of blessed memory, would visit us in Milwaukee twice each year. Their first stop en route from the airport was to the home of my elderly mother-in-law. My father suffered from heart disease and the trip was not an easy one for him, but he always insisted on making this first and primary stop because, as he put it, tradition demanded that we show respect and deference to those of advanced age.

Rabbi Yaakov Kamenetsky, a luminary of our time, was once on a plane flying from Israel to New York accompanied by a son. The Rosh Yeshivah was in business class and his son in coach. The son tirelessly propped up the great rabbi's pillow, served him drinks, and generally fussed over him the entire trip. A fellow traveler had observed the unbelievable care and attention given by the son with such love and reverence to his father.

Near the conclusion of the flight, with awe in his voice, the traveler asked how, in our day and age, it was possible to achieve a relationship of such deference by the young to the elderly. Rabbi Yaakov responded that the finest moment in collective Jewish history was the revelation at Mount Sinai, the giving of the Torah more than 3300 years ago. Hence, from a Jewish perspective, the closer one is to that source and defining event, the loftier and more spiritually exalted and connected is the person.

Therefore, explained Rabbi Yaakov, the younger generations look with great regard to those who preceded them. In contrast to that view, one who sees his ancestor as descending from the apex, sees himself as the advanced model, worthy of greater esteem than his elder. It all depends on your point of departure, Rabbi Yaakov concluded.

Inherent in this perspective is that there is more to life then the current value of "making a living." In fact, inherent in our Jewish legacy is the highest regard for family life, connecting with others, giving charity, giving of oneself, studying Torah, and learning the principles of our tradition. These are the real substance of life.

If one incorporates and cultivates these time-honored values as lifetime pursuits, one would not feel as diminished when the need to retire from the workforce is mandated. Conversely, the singular focus on "work" to the exclusion of the cultivation of other values and pursuits can be devastating on what should be the "golden" and "harvest" years of one's life.

SOME ADVICE

In coping with a retired husband, it is important to understand that he has a very difficult adjustment to make. A man's identity in our society is very closely related to his "work" and the loss of that "productive" stage in life is unsettling at best; this "stage" can be diminishing and devastating in terms of his feelings of self-worth. He needs more than ever to feel that he is still a desirable, functioning, and contributing member of the human race.

Toward this end, a wife can either "make him or break him." She needs to guard against confirming his greatest fears that his presence and his very existence are superfluous and a burden.

Here is some practical advice:

Even though he maintains that he has no interest, in deference to her wishes and desires, husband and wife could take a class together (spirituality, art, music, etc.). Encourage him to volunteer in places that would allow him to use or develop his specific talents, for example, tutoring remedial students, visiting the homebound, etc.

While excessive nudging and nagging in a spousal relationship doesn't work, it might be helpful to do some discreet inquiry and maneuvering behind the scenes. Consult a rabbi or the head of outreach centers or men's groups about your husband. Perhaps they can solicit his participation in either learning one on one, teaching, or whatever activities they might see as beneficial for him.

Family is always important, but at this stage in life it can be a soothing balm for the hurting psyche. If there are no biological grandchildren, "adopt" a grandchild. Set up time to spend in a park, playing ball, swimming, etc. These activities can infuse life with newfound energy and purpose.

Finally, I would like to share an encounter that shakes me up each time I think of it even though it actually took place more than 30 years ago. I was young and newly married. Martha, a cousin of my husband's, came to visit from England. She was an elegant aristocratic woman who was ordinarily very formal and reserved in her behavior. I was, therefore, surprised to find her in my kitchen one morning. She began to tell me about Harold, her late husband. He was a wonderful, gentle, and kindly man. She was the "strong" one in the family and he always deferred to her. She ran the show and he never demanded anything from her. She went about, day to day busily attending to the "important" things in her life, fully expecting that some day she would focus and spend more time with Harold, who she assumed would always be there. There didn't seem to be any urgency.

Then, without warning and totally unexpectedly, one day he collapsed and died. I can still hear her sobs these many years later. "Feigele," she cried, "I can perhaps come to terms with the fact that he died prematurely and left me alone, but I am haunted and inconsolable that I took him and his presence for granted. I will never forgive myself for not taking the time to tell him how much he meant to me."

I would remind the reader that while having a husband around 24/7 can be trying, she should not lose sight of the bigger picture. Many interests in life appear to be terribly significant, but the greatest gift by far is the presence and companionship of a spouse. Indeed, we must confront our issues, but at the same time we must work hard not to allow our "busy" schedules to obscure our greatest blessing.

Personal Growth

Personal Growth
Appropriate Guilt

It's hard for me to differentiate between guilt and self-improvement. I feel this especially now. There are three people in the immediate community who are seriously ill. The news is frightening. There are a few small things I have changed in the hopes that this will serve to benefit them. But in the scheme of things they seem minor. I sometimes feel guilty about feeling happy with my family and security when others don't have this. In another vein, does working on controlling anger count if after ten calm days one explodes?

There is a great difference between conventional guilt and the Jewish concept of guilt. Conventional guilt keeps one enmeshed in the past, wallowing and repeatedly obsessing about past wrongdoing and misdeeds. It leaves one feeling unworthy and unredeemable.

In contrast, Jewish guilt means regretfully admitting inappropriate behavior and moving on to assimilate and integrate the insights gained into one's ensuing daily living. It is present and future oriented. It maintains that to err is human and no experience in life is a failure if we learn from it and are modified by it.

Your sensitivity to the necessity for personal contributions to the troubling events of our times are right on target. We all desperately seek relief from the terrible darkness that surrounds us, both collectively and individually. It mandates that each of us light a candle, in our own way, given our unique resources and individual circumstances. Each of us has to assume responsibility to effect the change that we want to see.

In the Book of Ruth, we read of Elimelech, a wealthy leader of the Jewish people. At a time of his people's suffering and travail, he chose to distance himself and abandon them. Erroneously, he assumed that since the calamity had not affected him directly, he was free of responsibility for his fellow people. He paid with his life for this reprehensible attitude.

You have correctly identified a most critical area of contribution — the work we need to do in the inner landscape of our person. Working and effecting change internally on our character attributes and attitudes toward life is the most productive approach to creating a better world. Precisely because it is unquestionably the most difficult battlefront, the very Heavens stand in awe of every effort to confront our shortcomings and proceed to put forth the requisite toil to achieve personal change and growth. Rabbi Yisroel of Salant commented that the loudest sound in the universe is that of a person breaking old behavior patterns and putting constructive ones in their place. Every time we wish to respond in the predictable, unacceptable mode of old, whether in anger, pride, selfishness or excessive ego-involvement, and by dint of exercising control and invoking the better part of ourselves we hold our tongue or modify our reaction accordingly, it is of ultimate value.

Your concern that this position of control cannot be maintained 100 percent of the time and hence the subsequent outbursts invalidate the success of your resolve is unwarranted. In all of growth there are relapses. We move up a number of steps and then predictably regress a notch or two. This is the nature of human growth and should not discourage or dissuade us. We must persevere. Old patterns are not easily changed and every bit of effort exerted brings us closer to achieving the purpose and the reason that we were put on this earth. This is the case under all circumstances and most especially in our troubled times.

These are the best offerings that we can bring in an effort to promote healing and positive energy into the world. These are the loftiest expressions of self-sacrifice. As one of the commentaries notes, "To live with Kiddush Hashem, sanctifying G-d's Name, is an even greater achievement than to die with Kiddush Hashem. A lifetime dedicated to self-transcendence, dedicating oneself to the will of G-d, surpasses the once in a lifetime transcendence of martyrdom. Not to die for G-d, but to set our will and impulse aside in deference to Him and His understanding of the appropriate behavior that is ultimately in our best interest and should be our goal.

You write that under the circumstances you feel guilty about being happy with your family and your security. It is important to understand that from a Torah perspective that everything we are given in life, both the desirable and that which appears to be less desirable, are all part of Divine Providence and orchestration. Having "good" things in life is not arbitrary or a product of "luck." It is all part of the "tailor-made" context of our life, structured and prescribed by the Almighty as necessary for the unique challenges with which we must deal.

The challenge of adversity demands a perspective of courage and strength. The challenge of "good" demands a perspective of sharing, appreciation, and abiding gratitude. To sustain an attitude of feeling blessed is not an easy matter. Human beings generally focus not on what we have but what we would like to have. To enjoy security and family is not only appropriate, it is imperative. Our Sages teach us that one of the reasons we recite blessings throughout the day is to make us conscious of G-d's beneficence that surrounds us — food, clothing, fragrant flowers in bloom, milestones, holidays, and even life itself, as we recite the "modeh ani" blessing at the dawning of each new day of existence with which we are favored. These are all gifts for our enjoyment. As a matter of fact, we are told that after our mortal existence we will have to answer for the legitimate joys in life that were available to us and of which we did not partake.

Guilt is not a legitimate response to blessing. Redoubling our efforts to share our resources, gladdening the hearts of others, being a source of enveloping light and maintaining a positive stance for our family are the constructive and productive expressions of gratitude for the gifts granted and blessings rendered that the Almighty would hold most dear.

In the merit of the sincere quest to do what is right as you articulated so well, may G-d grant all of us the ultimate light that will illuminate our lives, individually, and the world as a whole.

Personal Growth
Inexcusable Behavior and Forgiveness

A woman came to me in deep despair, asking a very difficult question: "My husband has conducted himself in a way which has undermined and destroyed my trust in him. How can I ever forgive him and trust him again?"

hile every situation is unique and must be dealt with in its particular context, there are some guidelines in the Torah which can help lay the groundwork for how to approach such a problem and how to initiate the process of healing.

During this season of our religious calendar — between Shavuos and the High Holy Days — themes that jump out of the pages of Jewish history relate to the agonizing issues of commitment and betrayal, love and infidelity, greatness and disgrace, and ultimately the concepts of repentance and forgiveness.

The most striking is the incident involving the Golden Calf — a tragedy that occurred a mere forty days after the encounter with G-d at Mount Sinai. While awaiting the return of Moses from the mountaintop, the Jewish people miscalculated his estimated time of arrival and concluded that their leader had perished. In dread of having lost their intermediary to G-d, they fashioned the infamous idol to take his place (Exodus 32:1).

The Divine response clearly marks the episode of the Golden Calf of supreme betrayal and infidelity on the part of the very same nation that had, just a short time earlier, pledged their allegiance to G-d and His Torah. In the ensuing dialogue between G-d and Moses, the very viability of a continued relationship between G-d and His elect people seems to be in question: G-d wants to sever the relationship.

Yet Moses' unceasing and fervent petitions prevail and the process of repentance and forgiveness is begun.

· · · · · · · · · · · · · · · · · · WHAT REPENTANCE INVOLVES

Upon examination we find that the text articulates a three-tiered process:

• The first stage involved admission, whereby the Children of Israel acknowledged having done a reprehensible act. No rationalizations or excuses were allowed. We admitted the sin and said the equivalent of, "We did it and it was wrong!"

• The second step called for remorse, being truly sorry and regretful.

• For the third and final step, it was necessary that the nation put into place a program that would prevent the possibility of failure in the future. This demanded boundaries and safeguards to protect against the recurrence of such a lapse. It goes without saying that this mandated a formidable investment of arduous work.

In addition, the nation had to contend with loss of heart, disappointment in themselves, self-directed anger at the inability to have risen to the challenge, inordinate self-doubt, and a serious loss of trust in one's judgment. Before G-d would forgive us, we had to work through all these issues, so that first and foremost we could forgive and restore trust in ourselves.

In the end, forgive us He did!

Another example, on a more individual level, is the "sin" committed by King David, head of the royal line of Israel, and one of the most illustrious figures of all time.

Our Sages inform us that the popular perception of King David's "sin" with Bathsheba is in error. There was a rationale for what he did. Nevertheless, the way in which his actions are recorded (II Samuel 11:2) indicates that a serious breach of morality occurred.

G-d dispatches His prophet to confront the king. The prophet's rebuke leaves David devastated and anguished.

Following the pattern of repentance set by his ancestors at Mount Sinai, King David acknowledges his wrongdoing, confesses, agonizes, and soul-searches, resolving never to allow for the repetition of such behavior.

The Book of Samuel records that King David paid a bitter price, but most importantly, he was forgiven by G-d and reinstated as one of the spiritual giants of Jewish history.

THE PROCESS OF FORGIVENESS ················

From the examples above — and many others – we take G-d as our model and just as He forgave when there was genuine repentance, we must do likewise.

However, forgiveness of any serious violation of trust does not come easily.

How do we do it? How can we forgive?

Forgiving another has to begin with examining ourselves. We must look at the issues of our own complicity — real complicity or perceived complicity, for they are both variables of great moment.

Moreover, we need to confront our own vulnerabilities. Are there deep-seated insecurities and weaknesses that this betrayal has brought to the fore and that urgently demand our attention?

It is critical that we regroup — to strengthen and fortify ourselves. Another crucial objective is to center one's life, forging a relationship with G-d, our Higher Power. We can do this through introspection, learning, meditation, praying, and surrounding ourselves with people of genuine spiritual substance. When we begin to feel the comforting, loving embrace of our Creator, we will simultaneously experience a sense of healing and wholeness. We will know with certitude in the depth of our being that G-d, unlike mortals, will never betray us or abandon us.

Furthermore, we need to reach in and reach out, embarking on pursuits that will foster a positive self-image and make us feel healthy, competent, and sufficient. From this position of strength and self-esteem we can proceed to the next phase, which is to address the issue of the offending party.

This stage of the process asks: Has the spouse sincerely engaged in repentance as we understand the three-step process from the Torah model?

- Has he/she owned up to the infidelity?
- Is he/she genuinely contrite?
- Is he/she earnestly committed to moving forward in a positive direction? Is he/she committed to a lifelong investment in the relationship?

· AGENDA FOR COUNSELING

The response to the last question should include, among others, the willingness to obtain counseling. The agenda for counseling would be to:

- Deal with the pain and fallout.
- Improve communication skills. This means learning to talk so that we can listen, and listening so that we can talk.
- Clarify and better understand what we need from each other. What do I need you to do so that I can begin to trust? Is it to spend quality time together in order to communicate regardless of our hectic schedules?
- Share the spiritual centers of our lives, striving together to integrate transcendent values such as a relationship with G-d, learning Torah, charity work.

It should go without saying that forgiving, healing, and building trust take time. It requires consistent investment and hard work.

In the last analysis, hanging on to anger and resentment, obsessing and refusing to forgive is, as someone observed, letting someone live in our head rent-free. The greatest beneficiary of forgiveness is to the one who finds it within one's self to do so.

Most significantly, by forgiving we reach beyond our finite limitations and in the likeness of our Creator in Whose image we are fashioned, we become more exalted human beings, mending the broken, healing the wounded, and restoring the integrity of love.

Personal Growth
Sensitivity Training

Sensitivity to the circumstances and feelings of others is the cornerstone of human relationships. The seasons of sunshine and joy and alternatively the seasons of cold and suffering spare no mortal the desperate need for caring and understanding from his fellow human beings.

Rabbi Samson Rafael Hirsch, commentator and biblical linguist, notes that the Hebrew word for compassion — "rachamim" — shares the same root as the Hebrew word "rechem" which means womb. Compassion and sensitivity to others flows from the awareness that all of us share the same spiritual womb, the same history and fate — indeed, that our destinies are intertwined. Whatever happens to one of us must affect the other. Understanding this reality mandates not only participation and empathy in times of hardship, but gives rise to a sense of joy and delight in the good fortune of our fellow travelers in life's journey.

My father, of blessed memory, often encouraged us to become card-carrying members of the "farginners club" — the nonbegrudgers — a group dedicated to acknowledging and expressing our feelings of delight when others are blessed with good fortune in life, i.e., becoming engaged, birth of a child, building or expanding a home, marrying off a child, winning the lottery, etc.

It is important to note that sensitivity is not just an emotion; it must express itself in actions as well, especially when people we know are experiencing pain and difficulties.

The first task in sensitivity training is to climb out of ourselves and notice others. In describing the Egyptian bondage that is the prototype of all Jewish diasporas, our Sages inform us that it began when the "eyes and hearts of Israel were plugged up" (Genesis 47:28, Rashi). When Jews can't notice, see or feel for one another, darkness ensues. Conversely, the redemption was set in motion when "Moses grew up and saw their suffering" (Exodus 2:11). Despite his privileged status as a child of the palace, Moses became aware of and noticed the suffering of his brethren.

The next level is to respond. This can take many forms. One size does not fit all and often the same situation at different times requires different approaches.

1. The first step in any interaction, especially in delicate situations, is to press the internal "pause button"; i.e., not to shoot from the hip but to stop and think if what we are about to say is advisable.

2. Refrain from asking too many questions. Take your cue from the person in pain. People who are suffering find it especially offensive for someone who has not previously shown much interest in them to grill them on all of the private and often gory details of their situation. It makes them feel like they are the object of curiosity and gossip.

3. The Mishnah advises that one "should not try to console a bereaved person while the remains of the deceased are still before them." When pain is so new and fresh, a person is not in a position where he can hear moralizing comments such as "they lived a good, long life," or "left good children behind," etc. At this time these pronouncements are often premature. This is the time when the afflicted needs validation and affirmation. He will ask for perspective when he is ready.

A woman called me to speak on behalf of an organization of families with special needs children. I asked her what she wanted the thrust of my remarks to be. She answered, "Just don't tell us how special we are and how much G-d must love us to give us so much pain. We need validation and help in coping." I find that a good rule of thumb is that what works for me generally works for others. If the opportunity presents itself, it is helpful to gently remind the sufferer of the need to take charge of his life. No matter what the circumstances of a person's life the Torah's message of "choosing life" is extremely relevant. The Torah is, in fact, cautioning us against the inclination to postpone living until life chooses us — until a suitable match comes along, until we are granted a baby, until we are cured, until the dead are resurrected, until we regain our fortune, etc. Practically speaking, choosing life means that we have to have a plan for every day — what we are going to do, whom we are going to meet, what we are going to learn, etc. Life has to be productive and justifiable on its own terms, each day, one day at a time.

4. I have counseled many who confided in me that people shunned them during their hour of suffering. One woman who was undergoing chemotherapy recalled that her most painful moments were when people who knew her would cross the street to avoid having to greet or talk to her. She understood that it was not a malicious act. She knew that they were at a loss as to what to say or fearful that they might say the wrong thing. Nonetheless, it hurt her to the core. She felt like a pariah, alone and rejected. In those situations, one can simply say, "It's so good to see you," or "I've been thinking about you," or "I've been praying for you," etc. — without prying or asking for a medical report unless it's offered.

5. People cope differently. Some are "attenders" and others are "distracters." The "attenders" get comfort from discussing and sharing their issues. The "distracters" prefer to talk about other things to get space and relief from their woes. We need to take our cue from the person and not impose our preference.

The Mishnah wisely warns us, "Don't judge your friend until you find yourself in his place." This actually means, never judge another person as you can never find yourself in precisely his place. Michelle, a woman who had multiple miscarriages, told me that after many months in bed, she tried to find something that would motivate her to get out of her rut. A department store's advertisement for a free makeover caught her eye. Unfortunately, she refrained for fear of being seen and judged for indulging in so petty a pursuit. Even thinking that we can judge another person is terribly misguided. Every human being copes and deals with pain differently. We know nothing of another person's life and can never be in another person's shoes. Both externally and internally the worlds of two distinct individuals can never totally match.

6. Be specific in offers to help. Patty, recently widowed, shared that she immediately dismissed the offers of "call me when you need something." She felt they were totally unhelpful, if not insincere. A call asking her if today was a good time to take her shopping or to baby-sit or to pick up something for her rang true and more sincere.

7. Replacement strategies can be helpful. It is important to include those who have suffered losses into our lives, giving them space and letting them know they are welcome.

Carrie lost her mother at a very young age when she could barely remember her. When contemporaries commemorated the memory of their own loved ones, the pain of her deprivation would surface. Her therapist suggested that she keep a notebook specifically for communication with her mother, so that when anything significant would happen — i.e., when her baby took her first step, when she would celebrate an anniversary, or any other achievement that was a milestone — that she write and share it as a connection to her mother. The gist of it would be to tell her mother how proud she would be, and probably is, in the achievements and nachas of her family. Carrie found it tremendously helpful and therapeutic.

We would all like to see that final light at the end of the very dark tunnel of the last thousand years, to see the long-awaited millennium that signals the end to both collective and individual pain and suffering. Every act of reaching out with sensitivity, of sharing the joy and pain of a fellow traveler, brings us closer to that time of ultimate redemption.

Personal Growth
The Art of Giving and Taking Criticism

We live in Israel and our families, including two sisters-in-law, have very little contact with us. My in-laws are great, and are very supportive and encouraging of how we are raising our kids. My sisters-in-law, however, are another story entirely. They constantly offer "advice" that is actually not-so-veiled criticism, and this has gone on for years even though neither of them had children of her own. Nothing I do is right, and they are not shy about telling me what or why, and as one might expect, I find their "suggestions" impractical and unreasonable.

We've been told we aren't giving the kids enough time or material comforts. We should never criticize them. We should never get angry at the children (we try, we try, but everybody slips sometimes), and we should never punish, only explain.

I have tried smiling and saying nothing; I have tried saying that we will take their opinion into account. My husband has, on occasion, explained pleasantly that we appreciate their concern but that we see the situation differently, thank you. I now realize that it would have been better to have directly confronted the two of them years ago. Is there any good way out of this now?

A TOUGH CHALLENGE

efore addressing the issue at hand it is instructive to note that criticism is, at the very least, a very sensitive and delicate issue. The Torah states, "You shall surely rebuke your friend." The critical word here is "friend." The person reprimanded must feel that the rebuke comes from someone perceived as a friend, an ally, one who truly has his best interests in mind and someone whose words the individual can respect and want to heed.

If that criteria is not met, the Talmud cautions that just as it is a mitzvah to speak what can be heard so it is a mitzvah to desist from saying that which cannot be heard.

When there are in fact legitimate issues that need to be addressed, often we may have to disqualify ourselves and identify another person who does meet the criteria of the perceived "friend." That might be a rabbi, mentor, or another who is significant and held in high esteem by the party in question.

One of the toughest challenges to human beings is to receive criticism graciously so as to respond to it appropriately. It is especially challenging to accept criticism when it comes to child-rearing. We often see our children as extensions of ourselves, and our parenting as reflections of our most significant efforts. Overly critical comments in this area hurt us to the core and feel like an assault on our very selves.

The Sages comment that one who is able to handle oneself well and control a response at a time of criticism and contention with another is worthy of the world existing in his or her merit. That's how difficult it is.

PRACTICAL ADVICE

Practically speaking, I would think that the reader would be well advised to:

1. Be reassured that there are many schools of thought in child-rearing methodology. In fact, some of the most popular approaches of the past have been discarded, and new ones surface all the time. There is no one right approach that fits all situations.

2. To fortify yourself against criticism you would do well to seek the counsel of someone who knows you, your children, your values, and your situation. I would subject the critical comments to the scrutiny of such a person and ask him or her to determine, given your situation, if there are indeed any modifications necessary in your approach.

3. I would then tell my critics that I appreciate their good intentions, have explored their suggestions, sought counsel for my particular situation, and am satisfied that while their approach might be commendable, mine works best for me. As they say, "Different strokes for different folks."

4. I might also share my vulnerability with them; namely, that I need to surround myself with those who will be supportive and who would give me positive feedback. If they can provide that, we can co-exist and they can be part of my immediate world. The bottom line is: I cannot waste my precious and limited energy on detractors who would undermine my efforts in the area of life that is both most challenging and most sacred to me.

5. Where the criticism is unwarranted or inappropriate to your particular situation, you can either let it go in one ear and out the other, or say gently but firmly that it is your life and your family and you must make choices that are right for you, your husband, your children, and the society you live in.

6. My personal counsel to mothers of large families who juggle so much responsibility is to be mindful of the care, attention, and nurturing that they owe themselves. These moms need to eat well, exercise, be well groomed, make sure they take personal time for an exercise class, a learning class, an hour at the library alone, a solitary walk in the park, etc. This personal attention is a neces-

sity, not a luxury. It recharges the batteries and helps us access our internal energy.

7. And, as with all things, I would continue to pray. I would ask the Almighty, the source of all wisdom, to guide my steps and to help me to clearly see my way.

Personal Growth
Letting Go

How do I let go of the past? I have been married for a number of years with three beautiful children. My husband was a drug addict and has turned over a new leaf. I live in constant fear as to what he might do next. I consistently argue with him and bring up the past. I have a lot of pain and I don't know where to begin my journey on healing. I have a lot of bitterness and fear.

Although the circumstances may be particular to this reader, the theme of not being able to trust and let go of past hurts is a common one. Let us examine the solutions to this specific problem and then look at some of the larger issues as well.

The fear and anxiety felt on the part of this woman concerning her husband's relapsing to his former behavior is real and perhaps based on past patterns. But much can be done to assuage her apprehension.

One part of such a plan would involve a commitment to regular attendance in one of the well-known and respected 12-step programs, where people support one another to stay away from drugs, alcohol or several other addictive behaviors. Such programs offer professional supervision, skilled support, and inspirational resources for both the addict and his family.

Another facet of the multiphased plan would require immersion in spiritual pursuits — learning, prayer, and meditation.

A third dimension would demand a serious review of one's social milieu. Healthy, supportive, caring friends can act as a powerful bulwark against repeating harmful or negative behavior.

On another level I would suggest that it would be extremely helpful for the wife to avail herself of a good therapist. Her pain, anger, and resentment need to be processed and resolved so that the requisite energy to move forward can be liberated.

BLAMING OTHERS···································

Some of the considerations that are likely to come up in therapy involve fundamental life attitudes. When our lives aren't as we would like them to be, we tend to look for answers outside of ourselves. We blame circumstances beyond our control: our bosses, associates, spouses, parents, children, etc. It is usually only after a lot of pain and suffering, both our own and that which we afflict upon those to whom we attribute responsibility, that we come to the realization that the ultimate solution must come from inside ourselves.

Hanging on to anger and resentment assumes that we have control over the behavior of another person. Consequently, we believe, quite mistakenly, that if we refuse to forgive and forget that we thereby punish the perpetrator. Our illusion presumes that the offender will suffer and hence never repeat the offense.

While this conclusion may be common, it is incorrect for the following reasons:

1. In reality, we have no control over the behavior of another person. Moreover, one can be fairly certain that constantly reminding others of their shortcomings will be counterproductive. Repeated admonitions of others' indiscretions are guaranteed to motivate them not to change. Quite the contrary, it will more than likely reinforce their feelings of inferiority and inadequacy that prompted their addictive behavior in the first place. A return to consumptive behavior would be a more likely consequence of constantly rubbing their face in it.

On the other hand, if we can find it within ourselves to adopt a positive mode, it can be significant in affecting an enduring turnabout. "Look at a person as they are and that is all they will be. Look at them as what they can be and that is what they will indeed become."

2. From a faith prospective, no challenge in life is arbitrary or capricious. My life and the circumstances by which I am confronted are uniquely relevant to me and provide an invitation for me to grow on a personal level. As someone once said, we cannot control the images that appear on the canvas of our lives daily, but we are the ones who determine the colors that we will apply to the canvas — bright, positive, and life-affirming ones, or colors that are dark and grim, which dishearten and drag us down.

We make those choices and we live by those choices. Certainly, it is hard work to apply bright colors to challenging images, but in the end, we ourselves are the greatest beneficiaries. We will have reached deep into our very core and accessed the better part of ourselves. Rather than wallow in self-pity, we will have become bigger and better people. To travel this positive road requires conscious and deliberate effort. Rest assured that we are not going to wake up one fine day and have an automatic change of heart. We have to actively choose that change of heart. We must stop in our tracks the moment we feel anger and resentment welling up inside us and alter the words that issue our mouths.

A self-talking to is absolutely critical to the success of this endeavor. We are constrained to keep telling ourselves over and over again that we must "let go" and forgive. Self-exhortations rehearsed regularly will heal us. In addition, we need to be vigilant for positive and compensating behaviors on our spouses' part. We need to notice and acknowledge these gestures. Often these are made as conciliatory, and represent a sincere loving effort to make up for time lost. These gestures may take the form of wanting to spend more time with us, helping out with chores, making inquiries into our well-being, attempts to draw closer and more intimate. Whatever form they take, these overtures are indications of regret for the past.

Implied here is also the idea that however hurtful the past behavior may have been, it was not malicious or calculated on their part. We need to be open and to give them a fair chance. Negative thoughts need to be replaced by positive thoughts. The rule is that "no two things can occupy the mind at once." If we actively choose to travel an upbeat and constructive road invoking a positive attitude, we will ignite a flame that will banish the darkness from our hearts and minds. We will have chosen to move forward.

3. We serve as models for our children. They watch us carefully as we move through our daily trials and tribulations. They are registering our every response. We are their textbooks. What better legacy can we leave our children than one of coping? A legacy that says: Yes, life can be disappointing at times but we get up, brush ourselves off, and move on with strength and determination.

4. Every day is precious and life passes all too quickly. We must not allow yesterday to contaminate today. How sad it would be for us to miss today's beautiful sunshine, because we refuse to let go of yesterday's overcast skies. In Hebrew there is a saying, "Do not prolong the suffering beyond the time of pain."

5. The final point is especially relevant for this season, the High Holy Days, when we will stand in judgment and ask the Almighty to forgive us for past transgressions. And as a vote of confidence in our ability to change, we ask Him to grace us with yet another year of life. Can we ask forgiveness for ourselves and at the same time withhold forgiveness from others? Especially at this time of the year, a most powerful appeal would be:

"Almighty G-d, we are all mere humans, finite, limited, subject to error and weakness. As one of Your children You have watched me struggle to overcome the formidable barrier of resistance to letting go, forgiving and forgetting. In the merit of my effort, Benevolent

Father In Heaven, I ask You to hold my hand and extend Your compassion to assist me in my arduous journey. Please inscribe us all in the Book of Life."

The best of everything and have a happy and fulfilling New Year.

Personal Growth
Responding to Insults

How should a person respond to insults? I have read that a good way to treat an insult is as if it never happened, to disregard it completely, and not to share the incident with anyone. In the same article, I've read that insults somehow serve as atonement for our sins.

I would appreciate it if you explain further how one should respond to a situation where someone insults a loved one in my presence.

Lashing back when we are verbally assaulted is almost a reflexive act. The ability to control a hurtful retort under these circumstances is seen by our sages as an act of almost superhuman discipline. Their comment is that "the world would not exist but for the merit of those who hold their tongues (and shut their mouths) during an argument."

The following anecdote is one of our family's treasures. On one occasion, my father-in-law, of blessed memory, attended a Jewish city council meeting. Many heated issues were discussed and the evening soon disintegrated into angry denunciations and accusations flung in all directions.

By the time it was over, my father-in-law, Rabbi Twerski, was the only one who had remained silent despite the barrage of caustic remarks directed at him. The following morning, a senior rabbi, who had been at the meeting, wondered how it was that Rabbi Twerski was able to exercise such remarkable self-control while everyone else succumbed to such unbecoming behavior. Rabbi Twerski responded that his self-control derived from his desire to eat dinner.

Seeing the perplexed look on his colleague's face, Rabbi Twerski explained he knew that had he come home and reported to his beloved wife that he had taken part in a nasty and insulting battle of words, she would have reacted by saying, "You stooped to their level. No dinner tonight!" It was a simple matter of valuing my dinner, he modestly concluded. Obviously, my father-in-law was kibitzing. My mother-in-law was not a shrew, but dining in the presence of her disapproval and disappointment would have made his meal unpalatable.

Our reaction to situations would be tempered and defused if we would realize that most often it's not about us — it's the one who berates who has a problem and, indeed, we should not get sucked in or "stoop to his level."

There is a wonderful story of Rabbi Chaim Chizkiah Medini, known by the name of his scholarly work "Sdei Chemed." In his elder years, he recounted that as a young man of average accomplishment, he studied in a Kollel (post-graduate learning institution) funded by a philanthropist. One of the other students had a grievance against the Sdei Chemed, and maliciously contrived to defame him.

He bribed the cleaning woman to accuse the Sdei Chemed of immoral conduct, in front of all the students. The entire Kollel was aghast and the Sdei Chemed was mortified.

The philanthropist, however, believed in the Sdei Chemed's innocence and refused to dismiss him. Nevertheless, his sterling reputation was tarnished.

A short time later, the cleaning woman was fired. Ironically, she came to the Sdei Chemed, contrite over what she had done, and asked his assistance in convincing the philanthropist to rehire her. She promised that she would publicly admit her treachery and expose the perpetrator.

The Sdei Chemed, in relating the story, shared that he was sorely tempted to accept the offer, to expose the source of the evil plot and to be vindicated. He knew, however, that dredging up the whole incident would cause a "chilul Hashem," a desecration of God's Name. He vacillated back and forth between the sweet taste of revenge and vindication on the one hand, and the greater transcendent good of the Kollel on the other.

Finally, he called in the woman and told her that he would advocate on her behalf on the exclusive condition that she would never discuss any details of the ugly conspiracy that had transpired. He was willing to bear the shame, blameless though he was, rather than subject Torah scholars to public disgrace.

It was at that moment, the Sdei Chemed concluded, that an amazing thing happened. The instant he decided to set his own personal interest aside, wellsprings of learning opened up for him. He felt his abilities expand so much that precincts and sources of insights and illumination totally unavailable to him became easily accessible. That decision propelled him toward becoming a world-renowned scholar and author.

Feelings of victimization when we are the object of derision and insults are more than compensated for by feelings of mastery when we take the moral high road and assume a posture of dignity.

In response to the second part of the reader's question, it is true that we cannot stand by when a loved one is insulted in our presence. There is a principle in Judaism: "sh'tikah kehoda'ah," remaining silent is tantamount to agreement and affirmation. It is important to deal with a situation effectively. However, a sharp retort may provoke additional negative statements in support for the original insulting remark. That would certainly be counterproductive. It would probably be best to put an end to the conversation right then and there by insisting, without getting into specifics, that you find the comment unwarranted.

At a later time, you might want to discuss the matter with the wrongdoer, both about the statement and the context. If the insulting party is insensitive and a habitual offender, it might be an exercise in futility even to address the issue. In that case, it is best that you and your loved one keep your distance from this person.

The points to remember:

1. Don't stoop to the other's level.

2. Don't exacerbate the situation even if the motivation is idealistic.

3. If you must rebuke, do so in private.

4. Know to whom you are speaking. Don't waste your time and spin your wheels with those who don't have the capacity to hear you.

5. Remember that you cannot be responsible for another's behavior but you are always accountable for your own.

In conclusion, consider the inspiring example of our Matriarch Rachel. The Patriarch Jacob loved her and worked seven years for her devious father to earn her hand in marriage. Anticipating that her duplicitous father might attempt to substitute Leah for Rachel, Jacob devised a secret code between them.

On the wedding night, Rachel watched her father put his deceitful plan in place. Unable to tolerate the terrible embarrassment her sister would suffer when she did not know Jacob's password, Rachel revealed the code to her. The painful thought of her sister's shame took precedence over her own happiness.

Our Sages inform us that Rachel could not know that Jacob would ultimately marry her as well. She was prepared to live her life without marrying him, rather than have her sister humiliated. This is considered the ultimate sacrifice, even greater, some commentaries note, than the willingness of our Patriarchs to suffer martyrdom for the Almighty.

Dying for transcendent ideals, although a sublime act, is of a moment's duration. But, the willingness to live out an entire lifetime, day in and day out, deprived of the love and happiness that one might have had, is of the highest order. This is why the tomb of Rachel has remained for all time the hallowed shrine for all of our prayers, entreaties, pain, and yearning.

Mother Rachel remains the symbol of caring. She cared enough to sacrifice her needs then, and she continues to be our advocate in perpetuity. "A voice on high is heard, Mother Rachel is crying on behalf of her children." In response, the Almighty promises that in the merit of her deeds, all of us will eventually (hopefully, soon in our day) be returned to our rightful boundaries, to our homeland.

Personal Growth
The Terrorist Within

I recently heard an interview with a microbiologist who gave a frightening description of the new microbes, germs, and organisms that appear to be surfacing. He voiced great concern that, in large measure, due to the overuse of antibiotics, these agents have already become resistant to effective treatment. And as they mutate they will present an even greater threat.

Listening to these disturbing facts, the interviewer exclaimed, "Wow! How frightening must be your world of microbiology!"

To which the professor responded, "It is not only my world. It's your world, it's our world. The only difference between us is that given my expertise and resources, I'm able to see what's out there and you cannot. But nonetheless, you are subject and susceptible to the same dire consequences."

Terrorism has always been out there, but now it has tragically reared its ugly head on our territory. Gone forever is the golden age of innocence. Gone is our sense of security and belief that despite what goes on everywhere else, we are safe and invincible. We, along with the rest of the free world, have become vulnerable to the evil that lurks out there that can, G-d forbid, strike at anytime.

As we applaud President Bush's "war on terrorism," we wonder what might be our individual role in all of this.

The Jewish perspective has always been that when things occur in macrocosm, in the world at large, we need to look to the microcosm, into our internal world, for a corollary.

Many parallel insights have been offered. My son, Rabbi Ephraim Twerski of Chicago, suggested to his congregation that as we begin this new Jewish year, we need to combat the "terrorist" within. All of us, by the decisions we make in life, are major players in the structuring of life around us. When we make choices based on morality, decency and honesty we effectively build the structure of our world. Brick by brick we add to the strength and well-being of the context in which we live.

Bottom line, we are the architects of both the material and spiritual parameters of our existence. Toward this end we are invested with an inner compass, a pilot if you will, to keep us on course, to negotiate the turbulent winds, i.e., the alien values that threaten our values. All too frequently, the "terrorist" within seizes control. It comes as a voice inside of us that seeks to undermine and destroy that which we have built and that which we have the potential to build. It tries to convince us in subtle and not so subtle ways that we are failures, that we cannot rise above past mistakes, that our flaws and blemishes condemn us forever to the dark side.

The "terrorist" within knows our weak points and hence its arguments are compelling. It seeks to stifle our growth and viability. Our response needs to be swift and decisive.

The cardinal sin in Judaism is to underestimate our heavenly and incorruptible essence that exhorts us to lift ourselves out of our past mistakes, assume responsibility, and move forward toward the legitimate excellence and majesty that is our birthright as G-d's people.

Every positive act of compassion, empathy, guarding our tongue, resisting verbal assaults, curbing anger, diffusing envy, etc., is a brick bearing our name that contributes to the strength of the structural configuration that is our world. Conversely, a deliberate destructive deed, a negative belief about ourselves and others is an assault, an act of terrorism, an act of destroying our potential.

The war on terrorism needs to be waged on all fronts. But the global efforts will ultimately be only as effective and successful as the sum of its individual parts. And this means you and me — the struggle, the conquests, and the victories on our internal battlefield.

We may not have the power to determine world policy, but perhaps more significantly we *can* take charge of our personal landscape.

Consider the following:

1. Kate, a tall attractive 19-year-old blonde, considered herself a total failure. Her standing at college had not been the best. Her infrequent attempts at finding employment were not very successful. Her group of friends was, as she put it, "more messed up" than she was and her parents were sorely disappointed in her. Her greatest desire was to sleep all day.

Kate's "terrorist," the negative voice inside her, had taken control of her life, convincing her that the only refuge was a pillow. It cast a pall on every area of her life and she was in great danger unless and until she would rouse the pilot, the better part of herself, to take control of her journey.

2. Isabelle suffered the untimely loss of her young mother. At first, denial did not allow her the comfort of mourning. But this eventually gave way to a complete breakdown. She was unable to interact with people, to work, eat, or function in any normal capacity. Her "terrorist" consisted of her inability to open up and share her feelings. Her misguided "private" stance kept her bottled up with her enormous pain and grief unresolved. Healing, which is so dependent on openness and sharing of feelings, became impossible. Without immediate intervention, she was in real danger of self-destructing.

3. Joe had a chronic back problem that had worsened over the years. He had many surgeries and endless procedures that compromised him physically. Pain became his constant companion. Drugs and more drugs were prescribed and they became his steady diet. He developed a "victim" mentality — always in pain, always on drugs, and eventually he resorted to alcohol to dull the acute aware-

ness of how far afield he had gone. His "terrorist" had successfully convinced him that he was entitled to play the "victim" and that only addictive substances could bail him out.

Each of us has our own internal "terrorist" bent on thwarting the good and the positive in our relationship with ourselves and our relationship with others. If we are not vigilant and wise in identifying its tactics and rooting it out, our personal, internal world may be at great risk.

The war on terrorism begins on very personal ground, inside each one of us. As one world leader put it, "You have to be the change that you would like to see."

Faith
Perspectives

Faith Perspectives
Inspired by Judaism

I have a great difficulty with my spirituality. I am an observant young woman who has never really wavered in my belief. But now I am struggling to feel anything when I practice mitzvos (commandments). I don't find that I'm getting satisfaction, joy, or positive emotion. Rationally I know that I am leading a meaningful life, but I feel as though it is empty. I have tried learning about the mitzvos, putting in extra thought and intention, and have spoken with a rabbi, but none of it really seemed to help. Any input you could offer would be greatly desired.

The growth pattern of an individual is never a straight line upward. Movement in the spiritual realm is more like making our way up a mountain. Inevitably, there are times when we lose our footing and slip back. The challenge is not to lose heart but to strengthen ourselves, to pull ourselves together, and resume the climb.

The Baal Shem Tov teaches that G-d's relationship and interaction with us can be compared to parents' relationship with their children. Imagine parents relishing the milestone of their toddler's first attempt at walking. Typically, parents will stand reassuringly at a short distance and hold out their hands, poised to catch the child.

But as soon as the child comes close, they retreat a few steps so that the toddler will venture yet another step and continue the process of learning how to walk.

At times, the Almighty does the same with us, appearing to retreat and take a step backward, moving away from us, and making His presence elusive and more difficult to perceive so that His children might draw on their untapped resources to forge ahead and expand their growth horizons.

So one way to look at your present inability to feel is that G-d is trying to teach you to "walk."

Another point to consider is that the more precious something is, the greater the price. Spiritual journeys, as a rule, do not provide immediate gratification. There are usually some dark tunnels along the way. Only the investment of patience and perseverance will ultimately yield the rewards of acquisition and its concomitant joy.

·····SUPPORT IN MOMENTS OF VULNERABILITY

In every person's life there are moments when an individual becomes very vulnerable. Quite often this is due to an emotional trauma or some major disappointment. It is at this point that one is at great risk of sliding precipitously from "the top of the mountain to a deep pit."

Rabbi Chaim Shmulevitz (of blessed memory), a noted thinker and past dean of Mirrer Yeshivah of Jerusalem, draws on the events in the life of Saul, the first king of Israel, to illustrate this phenomenon. Saul was humble to a fault, an individual who resisted honor and eschewed positions of leadership. Ultimately, he was obliged to accept the crown of leadership, but unfortunately, because he disobeyed a mandate from G-d, the prophet Samuel informed him that he would lose his throne.

The consummately humble Saul responded to the situation in a most uncharacteristic manner. He pleaded with Samuel saying, "Hold onto me and give me honor in the presence of the nation."

King Saul, who had shunned honor all his life, suddenly needed it. Rabbi Shmulevitz poignantly explains that Saul's uncharacteristic request sprang from his acute sense of vulnerability and the concomitant need for compensation. What was required at this juncture was to break the fall in order to minimize the ground lost and the damage done. The "hold onto me" approach had to be invoked. In moments of vulnerability an individual needs someone to hold, who will give him support, honor, validation, affirmation, and counsel. Such is the existential human condition.

Inevitably, life serves up challenges of all kinds. Feelings of rejection and disappointment, whether they appear to emanate from our relationship with the Almighty or with others in our life, render us vulnerable to the slippery slope. One hope is to identify an individual whom we can trust to help us regain our footing. In the absence of such a person a sensitive, spiritual, and highly recommended therapist might fill the bill.

Rabbi Dovid of Tolna once remarked that the world is divided into two groups. Half are believers; half are nonbelievers. "This dichotomy," he explained, "accurately describes the conflict within the psyche of each person." A part of us believes wholeheartedly in G-d and His providence; the other part of us is in constant conflict, struggling with metaphysical issues of faith and practice.

It is important for my dear reader to know that she is not alone, that the struggle is not unique to herself, and the fact that she has reached out to seek guidance is much to her credit.

CONNECTING TO THE ELUSIVE SOUL············

Though I don't know the reader personally, her question resonates with much of what I see as the ubiquitous challenge of our time. While Torah and commandments are observed and "the form" of traditional life is engaged, for some people, the inner substance — the "soul" — seems to be elusive. It is akin to a body functioning successfully on a physical level, but without the inner light of the spirit.

This perhaps helps to explain the search for soul within the secular world and the appeal of "New Age Spirituality" and "Kabbalah." Misguided and limited as they might be, their burgeoning presence is indicative of a hunger, a search for the inner meaning of life and existence. One must be cautious, however, about where one seeks answers to these most important questions.

As Jews, we are aware that ideally we should "serve the Almighty with joy" (Psalms 100:2). This is generated by the perspective that being created in the image of G-d means, in no uncertain terms, that the Almighty has invested part of Himself in our very being and that each of us contains a singular magnificence. The description of the creation of man in Genesis asserts, "And He blew into man a living soul." Just as one who blows exhales part of himself, so too did G-d imbue us with exalted spiritual potential in "blowing into man a living soul."

Given this Divine investiture, we must constantly be reminded that we are positioned for greatness and that our potential is infinite. We rejoice in this knowledge and it should motivate us to become the best we can be. Assuredly, there is much work to be done, but it is in the supportive context of affirmation.

EXISTENTIAL SORROW

To balance out the compelling imperative for joy in life and in our service to the Almighty, there is yet another core insight that needs to be recognized. The Torah describes the poignant episode of the Matriarch Rachel naming her newborn son moments before she dies in childbirth. She names him "Ben-Oni," the son of my pain (Genesis 35:18). Jacob, her husband, modifies the name to "Binyamin," the son of my right hand. A contemporary thinker states the following: "Rabbi Samson Rafael Hirsch, in commenting on Rachel's use of the word "oni" (my sorrow) here, notes that it has to do with a pervasive sense of loss. He relates "oni" to a word that appears in Numbers 11:1 as a description of the Israelites' unhappiness in their desert wanderings: "misonenim." This expression is usually translated "murmuring," but Rav Hirsch renders it "as if in mourning over themselves."

The Israelites were disturbed, worried, grieved. This sorrow was a feeling that came over them despite being completely taken care of, surrounded in their travels by clouds of Divine protection. The commentaries make clear that this murmuring or mourning was different from mere complaint. It was a specific kind of disturbance, an existential sorrow over the suffering present in human experience, a suffering caused by a spiritual lack. Despite the care G-d was giving and the blessings heaped on the nation, they remained unconnected to their souls.

This disconnection happens to everyone some of the time, and to some people much of the time. Rachel seems to have been a person with an intense soul-hunger. She could not be satisfied unless earth and heaven were truly connected.

Rachel becomes, for us, the mother of sorrows, because she knew the passionate struggle for life, for completion, and the sense of loss or failure we feel when that which we sought, and which seemed just within our reach, is suddenly taken away. How apt that she should be the one whose prayers reach the Heavens for our redemption. Rachel understood that no earthly experience could be truly complete. Only at the end of the journey of the entire nation through all time could one hope for completion.

PRACTICAL ADVICE

With the backdrop of these possible components of spiritual detachment, the following will hopefully help you arrive at a more spiritually engaged posture.

Your question implies the need for an emotionally richer environment. As with everything else, it has to be a good fit. It has to resonate with you. There is never "one size fits all" in spiritual growth. You mentioned that you have spoken to a rabbi. Perhaps a woman mentor would more readily understand the undercurrents of your situation.

At times, it might be appropriate to evaluate the community one lives in. Is it the best context for your spiritual well-being? What are the values that drive those around you? What turns them on? The energy of our environment impacts tremendously on the affect of our lives, for better or for worse.

Our Sages teach that to make the learning of Torah most potent, it must perforce be accompanied by the "fire," the experiential component, its coming alive in every precinct of life.

I have found weekend retreats where one can immerse himself in learning to be powerful modalities for growth. Partaking in such an event, in a serene, quiet, and secluded setting provides an oasis in our hectic supercharged schedules that can be conducive to constructive inquiry, reflection, and soul-searching. In addition, the interaction, the give-and-take with others who, like yourself, are spiritually motivated can create a strong and enriching bond.

Reaching out to others in acts of kindness, i.e., visiting hospitals, old-age homes, cooking a meal for the needy, and efforts to alleviate the pain of others can be an antidote for spiritual malaise. It shifts the focus from ourselves to awareness that there is a world beyond the self that desperately awaits our contribution. Forward movement and positive behavior always create momentum in the right direction.

The women of my community, in pursuit of maintaining their spiritual well-being, have formed partners in learning. They have explored many significant works. Not only is the learning edifying, but perhaps more significantly, they draw on and share the rich and meaningful insights born of their own personal and individual life experiences.

Another wonderful tool for being "inspired" is to inspire others. The Mishnah attests to the fact that the greatest beneficiary in a teaching relationship is the teacher. "Much have I learned from my teachers, even more from my colleagues, but most of all from my students." Students challenge us and force us to explore deep places within ourselves we did not know existed. An appropriate teaching opportunity may well provide a source of inspiration.

We, as Jews, begin our day with the recitation of the brief "Modeh Ani" prayer. In these two verses we express "modeh" (gratitude) to G-d for returning our soul to us, so that we may enjoy the gift of another day. The word "modeh" shares a root with the word "hodaah," meaning admission and submission. In effect, we acknowledge, we submit that everything in life, all of our blessings, are a gift, a bestowal from the Master of the Universe. King David in Psalms exclaims, "Every soul will praise G-d." How? The word "neshamah," soul, is related to the word, "neshimah," breath. Every breath we take should remind us and give rise to songs and praise to the Almighty, Who invested our life-sustaining soul within us. Listen to your breath, observe the beauty of the exquisite functioning of the body, of the natural order of the world around you: the sky, the stars, the sun, the moon, the seasons, etc. "How magnificent are the works of the Almighty!" Living mindfully with awareness and consciousness can unquestionably move us in a spiritual direction.

Finally, pray. Before engaging in any mitzvah or endeavor that has not been giving you "satisfaction, joy or positive emotion," recite your own formulation of a short entreaty to the Almighty that He help you achieve fulfillment and connection through the deed that you are about to perform.

In conclusion, take heart from the profound insight of our Sages that encourages us to see the dark night of the soul as a springboard for spiritual growth. They said, "Had I not fallen, I would not have arisen; and had I not sat in darkness, I would not be the beneficiary of light" (Midrash, Psalms 22). Your honest quest and serious endeavors in the pursuit of clarity will, with G-d's help, propel you to higher ground.

Faith Perspectives
Acquiring Faith

As long as I can remember, I have had doubts about the existence of G-d, and confusion about how and whether the requirements of Judaism apply to me. If I knew for sure that G-d exists and that He wrote the Torah, obviously I would follow it. Unfortunately, as a person who isn't sure if there is a G-d, I cannot see any good reason for taking on all of the stringencies of Jewish observance. I keep a kosher kitchen, but cannot explain why, especially to my husband and stepchildren, who find it a nuisance and nothing else.

As the world has gotten to be a scarier and scarier place, especially for a Jewish American, I have felt envious of those who are sure of their faith in G-d. I long for the comfort and certainty that belief in G-d would afford. But how can I make myself believe, when I don't? I want to believe, but I don't know how.

A young man, a congregant in our synagogue, stood spellbound as he watched my brother-in-law Rabbi Shloime, of blessed memory, totally absorbed in and transported by the experience of prayer. At the conclusion of the services, he approached Rabbi Shloime and asked him how one can access the remarkable level of connection and faith that he had witnessed. Rabbi Shloime replied, "With a lot of effort and determination."

Most of us erroneously assume that the most important things in life such as spirituality, love, creative inspiration, etc., should be spontaneous — a flash, a gift, a bestowal. We are a culture that is paying dearly for the terribly misguided romantic notion that relationships can be engaged and based on the "love at first sight" premise. We believe that creative endeavor can be successfully negotiated by a mere flash of inspiration, without the requisite input of toil.

Determining the existence and nature of the Eternal Being, Who is the Source of our life and all life, requires time and effort to explore and learn. Moreover as intelligent people who pride ourselves in making responsible choices in life, we owe it to ourselves that our metaphysics be a product of an educated, well-informed decision.

For starters, I would urge you to consider the following points:

1. The defining moment of Jewish history, the revelation of G-d at Mount Sinai when He chose us as His people, was a national experience. There is no other nation in the world that claims a prophetic experience witnessed by millions of people. All other religions are based on the testimony of a small group (or a single person) bearing a message to the masses. The Jewish people would never have accepted G-d (and as you put it, "the stringencies of Jewish observance") had it not been for the indisputable certainty of their personal prophetic experience.

2. Jews in all four corners of the world, whose paths have not crossed in centuries, share the same concept of G-d and the same beliefs with only very slight variations in customs. The Jewish calendar has also been identically maintained by these disparate communities.

3. My husband has an impressive Jewish library. I often venture in to find him, sitting at his desk, surrounded by many treasures — the thousands of "sefarim" (holy books) of Bible, Mishnah, Talmud, Midrash, Maimonides, Nachmanides, and responsa and philosophic works, both ancient and modern. I think of all the bril-

liant minds throughout the ages represented in these works who have laboriously tackled the intricacies of an infinite Torah wisdom, who were transformed by it and proceeded to elucidate its teachings and illuminate Jewish learning.

And when doubts arise, as they invariably do in most people's lives, I think of our illustrious ancestors, the compilers of these magnificent works, of these minds that were far greater than my own. At given times, they too must have struggled with issues that challenged their faith, but their conclusions laid all doubt to rest. When uncertainty takes hold, I defer to the wisdom of the sages that preceded me, and to the understanding of those whose connection to and comprehension of the sublime far surpassed my own.

4. While very difficult, it is imperative to be intellectually honest. Maimonides (one of the greatest philosophers of all time) posits that idolatry, the rejecting of G-d and/or serving other deities, is not generally rooted in intellectual deliberation. It is emotional driven. He explains that a person who wants relief from the confines of a disciplined life, or who desires to partake of licentious or other similar pagan or secular practices, is loathe to admit these base desires. So the person will build an intellectual construct, an "ism" or belief system (or better said, "nonbelief") that not only permits but supports or mandates the given behavior. These are often sophisticated rationalizations for relieving oneself of "the stringencies of observance."

Consider this variation of the theme:

Janet, a tall attractive 20-year-old, came to see us. Despite the heartache she would cause her family and friends, she confided that she was seriously considering rejecting Jewish life. She had come to the conclusion that she could not believe in a G-d Who would allow the Holocaust or 9/11 to happen. As the session progressed, it surfaced that Janet came from a terribly dysfunctional home and had been abused as a youngster. She was harboring a great deal of anger and an enormous amount of pain. Early in her life, everyone who should have been her advocate and protector betrayed her. And most significantly, by extension, she was heartbroken that G-d did not protect her from her own personal holocaust.

My husband invoked for her the image of a drunk thinking that he was walking a straight line, as he stumbled and wavered in and out. Similarly, a person making ultimate decisions about whether G-d exists, while viewing life through the prism of pain and unresolved issues, cannot possibly negotiate a reasonable path. The decision, if it is to be intellectually honest and consistent with reality, must come from a whole and emotionally healthy person. Janet was advised to seek intervention to help her heal. She was also encouraged to pursue a course of study in consultation with scholarly authorities.

5. Finally, dear reader, the assertion that you would take on the "stringencies of Jewish observance," if you knew for sure that there is a G-d, is reversed in its order. While all of us would wish to be the beneficiaries of a revelation or prophetic experience where G-d appears to us in living color, that is not the way faith is acquired. "If I will have faith, I will observe" would be better replaced by, "If I observe, I will have faith." Many Jewish sages have noted that the Hebrew words "emunah" (faith) and "emun" (training) are derived from the same root. This shows that the soul must train itself in order to be capable of achieving religious experience and a relationship with G-d.

The mitzvos comprise a communication, a response to a higher law that we cannot totally identify with or comprehend. Initially, the would-be believer cannot expect them to flow from within, because their source is above and beyond. But through observance, slowly but surely, a relationship is forged. Our souls, the eternal essence of our being, will resonate with a thirst-quenching validation of being connected with the Source — much like a flower bud lifting its face to the sun for affirmation.

Tishah B'Av is the Jewish national day of mourning, marking the destruction of the Holy Temple in Jerusalem. We fast and recite the Book of Lamentations, describing the glory of old that is no longer ours. Realistically, comfortable, modern-day diaspora Jews can hardly relate to — let alone mourn for — an era we never knew and perhaps, for which at least until recently, were much too complacent to have any use. Still we mourn. The articulation and configuration of that mourning, the prayer that we recite is best expressed as: "G-d, I long to long. I yearn to yearn."

Similarly, your poignant longing for faith, as expressed by your words, "I want to believe, but I don't know how," is a wonderful and appropriate beginning for the journey toward faith.

I would suggest the following:

a. Take some quiet meditative time and address this yearning to G-d (even if initially it takes the form of "to Whom it may concern"). Tell Him that you would like a palpable sense of His being with you.

b. Look around, mindfully, at your blessings, your husband, children, friends. Observe the magnificent beauty of nature — the sun, trees, flowers in bloom, lakes, rivers, oceans, etc. Ultimately, you will begin to discern the Hand of the Almighty (veiled though it might be) in everything that surrounds you.

c. Faith, by definition, precludes open, obvious, and clear manifestation. It speaks of hiddenness, searching deep, stripping the facade, and cutting away the layers that obstruct a clear view. One can only achieve this through learning Torah, G-d's expressed will for us. Avail yourself of classes, lectures, and behavioral experiences, i.e., spending Shabbos and holidays with observant families, and networking with supportive communities of faith.

May God bless your journey.

Faith Perspectives
Hastening Mashiach's Arrival

*My teacher taught me that nothing stands in the way of a
person's will. I'm 16 years old and I want Mashiach to come
already, but I don't even know where to start.*

*So many great rabbis have pined for Mashiach's arrival
much more than me, yet he still has not come. Why should I
think that I could hasten his arrival?*

hat wonderful sentiments for a 16-year-old! Yearnings
of this kind most certainly impact the arrival of
Mashiach (Messiah).

An introductory note on the subject of Mashiach is in order.

Jews, since our inception as a people, in every corner of the
globe and especially in every generation since the destruction of
the Temple in Jerusalem in 70 CE, have awaited the coming of
Mashiach.

Maimonides teaches that Mashiach will be a living person, a
leader of stature, of royal lineage, descended from the house of
David. He will be an exemplary Torah scholar and an impeccably
faithful adherent of the mitzvos (commandments).

Mashiach will be Divinely inspired but will not be required to
perform miracles or supernatural feats to prove his authenticity.
Rather his credentials will be confirmed as he leads his fellow Jews

to a full commitment to Torah observance and to their responsibilities as "a light unto the nations."

In fulfilling his messianic mission, Mashiach must bring the Jewish people back to our homeland, the Land of Israel, and reestablish the Beis HaMikdash, the Holy Temple. He will usher in the long awaited millennium wherein the world (continuing in its current physical configuration) will be full of the "the knowledge of the L-rd like the waters cover the seas."

Enmity and discord will cease from the face of the earth. Isaiah's prophecy of the "lion lying down with the lamb" will finally be realized. Humankind will no longer be subjected to the tyranny of the wicked, and there will be neither famine nor war. There will be no envy or competitiveness, and prosperity will abound. G-d will wipe the tears from every face. Peace will reign and mankind, most especially Israel, will be free to pursue its spiritual goals and aspirations.

Despite a scientifically and technologically advanced world, there has arguably been little progress in the realm of human relationships and interactions. Hatred, wars, and conflict continue to rage out of control. In frustration, desperation, and feelings of total impotence, we throw up our hands and admit that only the redemptive force of Mashiach will bring sanity to our world.

But why hasn't Mashiach come yet? And what role can we play in expediting the process? The prophet says, "The smallest shall become a thousand, and the least, a mighty nation. I am the L-rd, in its time, I will hasten it [the redemption]" (Isaiah 60:22). There is an apparent contradiction: If there is an appointed time, how does "hastening it" help?

The commentaries note that there are two possibilities. The first is that if we are meritorious, the process will be speeded up. And if not, then there is a designated concluding point in the destiny of mankind by which the redemption must come regardless.

Yes, there is a designated time, but G-d allows for the possibility of a quicker redemption, thereby opening the door for human input.

It is also noteworthy to point out that we have here the assurance that the Almighty will not allow us to totally self-destruct. Taking the holiday of Passover as the model, when there was the danger of spiritual extinction (having descended into the 49th level of the abyss of the decadent Egyptian culture), the Almighty intervened and redeemed us.

Contrarily, if we should rise to the challenge and access lofty spiritual heights on our own, the footsteps of Mashiach will immediately be heard and redemption will follow.

It is impossible for a human being to fully understand the complexities of G-d's plan for His world. There are mystical intricacies far beyond our reach. For most who are presumptuous enough to claim access to the Kabbalistic works, consider the apt comment that "those who know don't talk and those who talk don't know."

Nevertheless, there are some fundamental concepts that inform Jewish living. We believe that G-d created the world with purpose and that each one of us has a unique role to play and a specific contribution to make to the ultimate destiny of mankind. Both collectively and on an individual level, the total picture will be incomplete if we don't achieve the objectives of our lives as mandated by heaven.

Thus the conclusion of history as we know it and the ushering in of the new millennium waits for our personal "tikkun" (reparatory work).

In the language of mysticism, these constitute the specific "sparks" that are assigned for our soul to claim. Moreover, our souls cannot access eternal peace without the completion of this mission.

The internal, mystical workings of G-d's world are unfathomably complex and defy conventional human understanding. Suffice it to say that Mashiach's tarrying presents us with the disconcerting but nonetheless compelling challenge to examine our lives, our values, and our behavior in order to determine whether perhaps it is our soul that has as not yet reached its potential.

Our sages exhort us to always view the universe as hanging in the balance as if it is our choices and decisions that determine its fate. If Mashiach and the redemption have to wait, let us make sure that we are not the ones who are holding up the process.

The Talmud teaches that one of the three questions the Heavenly tribunal will confront us with on our final day of judgment will be "Did you live with anticipation of that final redemption?"

The following incident elaborates. The renowned Rabbi Nachum Tchnernobler, one of the early Chassidic luminaries, found himself in the inn of a simple, hard-working farmer during one of his travels. The rabbi's custom was that at midnight he would arise, sit on the floor, and mourn and wail over the destruction of the Temple and the "Galus HaShechinah" (the Divine Presence in exile).

The farmer was awakened to the sorrowful sounds of crying and rushed into the rabbi's room to see what was wrong. He found the rabbi on the floor, tears streaming down his face. Fearful that he might be responsible, the innkeeper beseeched the rabbi to share the cause of his pain.

The rabbi explained that this was a nightly ritual to beseech the Almighty to send Mashiach to redeem His people and return them to the Land of Israel.

Moved by the rabbi's words and intense feelings, the simple innkeeper ran to tell his wife that they, too, must pray for Mashiach to come.

His wife proceeded to excoriate him, reminding him that they had just recently managed to pay off their debt and gain ownership of the farm and its animals. How terribly inconvenient it would be for Mashiach to come now! She then instructed her husband to make sure that the rabbi would stop praying.

The poor innkeeper ran back to the rabbi's room with his wife's message. The rabbi patiently reminded him that prosperity of any kind in the climate of the wicked Cossacks and their recurring attacks on Jews was very short lived and certainly could not be depended upon.

Impressed by this irrefutable point, the innkeeper ran back to his wife. She agreed that the rabbi's point was well taken, but insisted that instead of his praying for Mashiach to redeem the Jews and take them to Israel, Mashiach should take the vicious Cossacks to the Land of Israel, leaving the innkeeper to enjoy his newly acquired farm.

While humorous, the story strikes close to home. Indeed, how many of us, comfortable as we are in our surroundings, with homes, jobs, and a high standard of living, would be ready to pick up and move to Israel if Mashiach would come now?

A bottom-line requisite to bring about redemption is to eagerly "await" Mashiach with a genuine burning desire. Whether he comes in our time or, G-d forbid, does not, we are both held accountable and credited for the quest. Nothing stands in the path of willing. We must will, long, yearn, desire, quest, beseech, and pray. But as to the actualization of that long-awaited promise, we must defer to the unfathomable wisdom of the Almighty.

In conclusion, I would urge you, my dear reader, to consider the following points:

1. Be mindful of your own personal world by responding purposefully to the day-to-day choices that represent the "sparks" assigned for you to reclaim. Beware of your nemesis. Excessive pursuits of materialistic things sap the energy that is required to reach real goals and objectives. Only consistent immersion in Torah values will keep you in touch with true reality and sharpen your ability to keep your "eye on the ball." We impact the coming of Mashiach one soul at a time. Indeed, your achieving your spiritual goals is a critical piece of the puzzle put into place.

2. Pray
   a. for others to find their way and bring closure to their soul's unfinished business.
   b. for an end to misery and suffering that the new era will bring with it.

c. for an end to the pain of our benevolent Heavenly Father, Who suffers along with His children in their exile but Who simultaneously understands that dignity comes only in their earning their redemption.

3. Hope, yearn, anticipate, and have faith. Keep your desire alive and burning. "And even if Mashiach tarries, nonetheless, I will await him every day, fully expecting him to come."

Faith Perspectives
Terminal Life

*M*ichelle called me to share the devastating diagnosis of her father's terminal illness. The probability of losing him put her into an already full-blown, if premature, state of mourning. She was heartbroken, inconsolable, and determined to spend every remaining moment with him.

Predictably, she was deeply burdened with guilt based on hindsight of what she might have, could have, and should have done with and for him all the years that she was preoccupied with her own life.

From the moment he was diagnosed, her father, Sam, a vigorous, successful and active man, suspended all his business and activities, dedicating himself exclusively to the "truly important" people in his life — his children, grandchildren, and very close friends. He is now flying kites in the park with his grandson, taking boat rides with his granddaughter, and conducting long talks with his wife, things he wouldn't have considered previously, when his days were filled with work. He is putting his affairs in order, while Michelle is falling apart.

IMMINENT LOSS··

There is no greater source of pain than the imminent loss of a loved one. It hurts to the core. Upon the loss of his father, my husband commented that losing a parent is like challenging the assumption that the sun would rise in the morning. Unquestionably, parents will be there tomorrow just as the sun will come up tomorrow.

There are many stages in grieving. There is the unreality, the denial, the overwhelming pain, the guilt, and the anger. We have to allow ourselves sufficient time to experience all of these emotions. To deny and repress them in an attempt to hasten the healing process can be extremely detrimental. Ultimately such acceleration will prolong the effects, leaving unresolved issues with the potential of compromising relationships and situations. We have to give ourselves permission for as long as it takes — to feel, to cry, to mourn, to grieve — and not feel constrained to abide by someone else's timeline.

Simultaneously, we need a deep faith to sustain us with regard to mortality and ourselves.

ALL LIVES ARE FINITE

I gently suggested to Michelle that, in fact, each individual's time on this earth is finite. As one thinker put it, "If you're aware of death and the transient nature of your life — the fact that it's impermanent, intangible, and insubstantial — then your priorities are quite different. If you know that death is stalking you every moment of your life, you don't give importance to trivial things."

Facing our mortality would help us define what we would prefer our legacy to be. My husband has suggested that the Yizkor service, in which we remember our deceased loved ones, reminds us not only of those who preceded us, but also of ourselves and our own lives. If we ponder the legacy that we leave behind, then how we live becomes more urgent to us. This will enable us to focus on priorities and to pull our act together.

The Sages teach us that while other cultures celebrate and commemorate birthdays, Jews remember loved ones at the "yahrzeit," the anniversary of their death.

The Sages draw an analogy to a ship. Should we celebrate, they ask, when the ship sets forth on its maiden voyage as it is launched onto the stormy seas, uncertain of its ultimate fate? Or, is it more appropriate to celebrate when the ship returns to port intact, having successfully navigated its long, arduous journey?

As Jews, who view the challenging voyage of life, its trials and tribulations very seriously, we understand that choices we make in life render us either victors or the vanquished on this journey. We therefore regard its successful conclusion as cause for celebration.

DIMENSIONS OF GRIEF······························

Another dimension of grief is generated through missing our loved ones: the loss of their physical proximity. Sadly, we cannot sense their immediate presence in many precious ways: their embrace, their gaze, their kiss. We long to touch them, indeed to verify that they are still with us.

This is analogous to a plane as it travels into the distance and is surrounded by clouds. Would we question the airplane's continued existence as it disappears from sight, or do we understand that we cannot see it, because it has traveled beyond the scope of our vision? Obviously, regardless of our inability to see it, the airplane's flight continues.

Life is a narrow bridge between two eternities: the source from which we come when we are born and that to which we return when our journey ends. In eternity, we will find the loving embrace of our Heavenly Parent, Who will wipe the tears from our cheeks and Who will never leave us or abandon us. There, too, we will ultimately be reunited with all of our loved ones for all eternity.

The sobering postscript, however, is that though eternity awaits us, the nature of that eternity is defined by the choices we make now — our behavior, thoughts, words, and deeds — as we traverse the narrow bridge that we call life.

An inspired bon voyage to all of us.

Faith Perspectives
Judaism and Vegetarianism

The vegetarian diet enjoys a measure of popularity in the West. Some choose to be vegetarian for aesthetic reasons: they don't like the taste of meat, or they regard a meat-based diet as less healthy. Others are vegetarians because they find it morally wrong to kill an animal for food.

What does Judaism say about all this?

First, some background on the Jewish worldview:

Ideally there should be no barriers between one's physical and spiritual existence. Life should be a seamless expression of connecting to the Master of the Universe, the Author of our being. From the Jewish perspective, activities that present themselves as mundane — eating, sleeping, conducting business, relationships, etc. — are part of serving G-d, no less than the ritual observance of prayer, study, and giving charity.

Earthly activities are the bridge whereby we access higher realms. Therefore, the act of eating is not a meaningless, sensual indulgence, nor even a necessary means of maintaining our physical well-being. It can and should be the proverbial ladder to Heaven, a means of bringing holiness and sanctity into our lives.

The Talmud says that at the end of one's life, the first question G-d asks is: "Did you taste of every type of fruit that I put on Earth?" We are enjoined to appreciate all of life's bounty. Indeed, Maimonides deems it a mitzvah to partake of meat on the holidays, in order to increase one's pleasure and rejoicing. (In practice, this does not apply to those who do not enjoy these foods.)

In general, Judaism permits the eating of meat, provided that the animal is a species permitted by the Torah (Leviticus Chapter 11); is ritually slaughtered (shechitah) (Deuteronomy 12:21); has the nonkosher elements (blood and certain fats and sinews) removed (Leviticus 3:17; Genesis 32:33); is prepared without mixing meat and milk (Exodus 34:26); and that appropriate blessings are recited (Deuteronomy 8:10).

By eating in the Torah-prescribed manner, and with the proper focus and intent, says the Talmud, one's table can become a virtual altar in the service of G-d.

COMPASSION FOR ANIMALS ·

At the same time, the Torah stresses compassion for animals. Indeed, the Jewish forefathers are known affectionately as the "Seven Shepherds," and the Talmud describes how G-d chose Moses for Jewish leadership based on his tender care for the flocks.

Here are some examples of Jewish legislation regarding the ethical treatment of animals:

a. It is prohibited to cause pain to animals — "tzaar ba'alei chaim" (Talmud, Bava Metzia 32b, based on Exodus 23:5).

b. One is obligated to relieve an animal's suffering (i.e., unburden it), even if it belongs to your enemy (Exodus 23:5).

c. If an animal depends on you for sustenance, it is forbidden to eat anything until feeding the animal first (Talmud, Berachos 40a, based on Deuteronomy 11:15).

d. We are commanded to grant our animals a day of rest on Shabbos (Exodus 20:10).

e. It is forbidden to use two different species to pull the same plow, since this is detrimental to the weaker animal (Deuteronomy 22:10).

f. It is a mitzvah to send away a mother bird before taking her young (Deuteronomy 22:7).

g. It is forbidden to kill a cow and her calf on the same day (Leviticus 22:28).

h. It is prohibited to sever and eat a limb taken from a live animal (Genesis 9:4; this is one of the "Noachide" laws that apply to Jews and non-Jews alike).

i. Shechitah (ritual slaughter) must be done with a minimum of pain to the animal. The blade must be meticulously examined to assure the most painless form of death possible ("Chinuch" 451; Pri Megadim, Introduction to Shechitah Laws).

j. Hunting animals for sport is viewed with serious disapproval by our Sages (Talmud, Avodah Zarah 18b; "Noda BeYehudah," 2-YD 10).

To deal casually or cavalierly with the life of an animal is antithetical to Jewish values. This sensitivity is illustrated by the following story:

In a small European village, a shochet (ritual slaughterer) fetched some water to apply to his blade in the preparation process. At a distance, he observed a very old man watching him and shaking his head from side to side disapprovingly. Finally, the young shochet asked the old man for an explanation.

The old man replied that as he watched him prepare his blade, it brought back memories from many years earlier when, as a young man, he had observed the saintly Rabbi Israel Baal Shem Tov (founder of the Chassidism) doing the same thing. But the difference, he explained, was that Rabbi Israel did not need to fetch water in order to sharpen the blade; rather the tears that streamed from his eyes were adequate.

·HIERARCHY OF CREATION

While Jewish law protects the ethical treatment of animals, Judaism also maintains that animals are intended to serve mankind, as it says: "Let man dominate the fish, birds, and animals" (Genesis 1:26). There is a clear hierarchy of creation, with man at the pinnacle.

Maimonides identifies four levels in the hierarchy of creation, in which every creature derives its sustenance from the level beneath it:

> Level 1: Domaim — the silent, inanimate realm (i.e. earth and minerals) constitutes the lowest existence, and is self-sustaining.
>
> Level 2: Tzomei'ach — vegetation is nurtured by the previous level, earth.
>
> Level 3: Chai — the animal kingdom derives its nourishment mainly from vegetation.
>
> Level 4: Medaber — (lit., the speaking being) human beings derive nourishment by eating both vegetation and animals.

When food is consumed, its identity is subsumed into that of the one eating it. Thus the Talmud (Pesachim 59b) regards it as morally justified to eat animals only when we are involved in holy and spiritual pursuits. It is only then that the human actualizes his highest potential, and the consumed animal is, so to speak, elevated to the level of "human."

In Jewish consciousness, the highest level an animal can achieve is to be consumed by a human and used in the service of G-d. A chicken on a Shabbos table is a very lucky chicken! (See Tanya Ch. 7.)

If, however, the person is acting like an animal, then by what right may he consume his "peer"? What spiritual improvement can he confer upon this animal by eating it?

Therefore, before eating meat, we must ask ourselves the very sobering question of whether in fact, given who we are, are we indeed benefiting this animal?

When eating is not merely an act of "mindless consumption," but rather an act with clear intent that the strength and energy one derives from the food will be utilized to benefit the world, then eating has been sublimated to an act of worship.

·····················RADICALIZED EXTENSION

Animal rights can be a double-edged sword: While the animal kingdom is important and must be treated ethically, we must recognize that there is no equivalence of species. Among all living things, humankind alone is created in the "image of God" (Genesis 1:26).

When the lines are blurred, when both human and animal life is considered equally sacred, this can trigger a dangerous philosophy that regards killing a human being as no more heinous than killing an animal.

Rabbi Yosef Albo (14th century) asserts that this philosophy has its roots in the biblical story of Cain and Abel. Genesis Chapter 4 describes how Cain brought a sacrifice of grain, while his brother Abel offered animals. Rabbi Albo explains that Cain regarded humans and animals as equals and, accordingly, felt he had no right to kill them.

Cain then extended this misguided logic: If people and animals are inherently equal, then just as one could permit taking the life of an animal, so too could one permit taking the life of his fellow man. Thus Cain was able to justify the murder of his brother.

In modern times, the radicalized extension of Cain's philosophy came to the fore during the 1930's, when the Nazis passed a number of laws protecting animals, e.g., restricting the use of live animals in biomedical experiments ("vivisection"). All the while, the Nazis were killing millions of humans. (Actually, Jews were legally relegated to the status of "subhuman.") The lines between human and animal had been totally obscured.

Judaism's permitting animals for food serves as a pragmatic hedge against such extremism by constantly reminding man of his unique status among G-d's creation. The 18th-century kabbalist, Rabbi Moshe Chaim Luzatto, explains that all living things — humans and animals — have souls. However, not all souls are created equal. Animals have a soul which animates them and carries within it the instincts for survival, procreation, fear, etc. Only humans, with a Divine soul, have the ability to forge a relationship with G-d, the transcendent dimension. Only humans have the ability to choose higher "soul pleasures," like helping the poor, even at the expense of lower "body pleasures," like hoarding more food for ourselves. You'll never see a hungry dog say to his friends, "Let's not fight over this," or "Let's save some for the other dogs who aren't here."

Rabbi Abraham Isaac Kook writes that man was granted dominion over animals in order to underscore our spiritual superiority and heightened moral obligations. Were man to accord animals the same rights as humans, then just as we don't expect high moral standards from animals, we would, tragically, lower our expectations of humans as well.

HISTORICAL PRECEDENTS ·······················

Historically, Adam and Eve were vegetarians, as it says: "vegetables and fruits shall be your food" (Genesis 1:29). God first permitted meat to Noah and his descendants after the Flood (Genesis 9:3; Talmud, Sanhedrin 59b).

What brought about this change?

Some commentators explain that before the Flood, man was above the food chain, given the responsibility to take care of the world and everything in it. After the Flood, man descended a level and became linked with the food chain, albeit at the top of it. Mankind had fallen in its ability to influence the animal world through actions and deeds, and it thus became necessary to influence the animal world more directly by ingesting them.

Rabbi Yosef Albo asserts that Cain's misguided philosophy had been adopted by succeeding generations, and meat was permitted to Noah in order to emphasize the superiority of humanity over the animal kingdom.

Another commentator, the Malbim, explains the shift from a physical perspective: The post-diluvian era was marked by a general weakening of the human condition. As the quality of produce became nutritionally inferior, and as mankind became geographically dispersed and subject to varying climates, it became necessary to supplement the human diet with animal products.

Some cite the precedent of Adam and Eve as indication that in a perfect world, i.e., in the future time of the Messiah, humans will return to universal vegetarianism. The vast majority of rabbinic scholars, however, maintain that animal offerings will be resumed in the Messianic era. Indeed, the Talmud (Bava Basra 75a) states that when Mashiach arrives, G-d will prepare a meat-based feast for the righteous.

· SUMMARY

In conclusion, Judaism accepts the idea of a vegetarian diet, though dependent on one's intention:

Vegetarianism based on the idea that we have no moral right to kill animals is not an acceptable Jewish view.

Vegetarianism for aesthetic or health reasons is acceptable; indeed, the Torah's mandate to "guard yourselves carefully" (Deuteronomy 4:15) requires that we pay attention to health issues related to a meat-centered diet. Some points to consider include the contemporary increase in sickness in animals created by factory-farm conditions, and the administration of growth hormones, antibiotics, and other drugs. All of these may pose possible health risks to humans.

In addition, there is the possible violation of "tzaar ba'alei chaim" (causing pain to animals) resulting from mass-production methods of raising, transporting, and slaughtering animals. The great 20th-century American sage, Rabbi Moshe Feinstein, forbade raising lambs in cramped and painful conditions, and forbade feeding animals chemicals in place of food, since this would deprive them of the pleasure of eating (Igros Moshe EH 4:92).

Jewish consciousness requires constant attention to preserving and protecting our natural world.

Rabbi Benzion of Bobov was strolling with a disciple, deeply engrossed in scholarly conversation. As they passed a tree, the student mindlessly pulled off a leaf and unconsciously shredded it into pieces.

Rabbi Benzion stopped abruptly. The student, startled, asked what was wrong. In response, the rabbi asked him why he had picked the leaf off the tree.

The disciple, taken aback, could think of no response.

The rabbi explained that all of nature — birds, trees, even every blade of grass — everything that G-d created in this world, sings its own form of praise to its Creator. If they should be needed for food and sustenance, they are ingested and become part of the song of the higher species. But to pull a leaf from a tree for no purpose at all is to wastefully silence its song, giving it no recourse, as it were, to join any other instrument in the symphony of nature.

Yes, Judaism permits the eating of meat, provided that proper intent and mindfulness are present: to elevate the Divine energy contained in meat to a higher human level; to use energy derived from eating to discharge spiritual and moral responsibilities; and to serve G-d through the pleasures of His world.

This article was prepared with the help of Rabbi Shraga Simmons.

For further reading: "Vegetarianism and Judaism" by Rabbi J. David Bleich, Contemporary Halakhic Problems, Volume III.

Holy Days and Holidays

Holy Days and Holidays
Entering the Palace of the King

In recounting our many wanderings during the war years and the final journey that brought us to America, my father, of blessed memory, often related the comment of one of his fellow travelers. This man had lost everything during that fateful time. The Nazis had stripped him of his home, his wealth, his community, his relatives, and every member of his immediate family.

Left with none of the accouterments that generally identify a person, he concluded that it was here and now, on this ship, that he was obliged to determine where he would live, what he would do, and what the context of his life would be. In effect he would have to recreate himself — to be reborn — and start his life anew.

Rosh Hashanah, the Jewish New Year, marks the anniversary of the creation of man. Elul, the month prior to Rosh Hashanah, is designated as a time of inventory, a time to take stock of what was and what we want to perpetuate into the new year and of what we wish to divest ourselves.

It is noteworthy that the Hebrew word for year — "shanah" — has a dual meaning. It implies both "change" and "repetition," underscoring the task at hand of deciding what should be changed in the coming year and what behavior is worthy of repetition. This is the critical time on the "ship" between the world of yesterday and the tomorrow when we are given the opportunity to redefine or, if you will, "recreate" ourselves. When we appear before the Heavenly tribunal on Rosh Hashanah, the day that is both the birthday of man and the day of judgment, the brief we present should reflect a plan for the coming year that is an improved version of what was in the past.

The Almighty created us as unique beings replete both with our individual strengths, weaknesses, struggles, and challenges. Only the Almighty knows what we could be. Only He, by virtue of His personal investiture of potential into our person, has a true image of what we could be, and that is the benchmark for our accountability and for G-d's judgment of us.

However, it remains our prerogative, by dint of the life choices and decisions we make, to choose either to draw near or to distance ourselves from the realization of our potential self that was our "essence before creation."

During the month of Elul, the voyage on this ship mandates devoting our full energies to the existential crisis at hand that demands decisions and resolutions, mindful of the urgency to reach for the best in us — that which will resonate with the supernal image of us.

· CHANGING YOUR NAME

Maimonides, the great 12th-century commentator and teacher, instructs us on the necessary steps toward "teshuvah" (repentance) and returning to who we truly are. He identifies "changing one's name and stating I am a different person than the person who committed the deeds of the past year" as a requisite step in the process.

My husband commented that Maimonides was obviously not suggesting a change of ID, Social Security number or such. He explained that many of us have titles to our names. For instance, it might be a Ph.D. or M.D., so that it might read Paul Jones M.D., Alice Smith Ph.D. or Karen Hill M.S.W., etc. These are titles by which individuals identify themselves.

There is, however, other less formal but equally powerful titles that others or we ourselves assign to us. Examples might be: Betty the lazy, Harry the indolent, Jerry the selfish, Helen the disorganized, Abby the miserly, etc. As part of the introspective process on the "ship," Maimonides exhorts us to change our name, the title that will alter the perception of how we see ourselves.

Judy had always seen herself as incompetent and disorganized. She called to tell me that she had made a deliberate and conscious decision to change her name, and as a result woke up that morning energized and eager to begin life anew with her new self-chosen designation of Judy "the competent and the organized." She was determined to follow through with the behavior that would support and confirm her new name.

How we view ourselves, the labels, categories, and stereotypes clearly circumscribe our lives and impact our behavior. If our names reflect negative effects, we remain stuck in self-fulfilling patterns of behavior. If, however, we can convert them to reflect positive and affirming attributes, we will free up the necessary energy to access the best part of ourselves. Redefinition and substantive change of ID is a major step toward "rebirth."

THE BLACKOUT·······································

I was on the East Coast at the time of the blackout of 2003. Lakewood, New Jersey, the particular town I was visiting, was not affected but neighboring communities found themselves thrust into total darkness, some for a few hours and others beyond a day. It was a sobering experience to see New York City, the most powerful metropolis in the world, rendered impotent. The mighty cutting-edge world of technology in which we place such heavy stock proved useless.

Human endeavors, glorious as they may be, are limited and ultimately we must acknowledge that it is indeed G-d Who runs the world. Since no events in our lives are arbitrary, every occurrence invites scrutiny and should be gleaned for its message. The blackout, on the threshold of the month of Elul, conjured up the following image.

I saw myself in the vast theater of life, having come to experience the great play. It was intermission time and the throngs of people filed out to the lobby, heading to the refreshment stands. They sought ice cream, popcorn, drinks, and soon the ensuing socializing took on a life of its own. The lights began to dim and blink but the crowd was too engrossed, enjoying the pleasures at hand, reluctant to yield to the blinking dim lights.

What if they ignore the subtle reminders? What if they become so preoccupied in their current distractions? Will they miss the rest of the play: its culmination, its concluding point, and its message? Would it not be a shame if they were to exchange the purpose of their being there for the equivalent of popcorn and ice cream?

Jewish sources, similarly, relate a parable of a domain whose beloved and benevolent king announced that he would be available to meet his subjects on a designated day for a select few hours. The day arrived and the people flocked to the palace, eager to set eyes on their beloved monarch, the source of their bountiful existence.

The massive gates were thrown open and the crowd was blown away by the regal splendor of the magnificent grounds, the verdant gardens leading to the palace rich in flowers of every shape and color, their beauty and fragrance breath taking. Many in the crowd were so enchanted that they could not tear themselves away. Others made it to the first chamber where they beheld the most magnificent furnishings. Yet others were mesmerized by the awesome architecture of the palatial structure. Some were enthralled by the fascinating art, paintings, and sculpture. Then, there were those who stood transfixed by the sounds of the spellbinding music and melodies.

So enticing and totally absorbing were the endless fixtures and appointments of the palace that, sadly, most of the people forgot their mission, the purpose of their coming. And when, abruptly, it was announced that the time granted for his subjects to seek him out had ended, all too few had actually made it to the king's chamber. All too many, in their pursuit of the frills and nonessentials, had forfeited their dream of coming into the presence of the king and beholding his face.

Perhaps the blackout was a variation of dimmed and blinking lights, of reminders that intermission is over and we need to move on to the play, the purpose for which we came to this world. We need to make sure that we are on the path that will grant us proximity to the King.

ENTERING THE PALACE·····························

How do we merit the privilege of the King's presence?

Proximity to a Being Who is not bound by time or space can only be achieved by resemblance to His essence. G-d is perfect and all the G-dlike deeds that we perform make us more like Him and bring us a notch closer to His perfection and hence His presence.

A wonderful anecdote is told of a woman who, in preparation for the upcoming holidays, took her four children to a store to outfit them. She left the store with her family, all newly and completely attired, and stopped short at the sight of a young boy in tattered and ragged clothing wistfully looking into the shop window. The stark contrast between the lad's impoverished state and her privileged brood was more than she could bear.

She told her family to wait outside as she took the young lad inside and outfitted him from head to toe, just as she had done for her own children. As she was about to take leave of him, he looked up at her and asked, "Are you G-d?"

"No," the woman responded, taken aback. "I am not G-d; I am just one of His children."

To which the young boy, with tears in his eyes, replied, "I knew you had to be related."

G-dlike behavior brings us closer to G-d. It requires looking beyond ourselves, perhaps noticing and alleviating the pain and the burden of others: a kind word, a call, an inquiry, an act of forgiveness, getting beyond the petty, a charitable gesture. It just takes a little bit of caring to bring a smile and some sunshine into the lives of others. But it does require a shift in focus from "me" to "them," from "intermission" to the "play," and most significantly from the preoccupation with the accouterments and the trappings to remembering that we came to see the King.

We are on the "ship" that bridges the past and the future, and about to embark. What will be our resolve?

Holy Days and Holidays
Legacies and Luggage

$\mathcal{I}$ am writing this article on a Midwest Express flight en route from New York to Milwaukee. I have never enjoyed flying. Despite the fact that statistically it is assumed to be the safest mode of travel, I like to keep my feet on the ground. It gives me the illusion of control.

With air travel, I feel vulnerable, suspended in the air, despite the reassuring laws of aerodynamics. It reiterates with certainty the message that I am in G-d's Hand and at His mercy.

Intellectually, I realize this is the reality of our lives even as we assume mastery and move about managing and conquering the world. "Fill the earth and conquer it," was G-d's mandate to mankind at the very outset of creation. The implicit challenge in this command describes a very tenuous balance; to understand that although we are commanding conquerors, creators, and conductors, still the whole of our capabilities stems from the Infinite Source in the absence of which we are nothing and have nothing.

The approaching High Holy Days, Rosh Hashanah and Yom Kippur, should compel us to halt the rigorous efforts to control our environment, and rededicate our efforts to this awareness, the "coronation" of G-d as King and Master of our personal universe.

EXCESS BAGGAGE·····································

Yet another reflection from my recent trip might be instructive for our preholiday introspection. The zipper on my carry-on case, which has persevered through much duress, broke on this trip. Reluctant as I am, at this mature stage in life, to part with anything that has accompanied me for so long, I went to a luggage store to see if my bag could be repaired. They advised me that I would be better served discarding it and investing in a new one.

That's okay when dealing with "things." But what if our inability to let go extends beyond the "suitcases" in our lives? What if we retain excess psychological baggage and patterns of behavior, such as self-deprecating beliefs of our inherent worth? What if we unnecessarily debase our competence, goodness, etc.? Or perhaps, we maintain a negative attitude toward others; we are unfairly critical and disparaging of those around us.

An objective analysis of ourselves is especially germane at this time of year. Our sages advise that in our pursuit to improve our behavior, this period in the calendar is especially propitious. Heavenly assistance is readily obtainable and beneficial to those who choose to access it.

·············REPAIRING AND STRENGTHENING

A wedding took place many generations ago. The two sets of mechatunim (in-laws) gathered for the celebration. One of the proud fathers, a rabbi of prestigious lineage, arose, and consistent with his family's custom on such occasions, proceeded to enumerate at great length the names of all of his distinguished ancestors and the magnificent contributions they had made to Jewish life.

When he concluded, the other father arose and said, "My ancestors were not rabbis; they were simple tailors and craftsmen, but they too left a legacy. They taught that we are obligated to mend that which is broken and to strengthen that which is whole."

The first father embraced him, exclaiming, "I didn't realize that you had such an illustrious lineage!"

Coronating the Almighty as our Sovereign during this season requires us to scrutinize our daily activities and interactions, identifying that which needs to be mended and that which needs to be fortified.

My husband has suggested that the medical community's much-touted necessity for an "annual physical" examination should help us appreciate the even more critical and imperative need for an "annual spiritual." Rosh Hashanah needs to find us ready with our spiritual luggage in hand.

Some areas to consider might be:

1. Does our relationship with our Creator, our Source need enhancement, i.e., more Torah learning, and greater attention to the quantity and quality of our quiet time to meditate, to pray, to connect?

2. Our interpersonal relationships with parents, spouse, children, friends, and community. This might require that we subdue our egos and let go of negative attitudes; committing to guarding our tongues, being gentler, kinder, more compassionate, loving, understanding, etc.

We all have work to do. We may come from different places, different points of departure, and we may be at different stages in our life's journey or on the spectrum of personal development and growth. Yet we are all heirs to the legacy of this season, which demands that we take a spiritual inventory in order to mend the torn and strengthen the whole.

May it be a productive and meaningful journey into the New Year for us all.

Holy Days and Holidays
Leave It to G-d

The theme of the holiday of Chanukah is light, a theme that occupies a prominent place in Jewish thought and practice. In addition to the Chanukah lights, Jews kindle Sabbath candles, Yom Tov candles, and the Yahrzeit candles in memory of a departed soul. Indeed we are taught that creation of the world began with G-d's pronouncement, "Let there be light." Our Sages teach that a man's soul is the lamp of G-d. We are further advised that a little bit of light banishes a lot of darkness, and that it takes only one small flame to kindle many others.

The story of Chanukah commemorates the Jews' triumphant retrieval of the Holy Temple from the Hellenists. In meeting our ritual responsibility to light the Menorah, the candelabrum, the Jews found that there was only enough pure oil to burn for one day. And, as is characteristic of our people, we did not focus on how we would manage tomorrow, or what the next day would bring. We did what that moment called for! Miraculously the one-day supply sufficed for eight days by which time new pure oil had been pressed.

This serves as great instruction and inspiration for me. It says to me that regardless of the prevailing and depressing climate of darkness surrounding us, we need to celebrate the joys of every day and invest our moments meaningfully. We need to spend more time with our families and friends. Even if the brightness of the candelabrum of our existence appears to be diminished, we need to access even the smallest bit of available light. Regardless of the insecurity, unpredictability, and appearance of hopelessness, nonetheless, we as Jews need to do what we have always done, and that is leave tomorrow to G-d.

I am struck by another value highlighted in the story of Chanukah. The miracle of Chanukah included great military victories. The small Jewish army triumphed against the mighty Hellenist forces; the few vanquished the many. It is certainly a historically noteworthy fact, but typically not the focus of our celebration during this holiday. Wars and bloodshed have always been abhorrent to the Jewish people, resorted to only in defense and even then viewed as a necessary evil. We are the people of the book, not of the sword. War and killing violates our essence and even when, as in the story of Chanukah, it was unavoidable, for us as Jews it is not worthy of commemoration or celebration. Consistent with this value, on Chanukah, we don't have military parades or testimonials to war heroes. In the current idiom, Golda Meir expressed it well. She said, "We may someday forgive our enemies for killing our boys but we will never forgive them for turning our boys into killers."

Elie Wiesel once noted that upon the liberation of his death camp at the conclusion of World War II, many of the non-Jewish inmates of the camp celebrated their first moment of freedom by pillaging neighboring villages, thus taking revenge and settling the score with their oppressors. In stark contrast, the first act of freedom for Jews of the camp was to convene a minyan (a quorum of ten men) for a prayer service.

Jews all over the world will light candles — candles against the night and the darkness — and we will pray. We will pray that death and killing will cease to be part of the human experience. We will pray that the illumination of the Chanukah flames will spread to the four corners of the world bringing clarity, Torah values, G-d's wisdom, kindness, and compassion to fill the hearts, souls, and lives of all people on earth.

Holy Days and Holidays
Creating Peace

*T*he mutual love between G-d and His people is encapsulated by the names used to refer to the holiday of Passover. We, the children of Israel, call it Passover, commemorating His strong show of affection when, smiting the Egyptians' firstborn, He "passed over" Jewish homes.

G-d, conversely, refers to the holiday as "the Feast of Matzos, unleavened bread," attributing the cause of celebration to Israel's willingness to make haste, sacrifice, and make do with the bread of poverty, the barest of provisions, in order to follow Him into barren, uncharted territory, literally a desert, to become His elect nation. This marked the beginning of a glorious relationship that has spanned more than thirty-three centuries, surviving unprecedented challenges to the commitment of both our Heavenly Father and His often-wayward children to each other.

The Kabbalistic works offer yet another insight into the name of the holiday. "Pesach" can be split into two words, "Peh-sach," which means "a speaking mouth." This refers to the fact that the children of Israel had been brutally enslaved in Egypt and had not had the luxury of thinking, let alone speaking freely. With freedom came the liberation of the mouth, the signal human capacity to translate the language of the soul into comprehensible communication.

In Genesis, when God creates man and "breathes into him a living soul," Onkelos, the foremost Bible translator, renders this "man became a speaking being." The exclusive hallmark of humanity is speech, and when we were in bondage, our speech, likewise, was incarcerated and imprisoned. The breaking out of the shackles of servitude released our tongues and the expressions of our souls began to flow again.

In following the roller coaster of post-9/11 world events, I am struck by a virtual sense of vertigo at the runaway overhaul of our existence as we knew it. Moreover, when life moves at this rapid, fast-forward pace, it is almost impossible to get a clear perspective, a handle on what is occurring and perhaps, most importantly, what our response needs to be in this ever more insane state of affairs.

Recently I was asked by my community to give a class on "shalom bayis," domestic harmony and tranquility in the home, a refresher course on the relationship between husband and wife. I prefaced my remarks by sharing my sense of utter helplessness and frustration at being a mere spectator to events of such magnitude (i.e., 9/11) unfolding before our very eyes.

What power do we have to make a difference? What role can we play? What impact can we have?

I think it is fair to say that the world in which we find ourselves is a commentary, if not an actual reflection, of our inner landscape. Our Sages teach that every human is an "olam katan," a complete, albeit miniature, world unto himself or herself. The macrocosm is reflected in the microcosm and vice versa. This is most compellingly captured in the fact that G-d created "Adam," one single human being, to inform us for all time that the justification for the creation of the entire universe resides in each individual. Every person is considered a total world unto himself or herself.

When world peace and security are threatened, we need to look at our inner world and identify the corresponding issues. If inspectors are being dispatched to determine whether nations are in compliance or defiance of international norms, what about our personal domain? If what they are looking for is an arsenal, weapons of mass destruction, what about all the means at our disposal, in our own personal world, to build or to destroy? If we want shalom out there, perhaps the place to begin is shalom bayis, peace in our very own space.

At a time when we are approaching the holiday that celebrates liberated speech, are we not mandated to examine our use of that powerful "arsenal"?

"Life and death are in the hand (i.e., the power) of the tongue," our Sages inform us. Words can heal and words can devastate. Has there ever been a time when the term "verbal abuse" was as commonplace, almost a household phrase? How many people have been in the line of fire of our personal weapons of mass destruction? We are all familiar with these victims, those irreversibly scarred and mangled by those who could and should have been there to support and nurture. Their self-image will always be blackened by our ugly, verbal lashes.

It is so easy to destroy and so hard to rebuild. Those who are called upon to counsel others have tried to mitigate and assuage the pain of these anguished souls so that they can move on to forgive and trust in order that they might eventually engage in normal relationships. The poisoned word is as lethal as poisoned gas, and the ravages are no less extensive.

In reality, there is a greater body than the U.N. that sends inspectors to our homes, businesses, synagogues, and areas that we occupy. What will these Heavenly inspectors find? Are we in compliance with or in defiance of the Heavenly injunction to use our God-given gift of speech for constructive and productive purposes?

Rebecca, an accomplished musician, is a warm, highly intelligent, and competent member of our community. She called me, following my shalom bayis class and shared that her parents had divorced when she was very young. Her mother told her that the verbal carnage in the home left her with no recourse but to end the marriage. After all, her mother sadly concluded, cruel, hurtful words once spoken can never be retrieved and they continue to devastate and wreak havoc.

Rebecca has never forgotten her mother's comment. She resolved that this would never happen in her life. She married late but has a beautiful family and her resolve has remained steadfast and uncompromising. Indeed, before she utters a word, she consciously pauses for a moment to reflect whether this is a word to which she wants to give independent life and whether she wants to put it out there never to be recalled.

I was totally blown away. Rebecca's house may not yet be free of "chametz" (unleavened bread) prohibited on Passover, but she has already achieved the harder work of freeing her speech. Her arsenal is not one of mass destruction. It is affirmative of life. She brings shalom to her bayis, peace to her home and to the context of her world.

The positive and enriching energy that she and others like her create every time they comply with the innate rhythm and mandate of the supernal soul brings us all closer to the collective "shalom," the peace that we so desperately need.

We must not be helpless bystanders to a world bent on destruction. Liberating our speech, the greatest gift the Almighty has bestowed on humankind, will be our way, very literally, of converting our "swords into plowshares" and ushering in the long-awaited redemption.

Holy Days and Holidays
Personal Liberation

*P*assover is a physically strenuous and challenging holiday for women. In our community it is tremulously referred to as the "P" word. The prospect of searching every corner, nook, and cranny of the house for all chametz foods, crumbs, and residue — in addition to the chores for which we are already responsible — can be overwhelming.

The good news is that when it's all done and we sit down, thoroughly exhausted, to the Seder table, surrounded by family and friends, we do indeed feel exhilarated and liberated.

Passover, the historical event, and the spring season in which it occurs not only commemorate renewal and freedom, but bring with them the special spiritual energy that allows us, here and now, to achieve our own personal liberation.

As I clean my house of the chametz products, I realize that there is an even greater summons in all of this; that is, to purify my inner abode — my inner self — of any inclination that is spiritually undesirable.

Physical chametz is generally defined as leavened dough. As such, it implies a process of fermentation and distension that is out of proportion to its ingredients. Similarly, spiritual chametz signifies the kind of aggrandizement and distortion that impedes one's freedom to become the very best person that one can be.

A JOURNEY OF REDEMPTION· · · · · · · · · · · · · · · · · ·

Annually, the Hagadah reminds us that "in every generation each person should see himself as though he had been liberated from Egypt." This is a mandate to each of us to embark on a personal journey of redemption. Clearly, each of us has his own unique prison and his own individual Egypt.

We can understand this even better when we realize that the Hebrew word for Egypt is "Mitzraim," and that the root word of Mitzraim means "constriction" or "limitation."

Upon reflection, we discover that some of our limitations come from influences outside of ourselves: the environment in which we were raised, the people in our lives who have impacted us adversely. Moreover, there are the "pharaohs" we deal with daily; those who undermine us or attempt to dominate us. In some instances, the tyranny comes from within; self-absorption, hedonism, distorted needs, skewed values.

All of the above have the capacity to tie us up in knots and disable us from addressing the real things in life: relationships, family, community, and the yearnings of the soul.

Perhaps, most distressingly, our inner "pharaohs" keep us safely incarcerated by convincing us that the patterns of our lives cannot be altered, that we are too far gone to be redeemed. The voices within us whisper, "too much bad history," "too much water under the dam," "too much damage that can't be undone." We are intimidated into believing that we are a lost cause.

But it need not be that way.

GREATNESS OF POTENTIAL· ·

Three times a day, every single day, Jewish tradition exhorts us to remember the "going out" of Egypt. Our sages explain that the attention given to this event over any other event in our history is mandated as a response to the taskmaster within us who is determined to keep us enslaved forever.

It is supremely important to bear in mind that Jews in Egypt, preceding their redemption, had fallen into the deepest abyss of inner defilement, one degree short of total spiritual obliteration. Despite their personal despair, the Almighty knew that they were redeemable. He knew that their essence and core were incorruptible. He, the Creator of their majestic souls, understood the greatness that was their potential.

Three times a day we evoke the remembrance of G-d taking us out of that unforgiving abyss, so that we might know that no matter how lost we may consider ourselves to be, we dare not lose faith in our ability to lift ourselves to freedom.

This year as I ask G-d for the strength to appropriately clean and prepare my house for Passover, I entreat Him even more urgently for special assistance to help me identify my personal "pharaohs" so that I might set myself free of the shackles that inhibit my growth.

As I move closer, room-by-room, to the Passover celebration, I will hopefully, simultaneously, move step-by-step closer to putting my spiritual house in order. Then, and only then, will I know that I am truly free.

All the best, and happy Passover to all.

Holy Days and Holidays
Phases of Freedom

assover, the holiday of freedom, has come and gone. Children, relatives, and guests from near and far have returned to their respective homes. And, hopefully, we have settled back into our normal routines.

Our Sages advise us, however, that despite our having celebrated freedom, the work of setting ourselves free has just begun. Liberation from the bondage of Egypt, the ten plagues, the splitting of the sea, and all the myriad attendant miracles were gifts from G-d to give us a glimpse of the potential — a mere taste of freedom. But, the actualization — the making of freedom a reality in our lives — is up to each one of us. We have to earn it.

In effect, it is as if the Almighty said to us: "I took you out of bondage, removed your shackles, but that was just 'phase one' of freedom. True, ultimate freedom will be achieved only after you successfully master 'phase two' — which means accepting the Torah, living by its precepts, and leading a decent, moral, and Divinely mandated existence."

Toward this goal, as a newly born nation, we were advised that we would have 49 days, bridging Passover to Shavuos, to prepare ourselves for receiving the Torah, the awesome event that we celebrate on that holiday. Forty-nine days, wherein day-by-day, step-by-step, we would steadily elevate ourselves, ascending from one level to the next on the ladder of spiritual attainment so that when the

50th day would arrive we would be worthy beneficiaries of G-d's revelation.

Our sacred texts emphasize that this threefold configuration — Passover, the 49-day count of the Omer, and Shavuos — comes to teach us an essential lesson in life. And the lesson is this: Freedom *from* is not enough. It must be followed by freedom *to*. We learn that escaping oppression externally imposed, or, for that matter, extricating one's self from tyranny that is self-imposed (such as an addiction), is but a necessary first step toward liberation.

If, however, one has merely fled subjugation, but has not substituted a positive force in its place, it will just be a matter of time before one is again claimed by the same or another form of bondage.

A NEW FORM OF BONDAGE

Nature abhors a vacuum. Consequently, the vacuum created by leaving Egypt had to be filled by a positive commitment to a Higher Authority and to Torah and its commandments.

As one psychotherapist put it, "we must replace the demon with an angel," otherwise, we revert back to a prior affliction or seek a new one in its stead. Indeed, it is only when we simultaneously purge ourselves of the negative, while filling our lives with purpose and meaning, that we can begin to experience true freedom.

Some actual cases might best illustrate this principle.

Andrea, a mother of six, was a top executive in an accounting firm, and was considering leaving her job to become a full-time homemaker. She called to ask my advice about her plans, commenting that this had been her dream since her marriage. In addition she hoped that it would motivate her husband, as the sole breadwinner, to become more responsible and ambitious.

I thought that her reasoning was clear and compelling. I cautioned her, however, that she needed to sit down and carefully think through how she would fill her days. I suggested that she identify the pursuits she deemed respectable and desirable. I enumerated for her consideration: Torah learning, exercise classes, homemaking, courses of study, quality time with her children, volunteering at their school, writing a book, and upgrading her spirituality with prayer and meditation. I further proposed that she needed to structure a plan of how her goals would become a reality. I tried to explain that extricating oneself from an unacceptable place can be liberating only if the void is filled by constructive and productive pursuits.

Another instance involved Marsha, a student of mine, who approached me with her desire to disabuse herself of the propensity to gossip and find fault with others. Jokingly she remarked that she had heretofore defended this practice by calling it "character analysis." She realized, as she matured religiously, that this was a mere rationalization. Marsha appealed to me to help her actualize her resolve.

In response, I immediately invoked this very principle: If she were to be successful she would need to replace her present negative practice with a positive one. In place of gossiping, I recommended she spend five minutes on the phone with a friend reviewing the laws of acceptable and prohibited forms of speech. Or perhaps, when she felt the urge to deliver a juicy bit of gossip, that she instead lift the phone and place a call to a "shut-in." She would thus bring caring and sunshine to someone's life. I reminded her that eliminating the objectionable has staying power only if it is replaced by an act of virtue. As a foremost therapist argues, "You simply cannot banish a bad habit by an act of will, no matter how resolute. It requires coaxing it toward the door, while inviting an honorable and righteous guest to take its place."

MAKING EVERY DAY COUNT······················

This principle helps us understand the period of "Sefiras Ha-Omer," counting of the Omer, the countdown toward Shavuos, when we receive the Torah and ultimate liberation becomes possible. Every day we mark off is a day closer to our goal. Not only is every day counted but every day must count. It has to be focused on improving ourselves, on reaching beyond where we are, in character, learning, interacting, and relating. We need to become, by dint of our own hard work, people of greater substance.

As such, this season highlights for us the crucial, significance of time. Daily, it asks of us:

- "How did this day differ from yesterday?"
- "In what way am I a changed and better person than I was a day ago?"
- "What am I striving to have achieved by tomorrow?"

For Jews, the moments of our lives are our most precious and treasured gifts. The Kabbalah, the writings of Jewish mysticism, tell us that every moment of life cries out to us to fill it with meaning, because that meaning will define that moment and give it life. If that moment is wasted it will disappear for all of eternity.

"Killing time," as it is popularly known in our culture, is anathema to the Jew, and particularly in this season, it is a cardinal violation of the soul of our nation.

Reassessing how we spend our time and rededicating ourselves to investing the moments of our lives appropriately will certainly bring us to the successful conclusion of the "countdown." Thereby we will be privileged to hear, as we did over 3000 years ago, the sounds of revelation that sanctified us as a nation at the foot of Mount Sinai.

Authentic and total freedom will, with renewed force and relevance, resonate in our lives once again.

Holy Days and Holidays
Connecting: Passover Reflections

*P*assover is a family holiday; a time when nostalgia pervades as we dig deep into our rich past and uncover memories — both joyous and painful.

A dear friend tearfully shared with me how difficult it is for her to face yet another Passover without her beloved husband. Shortly thereafter, a young man from Israel contacted me. He was preparing for and anticipating the upcoming holiday. He wanted to know why the year of mourning for his mother had not mended the void he felt in his heart over her untimely passing.

As for myself, I move through my kitchen, stopping in my tracks as I find myself uttering the very comments my mother, of blessed memory, used to make at this time of the year. Without question I am thinking her thoughts and doing what she did. As I juggle four frying pans, flipping crepes for blintzes in the air, I turn the pages back in my mind some 45 years and see my grand-mother doing the same. My married daughters, whether they live in the United States or abroad, call almost daily in advance of the holiday to check if their memory serves them well as they recreate the Passover customs and delicacies with which they grew up.

The rhythms of past, present, and future converge to become one on this holiday. It is indeed a seamless fabric transcending time and space.

"Each and every person should see himself as though he or she was personally redeemed, leaving the bondage of Egypt," the Haggadah enjoins. It is as though we are being told if we go back far enough in our collective memories, beyond the immediate conscious recall of wives, husbands, mothers, fathers, and grandparents, we might access and touch — deep within the recesses of our soul — the biblical Exodus experience.

OUT OF BONDAGE

We should literally see ourselves being lifted out of bondage into the loving embrace of our Heavenly Parent, redeeming us out of His love for us; choosing us to be His very own people. These pronounced seasonal longings and recollections and the desire for connection are an internal expression of the deep need to connect at the very Source of all connection.

Rabbi Elimelech of Lizhensk informed his disciples that all of us have etched into our memory the milestone events in our history, such as the giving of the Torah at Mount Sinai. He goes so far as to assert that, by putting forth the requisite effort to access that event, he was able to recall who had been standing next to him during that experience.

Perhaps this level of connection is beyond our scope, but consider the following anecdote witnessed by my brother-in-law at the Kosel, the Western Wall, in Jerusalem. An older man standing at the Wall was passionately pouring out his heart and gesturing with his hands. My brother-in-law moved closer, curious to learn more about the nature of this elderly man's communication with the Almighty. The man cried, "Dear G-d in Heaven, You know my son's problem ... his health ... his heart ... he went to the cardiologist ... he sent him on to ..." The man paused, interjecting, "Oh, I am so sorry, dear G-d in Heaven, I already told You that yesterday. Forgive me for repeating myself." We can ascertain this aged individual's connection to G-d is authentic. G-d is right there for him, interested in and caring about every detail of his life.

This year, as we sit at our respective Seder tables, surrounded by family and friends, there will invariably be a moment of longing within each one of us. This moment may present itself as personal or collective. It may not be clearly identifiable, when we initially sense it, that we are really yearning for what once was. Let us understand and take it as an invitation, an opportunity, and a propitious moment to, with this longing, reach for the Being Who connected us to Himself at the very moment in history we commemorate and celebrate on this night.

Only the Almighty can assuage our longing and wipe away our tears of loss, pain, and suffering. Only He can bring the ultimate redemption. He is the ultimate loving Parent there for us at our Seder and every time we choose. And, it is through Him that all of us — living in the past, present or future — are forever joined.

Holy Days and Holidays
Counting Every Moment

The gift of life is experienced by all of us in segments of years, months, weeks, days, and, ultimately, moments. Every moment is to be treasured as an entity onto itself. Hence, there is great value in being "in the moment" — relishing, savoring, and appreciating the now, regardless of what preceded it or what might follow it. A little boy, in a cartoon I once saw, observed that yesterday was the past, tomorrow is the future, but today is a gift, so we call it the present.

To separate the present from a painful past or from anxieties about the future is a formidable challenge for anyone. Many of us have witnessed the phenomenon of some survivors — of the Holocaust or of other losses (widows, widowers, children, parents, etc.) — who find it almost impossible to be joyous in the present because of the lingering shadows of the past. In many instances, they feel that it would be a betrayal of the memories of their loved ones if they would find happiness in their present lives.

The Torah gives us wonderful insight into this dilemma. In Genesis, we read the tragic account of Joseph being sold into slavery by his brothers. They see him as a usurper of power and judge him guilty of treason, a capital offense. Rather than execute him, they choose the alternative of selling him into slavery, turning him over to a caravan of merchants traveling to Egypt. The text tells us that the caravan, into whose care Joseph was delivered, carried a cargo of aromatic spices.

The Midrash says this is noteworthy since most caravans of this nature carried foul-smelling merchandise, such as animal hides, etc. The question arises as to why the Almighty would orchestrate events so that a caravan with aromatic spices would appear at this particular time and place. Our Sages respond that the Almighty didn't want Joseph to be subjected to an offensive odor for the duration of his journey to Egypt.

This begs an obvious question. Having suffered the horrific trauma of betrayal by his brothers, could Joseph really have cared about such a seemingly insignificant detail as the smell of the caravan? It reminds one of: "Aside from that, Mrs. Lincoln, how did you like the play?"

The message, however, is a very important one. Despite all the painful events that had transpired, G-d wanted Joseph to know that He still cared about him and was concerned with even the most miniscule detail of his life. G-d wanted Joseph, all his suffering notwithstanding, to grasp and appreciate the blessings of the moment, not allowing the darkness of the past to obscure the light of the present.

My mother, of blessed memory, was a wife whose devotion was of legendary proportions. During one of my father's hospitalizations, I had occasion to be with her. As we left my father's side to go to our place of residence, we passed a mall. A beautiful sweater in a store window caught my mother's attention and she remarked, "I wonder if they would have it in my size." Although I was taken aback, I was eager for her to have a distraction, and suggested that we check it out; indeed, she purchased the sweater.

When I shared this incident with my sister, she thought it inconsistent with my mother's self-sacrificing devotion that she should care about a sweater at such a time. Upon reflection, I realized, however, that there was absolutely no contradiction. My mother was a woman of faith who understood that life comes from the Almighty with a mandate to live every moment to its fullest. Buying the sweater, on my mother's part, was a vote of confidence in life, in Divine Providence, and His benevolence. It was for her an echo of Joseph's "aromatic spices" in her journey through her personal "Egypt."

Every moment of life is a gift, an embrace of the Almighty. Too many of us are bogged down by what was and too obsessed with what will be. In the process, we lose sight of the present.

This season of "counting the Omer" invites us to stop and take notice and make every moment count for us.

Women's Issues

Women's Issues
Where Is Home?

There is something compelling about "going home." "Home" immediately conjures the image of a safe haven, bringing to the fore feelings akin to what it must have felt like in the womb: warm, secure, cared for, a sense of belonging to something greater than oneself.

For those of us who cannot conjure up such an image, there is an unfulfilled yearning, a "homeless" feeling for that which we were not privileged to have.

I was one of the privileged. And for 30 years of married life, while my parents were still alive — and I lived a thousand miles away from them, nurturing my own family — whenever I went to visit them, I was still "going home."

While some spouses take exception to that sentiment, it was not, for me, an indictment of my current domicile, so much as a recognition that the child within me was still alive and in need of reassurance.

My husband confides that he often drives miles to a distant neighborhood, parking adjacent to a vacant lot where his childhood home stood years ago. There he recalls events that warmed his heart as a child and that refresh his spirit even today.

"Home is where the heart is" proclaims the popular adage. But why is it that even as we move on to supposedly bigger and better things — careers, marriage, children, and grandchildren — the longing for one's childhood "home" persists?

Indeed, in the dark winters of our lives, we draw strength from our young formative years, and in the waning sunset years, when other forms of cognizance fail us, memories of "home" are the last to go.

Technical, physiological reasons are given to explain this phenomenon but I am convinced there is more to it than science has to offer.

HOUSELESS BUT NOT HOMELESS

An anecdote is told of a postwar refugee family transferred from one location place to another in search of a place to settle. On one occasion, the family was standing in a train station surrounded by their tattered suitcases, boxes, and bags when a bystander approached the 6-year-old daughter and remarked, "You poor darling, moving about so much with no place to call home."

The little girl looked up in surprise. "You are mistaken," she replied, "I do have a home. I just don't have a house to put it into."

I personally could have been that little girl. I was born in Romania during the terrible Holocaust years. My family was expelled from the house in which we lived, forced to seek shelter wherever we could. We became refugees, fleeing for our lives.

After the war, we boarded a ship and set sail for what was then Palestine, only to be turned away by the British at the shore of Haifa. We moved on to Cyprus and then to Italy. At long last, we received papers to immigrate to the United States. Throughout the entire ordeal, though I was "houseless," I was never "homeless." I lived in the supportive embrace of my family, nourished by their love and faith.

Clearly, a "home" has little to do with structure, bricks, and mortar or the accouterments of furniture, draperies, etc. It has everything to do with the spirit with which it is filled.

The Midrash teaches that our Patriarchs perceived Mount Moriah, site of Israel's Holy Temple, in different ways. Abraham, the first of the Patriarchs, called it a "har," a mountain — an awesome place that would challenge his descendants, test their resolve, and evoke the greatness within them.

The second Patriarch, Isaac, called it a "sadeh," a field where one might, in the context of undisturbed nature, seek the solitude that would enable one to access a relationship with the Infinite.

Jacob, the third Patriarch, and father of the twelve tribes, designated this holiest space on earth as "bayis," a home.

In referring to the Temple Mount as a "bayis," Jacob defined its essence. In describing the place where God and man would meet, as a "home," Jacob acknowledged the validity of both of his predecessors' views, but insisted that challenge and solitude require the support of a home to ensure success.

The Midrash concludes that the Almighty preferred Jacob's designation above the others. And so, a home it has been ever since.

HOME IS A SANCTUARY·····························

Indeed, more than anything else, a home is a sanctuary for the spirit, where one's soul can touch base with its Source, the Master of the universe.

Today, while we no longer have our "Bais HaMikdash," the Holy Temple, we do have our homes.

Our Sages advise that in the absence of the Temple, the special vessels that were utilized in the historic House of God in Jerusalem be symbolically replicated in our individual homes:

• The "Menorah," the Candelabrum of the Bais HaMikdash, symbolizes the oral tradition, the creative moral energy that maintains the contemporaniety of Jewish values in our abodes.

• The "Shulchan," the golden Table with the wondrous, ever-fresh showbreads, represents our worldly needs, the material sustenance whose acquisition requires integrity and balance, and whose blessings mandate that they be appreciated and kept fresh so that we have no need to indulge in excess.

- "The Mizbeiach," the Altar, site of the daily offerings, signifies the necessary sacrifices demanded of family members to transcend their personal desires in deference to the needs of others.
- Finally, there is the Holy of Holies, the sublime inner sanctum, which speaks to immutable moral principles, and through its cherubim symbolizes the intimate relationship between husband and wife, the energy of the home fires.
- Of singular relevance to women is the critical service performed by the Kohen (priest), the religious functionary who was responsible for the Temple's day-to-day functioning. In its current manifestation, it is the woman who, in large measure, has assumed the duties of the Kohen. She is the caretaker of the lofty center of life, and like the priests of old, creates the spirit, the ambiance, the quality and energy of the tabernacle entrusted into her care. How awesome a role it is!

HOME-MAKER

The Talmud explains that when the Almighty created woman, He invested her with a "binah yeseirah," a special dimension of understanding and intuition.

The contemporary thinker, Ashley Montague, in his book The Natural Superiority of Woman echoes this thought referring to woman's "genius of humanness."

By all accounts, G-d graced women with a special capacity for relationships, thus equipping them to be His delegates, the builders of the most sacred spaces on earth: our homes.

Throughout the ages, over our long and tortured history of persecution in the many lands of our dispersion, the Jewish home was an oasis, a quiet harbor in a stormy world.

Though oppression and deprivation afflicted the Jew in the streets of the diaspora, the moment he stepped over the threshold of his modest home, he entered a veritable palace where he was made to feel like a king.

He was surrounded by a loving wife and children and above all else, a way of life and purpose for living that nothing, not even a bigoted, hateful world, could take away from him. His home gave him a raison d'etre. His downtrodden spirit was uplifted, his soul soothed and quickened to life.

History has proven time and again, that the home is the pivotal factor in our national survival and the key to the redemption of our people. Our Sages teach that it was in the merit of Jewish women that our forebears in Egypt were redeemed. Despite years of slavery in the decadent Egyptian society, all attempts to acculturate and demoralize the Jews were to no avail because Jewish wives and mothers had transformed their homes into bastions of strength, courage, and morality.

HOMESICK SOCIETY·······································

All of which begs the Question.

How is it that we have allowed this most remarkable agency, the home, to become devalued in our time? How is it that we have allowed the role of women, the home's primary force, to be denigrated?

How have we allowed the secular world with its idolatry of self to convince us that there can be a more worthwhile calling than creating places of loving, caring, and belonging? How have we permitted our culture to convince us that a role that creates a link in an eternal chain can be an inferior vocation? How did they persuade us that bringing redemption to humanity is not the ultimate in gratification?

The need to "go home" is part of the human condition and will inevitably confront all of us during our life. Whether it is a "homesick" feeling, a yearning for that which we had or a "homeless" feeling for that which we were not privileged to have, our home experience needs to be dealt with if we are to lead productive lives.

In the final analysis, home exerts a powerful influence, shaping past, present, and future. The implication for women, who are G-d's appointed stewards over this sacred space, is that they hold the vital key to mankind's success and the realization of the world's destiny.

Women's Issues
The Inner Stage of Life

I converted over three years ago and have been married now for a year and a half. There are a few areas of halachah (Jewish law) I struggle with but the one that sticks out as being the hardest is covering my hair.

Right now, when I go to a religious function or to the synagogue, I wear a hat over my shoulder-length hair. At work I do not cover my hair. Aside from the issue of if I should be covering my hair, I am feeling that I am consigning myself to a certain social circle for how I cover my hair. I have also heard that the extent to which one keeps kosher can be "viewed" by whether one covers her hair. All of this saddens me and makes me reflect on how we as Jews do not love one another the way we should.

I can also add that people in my life who are not Orthodox (i.e., my mother, some friends who are Jewish but not observant, and colleagues at work) would react negatively to my covering my hair. I tried making a start by covering my hair all day Friday — I work at home and run errands at lunch. One nonobservant acquaintance saw me and in the middle of the kosher market said, "Since when are you covering your hair? Is this something new?" I felt so embarrassed as other women in wigs began to look closer at me. I just shook my head and changed the subject.

I am torn. Part of me wants to cover my hair, but part of me does not. All this makes me feel guilty for not covering my hair, and I wish there was a solution.

I worry that my career path will be hampered if I suddenly chose to cover my hair. I hate to call attention to myself and I feel in a way it's not modest since people will be drawn to looking at me to examine how I changed.

Finally there is my mother, who takes it all so hard, and being an only child I feel guilty that I am making her feel uncomfortable and angry, and I feel resentful that I still care about what she would feel more than what G-d asks of me.

Thankfully my husband is understanding and has indicated that when it is right for me, if it is right for me, it's all up to me; his mother did not cover her hair until later in life.

I would appreciate any words or comments you have about this particular law and also the bigger picture that perhaps everyone can relate to: being observant in the face of society's "approval."

The first note of clarification needs to be that the objective of G-d's commandments is not solely the betterment of society as a whole or how we might appear to others. Of at least equal importance is how the mitzvos (commandments) speak to us personally, and how they enhance and promote the requisite spiritual growth of the individual who observes them. A mitzvah (commandment) is a communication between the "Metzaveh," the Commander (G-d), and the person who has wisely chosen to observe His Expressed Will, thereby forging a personal relationship with the Master of the Universe.

As you correctly noted, covering the hair for a woman is indeed only part of a bigger "picture."

Philosophically, the issue at hand is the existential struggle between focusing on the external dimensions of life or the internal ones. The external cycles on the physical, material world of appearances that beckons to us compellingly and incessantly, moment to moment.

This includes the never-ending drive to sate our appetites. It encompasses the needs of eating, drinking, sleeping, clothing ourselves, careers, acquisition of money, buying bigger and more beautiful homes, cars, vacations, etc. All of these drives are part of the world of the proverbial hunt. Arguably, the pursuit of the blandishments of the external world can be all consuming and as such can conceivably take us far afield from a life of purpose and meaning.

In contrast, the internal world is the world of the spirit. Its voice is quieter and its demands on the human being more subtle and admittedly drowned out by the loud chatter of external pressures. But to ignore the needs of the soul ultimately is to deny our raison d'etre, the reason for our being on this earth.

The Almighty, in His great Wisdom, has provided us with the laws of "tzenius," variously translated as modesty and privacy. Better yet, tzenius is the deemphasis of the outer self, so that the essential self might emerge. Practically speaking, this means that our behavior in speech, dress, and in the way we carry ourselves should convey the message to ourselves primarily and to others secondarily, that I need to be attractive but not attracting. Attracting undue attention to one's physical self proclaims that what you see is what you get; that the totality of our person inheres in the physical presentation. In contrast, when one is private and modest in demeanor and in the extent to which one exposes only that which is appropriate, the statement is that the body, important as it is, is no more than a vehicle for essence, that it is indeed character, personality, and one's attributes that are the expression of the image of G-d in which man is created.

Consider the absurd end of the spectrum, that of the tabloids and the various magazines at the checkout counters—the flaunting of flesh that screams "look at me," "this is who I am" — with no sense of the greater dignity emanating from the fact that one's essence is drawn from G-d Himself. Clearly, there is no appreciation that there is so much more to a human being than their physical configuration that, no matter how impressive, ultimately has no enduring existence. In the end, everything that is corporeal wanes, dies, and decays. It is only the spirit, that is part and parcel of the Almighty, and as such His treasured embassy inside of each of us, that is eternal and timeless.

The external world of the marketplace, the contemporary version of the jungle, is primarily a man's domain. It's the sphere in which man exercises his power and finds fulfillment. It is he, though not exclusively, who has historically been responsible for going out to make a living by manipulating and exploiting the external environment.

The thrust of a woman's life is best captured by King David in the book of Psalms, who states, "the dignity of the daughter of a king is her inwardness." Hers is the inner stage of life, the private sector, the personal, the home, and by extension the one quintessentially able to connect with the inner wellsprings of her person. Her inner place is the source of her superior ability to relate, to intuit, to perceive, to care, and to nurture. A woman has the greater wherewithal to look inside of herself for fulfillment and true gratification.

Anne Lindbergh, in her book *Gift from the Sea*, writes, "Woman must be the pioneer in the turning inward for strength. In a sense, she has always been the pioneer. Less able until the last generation to escape into outward activities, the very limitations of her life forced her to look inward. And from looking inward she gained an inner strength which man, in his outward active life, did not as often find. But in our recent efforts to emancipate ourselves, to prove ourselves the equal of man, we have naturally enough perhaps, been drawn to competing with him in his outward activities to the neglect of our own inner springs. Why have we been seduced into abandoning this timeless inner strength of woman, for the temporal strength of man? The outer strength of man is essential to the pattern, but even here the reign of purely outer strengths and purely outward solutions seems to be waning today.

Men, too, are being forced to look inward, to find inner solutions as well as outer ones. Perhaps, this change marks a new stage of maturity for modern, extrovert, activist, materialistic man. Can it be that he is beginning to realize that the Kingdom of Heaven is from within?"

Often times, the stimulus for a woman to go inward and to connect to her core are life-changing events, such as life-threatening illnesses (G-d forbid), losses, and various forms of adversity. Something that challenges the status quo motivates her to take stock and evaluate the authenticity of her life.

For observant women who are tuned in and listen carefully, the mitzvah of tzenius — of dressing modestly and covering one's hair upon marriage — serve as a powerful medium to raise our consciousness and maintain our awareness that we must be inner directed. The hair, which is a woman's "crowning beauty," is covered when a woman leaves the confines of her home. In a sense, her full beauty is reserved exclusively for her husband. The foreign object, be it a hat or wig, no matter how attractive, is foreign, nonetheless, and constantly reminds a woman to focus on the inner beauty inside her. In a behavioral way, when we go out to interface with the powerful world of illusion, we center ourselves with a reality check. We cover our hair in an attempt to somewhat conceal our external selves, so that we might reveal and connect to the internal. The commentators note that a woman covers her eyes when she lights the Shabbos candles, to block out the external world — that which is only virtual reality — so that she might apprehend the true, real world of the spirit. Similarly, when we recite the Shema, our ultimate statement of faith in G-d, we cover our eyes to our immediate external surroundings and move deep inside of ourselves to get in touch with that which is real and enduring. Assuredly, observant women must take care to always look pleasant, clean, and appealing. Not to do so would reflect negatively on the G-d Whose imprint she bears.

Bottom line, the concept of tzenius cautions us that to allow ourselves to be seduced by a culture that is obsessed with externalities is to abandon our very core and essence.

My husband has suggested the following additional philosophic framework for covering one's hair. Hair, in Jewish sources, is representative of the "yetzer hara," the base inclination. Consider Esau, Jacob's evil twin brother who was born "sei'ar," hairy, furry, animalistic. Hair grows in the areas of our body that are most closely associated with appetites that require discipline and self-control; the mouth, pubic area, the head, the brain. While we cannot control whether hair will grow or not, we can choose our response to the challenge it represents.

The domain of the male in his service to G-d is within the sanctification of "time." It is preferably he who should usher in the Sabbath and holidays by the recitation of the Kiddush. The nazir who lets his hair grow does so for thirty days. Hence, in responding to the challenge of hair which represents unbridled appetite, a man is required to deal with it in "time." The Shulchan Aruch (the Code of Jewish Laws) provides that a man should cut his hair before the festival holidays. A Kohen Gadol (High Priest) was obligated to cut his hair once a week. A king was required by Jewish law to cut his hair every day. All of these are "time" connected.

The Jewish female's role is seen within the sanctification of "space" — the space of the home, the workplace, etc. The woman expresses her understanding of the need to govern her yetzer hara, i.e., the growth of hair that symbolizes appetite, by creating a space around her head. Thus, by exercising her prerogative, as the sanctifier of space, she creates a boundary around her head, by the covering that she wears on her head.

Whether this approach resonates with you or not, when a married woman chooses to abide by the requirements of halachah (Jewish law) to cover her hair, when she leaves the context of her home, one thing is very clear, covering one's hair is a very cogent reminder, moment to moment, that she is a married woman. Regardless of how attractive that hair covering might be and perhaps even more so than one's own hair, it is nonetheless a foreign object which creates an undeniable awareness of one's marital status. Especially in our times when the barriers to the genders interacting freely have been removed and the opportunities, both socially and in the workplace, abound, there can never be too many reminders that we are committed to the exclusive covenant of our marriage.

Dear reader, your taking into account everyone else's reaction, sensitive as it might be, does not serve you well or give you peace. "To thine own self be true"; everyone else will ultimately adjust. I sense that your level of observance and the kind of conversion to which you committed your life involved the acceptance of all mitzvos (commandments). You will feel best honoring the totality of your commitment.

Those who question the level of your kashrus (observance of dietary laws) or that of others, based on whether they cover their hair, are merely stating that since they have neither the time, inclination nor the opportunity to investigate every home in question, they can safely assume that those who commit themselves to all of the mitzvos can also be trusted in the standard of their kashrus. It's not a value judgment of their personhood. It's merely a way of attempting to maintain the integrity of a commitment that, to them, is very precious.

All of us, dear reader, are on a journey toward becoming the best we can be. There are times in everyone's life when we are torn. We hear conflicting voices inside of us, urging us simultaneously in different directions. There are times when we have to keep moving up the mountain and other times when we need to stop and catch our breath. This might be a good time to enlist the guidance of someone you respect to help you gain some clarity and perspective.

Your husband is wise to leave it up to you. He knows that your agonizing is a product of a desire to do the right thing. And I am sure that you will. Good luck.

P.S. If you wish, you can ask Rabbi Coopersmith for my home phone number and we can continue our discussion.

Women's Issues
Women and the Workplace

I am about to re-enter the workforce, and I am concerned about how this additional point of emphasis in my life will affect my family and my self-definition as a woman. Are there any guidelines you can offer? What are some practical suggestions and tips I can take with me?

Indeed, more women are entering the workplace than ever before, citing economic, psychological, and other reasons. As more women find themselves in the public arena, it is important to remain keenly aware that inwardness, privacy, and family relationships must dominate our personal domain, and are the values that form the core of our existence.

Although the "woman of valor," depicted by King Solomon, buys and sells fields and manages merchant ships from afar, the overriding focus of her existence are her relationships with her husband, children, and family.

Ann Richards, former governor of Texas, confirmed this concept in an interview. She acknowledged that, in her own very public life, financial and political setbacks paled when compared to failures in her familial relationships. She discovered that it was her private life, not the public one, which was the core of her feminine reality.

This holds true for any working mother, who must struggle constantly to keep priorities in order.

Take Susan, for example, an asset manager for a multinational corporation, working at her computer negotiating stock deals. Every few minutes, busy as she is, her eyes dart to the adjacent large bay window through which she can see her toddler swinging happily in the backyard playground. It appears as though Susan is watching her child while she is conducting business. In reality, she is conducting business while she is watching her child. Her emphasis is on the child; he is her priority.

Clearly, it's easier to remain focused on what's important to our feminine reality when we can remain within the home environment.

·······THE ESSENTIAL SPIRITUAL CONNECTION

The Patriarch, Jacob, was the first to blaze a trail for us in our journey to the working world. He left the spiritually supportive context, built by his grandfather and his father, Abraham and Isaac, on a journey that led him to Laban, his future father-in-law. His world was suddenly filled with deceit and treachery, the antithesis of that which had nurtured him in the "tents" of his childhood. Undeniably the 14 years he spent in the study halls of "Shem and Ever" adequately fortified him to withstand the odious temptations he would subsequently face in his new environment.

When we go out into the workplace, we too must be strengthened by immersing ourselves in spirituality. Toward this end, we need to surround ourselves with like-minded friends and associates. We need to take advantage of breaks in the workday and fill them with as many Jewish learning experiences as possible.

To maintain our integrity in the workplace, we must present ourselves as a countermessage to the unending bombardment of Madison Avenue hype and promotion that dictates the American lifestyle.

Abiding by kosher dietary standards, as inconvenient as that might be in the workplace, proclaims loudly and clearly that one marches to the beat of a different and transcendent drummer. The way we dress and our speech, the choice of verbal expressions, are reminders to ourselves and statements to others of who we are.

Several years ago, my husband and I conducted a weekend retreat in Oxnard, California at a lovely resort hotel on the marina. Passing the pool area on our way from one of the sessions, one of the guests — looking like Mr. Cool with a towel flung over his shoulder and gold chains gleaming in the sun — confronted my husband, who despite the warm California weather was dressed in the traditional Chassidic garb. "Why do you insist on dressing in those clothes of yesteryear in this modern world?" snickered Mr. Cool in an obviously antagonistic manner.

Nonplussed, my husband took the opportunity to explain that policemen wear a uniform in order to identify themselves as figures of authority. In much the same way, a rabbi — indeed, every religious Jew — wears a uniform so that he is identified as an individual with a sacred calling. More importantly, my husband asserted, his dress was an undeniable statement to himself and to the world that he was not buying into the pathological and immoral fabric of our society.

MAINTAINING FEMININE QUALITIES ···········

Perils of the workplace abound for women eager to be successful while still maintaining their singular feminine qualities.

When Charlotte began her career 15 years ago, she believed she could use her feminine attributes of kindness, caring, sensitivity, and gentleness in her quest to succeed in the male-dominated workplace. Instead, slowly but surely, her essential feminine qualities were replaced by callousness, opportunism, and ruthlessness — the signposts of corporate male America. True, she was one of the most successful women executives in the game, but she was feared and hated by everyone who worked for her — female and male alike. She wonders how it happened; how she had lost her feminine essence, how her dream had dissipated.

Jewish women, whether entering or firmly entrenched in the workplace, must be ever diligent to uphold the wisdom of Torah guidelines circumscribing relationships between the genders.

From local to national news, we read constantly of public figures engaged in affairs and harassment. It is essential to put safeguards in place, especially in today's open society where men and women work closely together. There indeed will be times and circumstances in each of our lives that may make us particularly vulnerable. Jewish law provides strict guidelines and precautionary measures so that women and men can avoid compromising situations.

STAYING FOCUSED

After 20 years spent working for the deceitful and dishonest Laban, Jacob gathers his family to head back home. "Behold I see the face of your father Laban and it was not toward me as in earlier days." This is how Jacob explains his leaving. Literally, we understand this to mean that Laban wasn't as kindly disposed as he had been in the past. My father, of blessed memory, had a deeper insight into this passage:

Up until that time, Jacob had seen Laban for what he really was, a scoundrel garbed in a presentable demeanor. Jacob knew it was time to leave since he could no longer see through Laban. All at once, Laban didn't seem as despicable as he had in the past. Jacob had become desensitized, and he recognized that it was too dangerous for him and his family to remain in Laban's presence any longer.

When we find ourselves justifying what heretofore was unacceptable, it is indicative of an erosion of values and sensitivities. It is time for us to run our life's scenarios past an expert, to reassess and to reevaluate. It is time for us to find a mentor and have a "spiritual checkup."

Women are blessed with special talents to create positive environments wherever we find ourselves and with whatever we are doing. We can accomplish this by incorporating the lessons mentioned above:

1. being ever mindful of our primary role as women;

2. fortifying ourselves with the necessary values for our venture into a valueless world;

3. never compromising our standards of behavior;

4. maintaining our unique feminine attributes which have been described by anthropologist Ashley Montagu as the "genius of humanity";

5. taking Torah-mandated precautionary measures in dealing with the occupational hazards of intergender relationships;

6. cultivating a relationship with a spiritual guide, a mentor who will help us take periodic "spiritual checkups" to verify that we are accomplishing the goals of our personal lives' mission statement.

Women's Issues
A Woman for All Seasons

*T*here are many different seasons in the life of a woman. While the substance of our relationship to G-d need not change, invariably the form of the relationship will.

One such season finds us involved in the pursuit of personal fulfillment such as school, professional training, and career. Finding, perfecting, and developing ourselves is the primary focus of this time of our life.

This season might also be utilized to foster a relationship with G-d through reflection, introspection, studying, and prayer.

Women tend generally to move onto the next stage, one of looking for the spouses with whom to share our lives.

Often, despite our efforts, success in this area is elusive. For those who are successful, conception and bearing children do not necessarily follow as readily as one might hope for.

When, finally, the goals of marriage, children, and creating a home are realized, we discover that the demands of our new roles cut heavily into what we perceive as our spiritual growth and connection to G-d. The many expressions of our personhood seem to fall by the wayside.

The core issue is that heretofore, the focus was on the self — self-fulfillment, self-gratification, self-growth. But now the "self" has to defer to the needs of the family.

The wife and mother may feel that she has lost her "self" — physically, spiritually, and, at times, even mentally.

As a result some women berate and denigrate themselves for what they perceive as the waning state of spirituality following marriage and motherhood.

A NEW CHAPTER ···································

It is important to understand that while every new chapter of life appears to close the door to what was, it does open a new door for us. The contrast with what was should be seen not as a diminution but as a challenge to find new avenues of expression and connection.

We need to understand that for women, our relationship to G-d is one seamless piece; it cannot be compartmentalized.

Clearly, time for formal prayer is harder to come by when our daily schedules necessitate carpooling, working, cleaning house, cooking, etc. We do need to recognize, however, that these are not mere mundane activities that distance us from our spirituality. Quite the contrary. If we invest them with awareness and see in them G-d's blessing and opportunities, they become vehicles for the highest form of worship.

It is all a matter of perspective and attitude. G-d does not reside exclusively in the formal prayer book. As King Solomon exclaims, "Know Him and relate to Him in all your paths." Whatever the stage of our life or the path of our journey, we can invite the Almighty into our life and make Him a constant Companion at our side.

Indeed, what we have learned from our single life, we can apply to our married life.

THE NEW SHAPE OF GRATITUDE ···············

When I passed my entrance exams I thanked Him. When I successfully negotiated my doctoral dissertation I was grateful. When I got the promotion I had hoped for I acknowledged my appreciation for His assistance.

No less so when I am in the kitchen. It is totally appropriate to ask Him to please make my cake rise and to thank Him when indeed it does. When I diaper my baby and behold this most precious of all gifts, I let myself feel embraced by Him. When a tired husband comes home, I count my blessing: we are a couple!

The cup filled by my Heavenly Benefactor runneth over. Every aspect of life itself — waking up, seeing the sun shining, trees blooming, feeling healthy, my limbs moving, my body functioning — is an opportunity for making a meaningful connection with the Sovereign of the universe.

Every season of life has both limitations and opportunities. Sadly, at times it is only through the wisdom of age and retrospection that we come to realize just how uniquely precious the years of raising a family were, despite the many difficulties we encountered.

· SOME SUGGESTIONS

Here are a few suggestions to effectively navigate through those challenging years of marriage and motherhood:

1. Move through your days with your eyes and heart open to "ordinary blessings."

2. Surround yourself with people of like mind and values, so that you can encourage each other, especially when the going gets tough.

3. Steer clear of self-pity. Put on lively and inspiring music or whatever it takes to create a happy environment and keep moving.

4. Take care of yourself physically: eat well, exercise, and take a little time off whenever possible.

5. Go to classes, listen to tapes, grow, learn.

6. Seek professional help when necessary to deal with the adjustment to the perceived loss of "self-hood" and the concomitant challenge of constant giving.

7. Make time (as limited as it might be) for creative modes of self-expression such as writing, painting, etc.

8. Above all, ask G-d for clarity, for help in keeping your head on straight amid all of the tumult. Finally, tell G-d how desperately you need to feel that He is holding your hand. Ask Him to help you understand that, despite your perceived feelings of being spiritually diminished, in your role of partner and nurturer you are, in fact, spiritually elevated, and more closely connected than ever.

Women's Issues
Challah and Candles

Can you elaborate on two of the rituals that are most significant to women — baking bread and separating challah, and lighting the Sabbath candles?

ecently, I was asked to speak to a group of professional single women who had strong nostalgic ties to Judaism, but very marginal connection to actual Torah observance. As a lead into our discussion, I asked them to share their background with the group, focusing on which member in their families had had the greatest impact on them.

Invariably, there was a bubbie in each of their experiences. Sherri, one of the young women present, pointed out that, to her mind, there is a clear and strong distinction between a bubbie and a grandmother. She claimed to have one of each:

- Her grandmother was a nice enough woman, but she had a very busy, independent life of her own. She worked, played bridge, golfed, etc., and occasionally "made time" for her grandchildren.

- Her bubbie, in contrast, was always available. Her home was always open and welcoming. At this point the tears flowed down Sherri's cheeks. She spoke longingly of the aromas of freshly baked delicacies that without fail awaited her every visit to her bubbie's house. It was clear that in Sherri's mind the aromas of her bubbie's home would always be associated with an expression of her great love for Sherri. They confirmed for Sherri that nothing mattered to her bubbie more than she did.

There are many jokes that circulate about the Jewish mother's preoccupation with food. From a traditional perspective, the preparation of food offers many opportunities and possibilities. The investments of time, effort, creativity, caring, and yes, even prayers, are connected with this seemingly mundane activity.

BAKING BREAD ···

Jewish law provides that when we bake a given quantity of bread or cake, we remove a requisite-sized piece of the dough, called "challah," recite a blessing, and set it aside. Historically, when Jews lived in Israel in Temple times, this consecrated piece of dough would be given to the Kohen, the priest, designated by G-d to officiate in the Temple service. In the absence of that context, this consecrated piece of dough is nowadays burnt in the oven. But the rite of setting aside, separating, consecrating, and hallowing the piece of dough informs us that nothing we do is pedestrian or mundane. A portion must be given to G-d (through the Kohen at the Temple, His representative).

This ritual is an acknowledgment that though we work hard, sustenance ultimately derives from the Almighty. The awareness that flows from this act elevates the physical practice of preparing bread (symbolically the staple of our sustenance) to a spiritual realm.

Thus, the preparation of food, by a Jewish woman following the ideals of Torah, leads to much more than merely nourishment for the body, it actually becomes nourishment for the soul.

To raise the consciousness and awareness of the tremendous G-d-given power inherent in women to influence and enable our loved ones in a positive way, we bake bread. As we knead our dough, we can choose to focus prayerfully on a personality characteristic of a loved one that would benefit from some help from Heaven.

Perhaps a son is quick to anger, a husband is limited in his ability to verbalize compassion, or a daughter is self-involved. With love, tears, and prayers, we knead the dough, mindful of our responsibility to use the special powers given to us by G-d, to knead the "dough" of our family toward growth and perfection. The bread thus enjoins us to influence, shape, form, and mold those entrusted to our care that they may reach their greatest potential.

The Lelover Rebbe, a man of great note, traveled to a distant village on an urgent matter. The rabbi of the village greeted his distinguished colleague and invited him to his humble abode. In great excitement, the rabbi ran into the kitchen to apprise his wife of his honored guest's presence and requested that they serve the Lelover Rebbe appropriately. She woefully shared with her husband that the only ingredients they had at their disposal were a bit of flour and some water. He said, "We'll have to do the best with what we have." She made a pancake and served it to the Lelover Rebbe, who was extremely effusive in his appreciation of the extraordinarily delicious taste of the pancake and thanked her gratefully.

Several weeks later, the rabbi's wife received a letter from the Lelover Rebbe's wife telling her that the Rebbe, who never takes note of mundane things such as food, had repeatedly raved over the delectable pancake she served. Could she possibly share the recipe?

The rabbi's wife replied immediately, "To tell you the truth, we were mortified that we had so little to work with for so esteemed a guest. I mixed bits of flour with a mixture of water and tears and said to G-d, 'I am contributing all I have — a meager bit of flour and water — and You, G-d, spice it with the flavor of Paradise, as only You can.' I guess that explains the Heavenly taste your husband experienced."

A rose is a rose is a rose, perhaps. But clearly, the results of our labor are dependent on the insights, emotions, and prayers we invest in them.

LIGHTING SHABBOS CANDLES · · · · · · · · · · · · · · · · · · ·

In Jewish tradition light represents illumination, direction, clarity, and vision, the ability to see clearly. Torah is seen as the ultimate light. It teaches morality, decency, values, and propriety. The Talmud tells us that the objective of lighting Shabbos candles is "shalom bayis," harmony in the home. The commentaries note that the word "shalom," meaning "peace," and the word "shalem," meaning "whole," draw upon a common root. This offers the additional insight that peace in the home derives from the creating of a "wholesome" environment for the family.

Women kindle the light because, as the primary nurturers, they determine the spiritual and emotional climate of the home. When we light our Shabbos candles we celebrate our role. We acknowledge our sacred trust as guardians of the light. As we stand before our Shabbos candles, we can grasp the awesome reach of the power G-d has invested within us. With this understanding, we commit ourselves to use our strength constructively.

It is customary after we recite the blessing over the candles to entreat the Almighty on behalf of the members of our family. We pray for Heavenly assistance to use our uniquely feminine endowments of insight, wisdom, and intuition to illuminate the lives we touch.

My daughters left Milwaukee to attend school in New York at the age of 12. They lived with my parents, of blessed memory. Their most cherished memory is of their bubbie lighting Shabbos candles at the conclusion of a hectic Friday. A tranquil sense of peace and serenity replaced the frenetic pace of the workday week. Bubbie would, at long last, rest her weary feet and sit down in her favorite chair by the window. My daughters gathered around her, and in the glow of the flickering Shabbos lights, she would recount stories of the Old Country. My daughters never tired of these stories, the embellishments, the images, the characters of a world they otherwise would not have known.

My brother-in-law, a psychiatrist of note, often illustrates the important impact parents have on a child's self-esteem with an anecdote from his childhood, when he was 5 years old. On one particular Friday, at candle-lighting time, his mother, of blessed memory, pointed out a particular candle. She said to him, "Shea, I light this candle for you because ever since you were born, I celebrate the gift of you. Your presence has brought more light into my life, the life of our family, and hopefully someday the life of the world." When he tells this story, my brother-in-law concludes that there is no amount of money you could pay a therapist to boost your self-esteem that would come anywhere close to what he felt at that moment.

The kindling of the Shabbos candles symbolizes that our teachings and our example can illuminate and bring wholeness and peace to all of those whose lives we touch.

Avodah: the G-d, Man Connection

Avodah; the G-d, Man Connection
Is G-d Comfortable Here?

A chassidic tale relates that the Rebbe of Kotzk once summoned his chassidim and challenged them, "Where can you find G-d?" One disciple volunteered, "His glory resides in Heaven." The Rebbe frowned with displeasure. A second disciple offered, "The entire world is filled with His glory." Once again, the Rebbe shook his head in disapproval. Anxious to understand, the chassidim implored the Rebbe, "Please, tell us where can we find Him?" The Rebbe said, "Wherever you invite Him in!"

All of us at some point in our lives struggle with the need to make G-d a more integral part of our lives. As such it is imperative that we understand how the Rebbe's counsel can be translated to impact upon our day-to-day lives.

Interestingly enough, and contrary to what we might think, making G-d a real part of our ongoing, moment-to-moment existence does not require an overhaul of our lives. It does, however, demand something that is very hard to come by in our hurried and driven society: focus and mindfulness.

Most of us move through life, day after day, in a predictable, robotlike way, hardly giving what we are doing a second thought. To most of us, the words of the Psalmist, "I have G-d before me always," represents a remote and wishful goal: an ideal accessible only to the very holy and saintly of spirit.

Such, indeed, was my thinking until the following realization hit me like a thunderbolt.

·············TAKING STOCK OF EVERYDAY LIFE

When I took stock of my normal everyday life, I realized how very mundane it was. I would wake up, get the kids ready for school, serve breakfast, carpool, clean up, vacuum, make lunch, make supper, carry on with telephone conversations, with familial interactions, help the kids with their homework, get them to bed, etc. — all in the context of a typical day. How much spirituality could there be in a day consumed primarily by physical and material concerns?

The scariest part, I realized, was that those activities that are purely physical are limited, moribund, and perishable; they die, never to be heard from again. How could I justify a life where the majority of my most precious moments would be relegated to oblivion?

Would the better part of my life be buried at its conclusion, like an animal? Would it be summed up with "been there, done that, and gone forever"?

In my heart of hearts, I knew it couldn't be. The moments of my life were too dear and meaningful —yes, even those spent baking, cooking, cleaning, and diapering babies — that I should consign them to nothingness.

The Rebbe had advised, "Invite G-d into your life. He will come when He is invited." I realized that what it takes to transform a "mundane moment" into a "spiritual moment" is the presence of the Almighty.

As soon as one introduces G-d and His Eternal Essence into the picture, His being there transforms the moment into something immortal and timeless, into a moment that will never die, a moment that lasts forever.

································INVITING G–D INSIDE

How do we do this?

Quite simply! Whatever it is that we are doing, we stop for an instant to ask ourselves the question, "Is G-d comfortable being here now?"

As I talk to my friend on the phone, I pause momentarily to reflect: Is the nature and the content of my conversation such that it invites His presence or banishes it? Is my conversation gossipy or is it positive and uplifting?

As I clean, vacuum, and care for my children (all clearly "mundane" activities), am I resentful or do I recognize that this is all necessary for the creation of a sacred environment, conducive to spiritual growth? In other words, given my present attitude, would G-d be comfortable being with me or not? If the response is affirmative, then I have captured the moment for eternity.

Commerce is clearly a weekday endeavor, but by applying the Torah's ethics to our business transactions, we can invite the Almighty to join us, thereby claiming these moments for all of time.

The same holds true of personal interactions and spousal relationships, if they are sufficiently sensitive such that G-d would relish being there.

When we sit down to eat, do we exercise our unique prerogative of choice to ask ourselves, "Is this what G-d would want me to eat? Does it meet His standards? Is it kosher? Is it healthy? Will it give me the requisite energy to do that which I need to do in order to fulfill His will? Is it the right amount? Did I remember to express my gratitude by reciting a berachah? Bottom line: Would the Creator be comfortable sitting at my table?"

The Psalmist's exhortation that "we have G-d before us always," when applied to our daily lives means focusing constantly on the opportunity to have G-d accompany us in everything that we do. No moment of our lives need be written off as "time killed."

For those of us who aspire to invite infinity into our finite lives, all it takes is asking the simple question: "Is G-d comfortable here now?"

Avodah; the G-d, Man Connection
Apathy and Indifference

isconsin is beautiful this time of year. In magnificent autumn hues all of nature presents endless variations and combinations of rich reds, oranges, and brilliant greens and yellows. The breathtaking beauty brings a sobering awareness with it, however. It is the prelude to the cold, chilling winter that renders the trees and countryside barren and sterile.

In our neck of the woods, it also heralds that the Jewish month of Cheshvan is upon us. This month is referred to by our Sages as Marcheshvan or the "bitter month." It represents a letdown from all the frenetic activity of its preceding month, Tishrei. But, why does this pause in time warrant a designation of "bitter" more so than even Av, the month in which we commemorate the destruction of our Holy Temple and many other "bitter" events? Our sages note that Cheshvan, in fact, is the only month in the Jewish calendar that is unmarked by any event, joyous or tragic. Events in the Jewish calendar mark the history of G-d's loving relationship with us. Even the commemoration of tragic days reminds us there is a Heavenly Parent, nudging us to "get back on track," so as not to repeat the wrongs and misdeeds of our forefathers. In the month of Cheshvan, there is only silence. It is this lack of communication between G-d and His children during this month that warrants the addition of "mar," bitter in Hebrew, to the month of Cheshvan.

I am keenly aware of the bitter quality of Cheshvan in a very personal way. Both my parents (of blessed memory) passed away in Cheshvan (one eight years after the other). A desolation spread over the landscape of my life. No matter how sick or infirm they were in their later years, for better or for worse, I was grateful to have them. In Yiddish it is said, "So long as one has a parent, one can still feel like a child." As long as there is a loving parent in one's life, though there may be times of rebuke or chastisement, one feels cherished and thus connected. Having lost that tangible bond, Cheshvan brings to me a chilling loneliness.

The commentary, Sfas Emes, shares a marvelous insight into the meaningfulness of our bond and relationship with our Heavenly Parent. For his role in convincing Eve and hence Adam to eat of the forbidden fruit in Paradise, the Almighty punishes the snake to crawl and eat dust. Is this an equitable punishment, asks the Sfas Emes, as compared to Adam's sentence to eat bread by the sweat of his brow; or as compared to Eve's punishment of pain and sadness in bearing and raising her progeny?

The Sfas Emes explains that the physical and emotional difficulties a person encounters as a result of this ongoing sentence forces the individual to look Heavenward for assistance. In so doing, the lines of communication between man and his Heavenly Creator are opened, thus fostering a loving, caring relationship. The snake may indeed have been provided with all the dust he would ever need for his physical well-being. At the same time, however, the snake was condemned to face downward and was given abundant sustenance so that he would not need to turn to G-d for anything, thus denying him the precious relationship Adam had been afforded with the Almighty. The snake's punishment is, clearly, the most severe and hopeless of all.

In an interview with a member of the Jewish Welfare Board of America, Miriam isolated the Friday-night Sabbath celebration as the singular event in her formative years that ultimately led to her positive feelings about being Jewish. She didn't grow up in a "religious" home. And, her parents, quite liberal for the times, gave her the freedom during the week to make her own choices regarding how and with whom she spent her time. But, Friday night was non-negotiable. Her parents insisted that come proms, ball games, school theater productions, she and her siblings would be home sharing "Shabbat" dinner together. Miriam admitted that at the time she was resentful of her parents' rigid enforcement of this family rule. She recognizes in retrospect, however, that her parents' strong and passionate stance conveyed a deeper message of caring, both for her and for the sanctity of the Sabbath.

Linda, a woman married for a number of years, confided that she was leaving her husband Howard because she felt no commitment. Her husband was a nice man, and denied her little, but at the same time, he was apathetic and indifferent. He seemed to avoid feeling passionate about anything, even his wife, and thus a chasm of emptiness and silence grew between them over the years. Without knowledge of the specifics, this would seem to be inadequate grounds for divorce. However, Linda, hopeless for quite sometime now that things would change, had finally given up completely.

Apathy and indifference, not caring one way or the other, lacking passion, an unwillingness to invest in relationships, self-absorption, and disaffection are the guarantors of a lonely, uninspiring existence. It is true that caring deeply about something carries with it a greater risk of being hurt. The lesson of "Marcheshvan" teaches us that if we don't accept the risk, for better or for worse, we may be faced with a more "bitter" alternative.

Avodah: the G-d, Man Connection
The Power Source

The first Seder this past Passover took place on a Saturday night. The timing compelled us to be organized in order to complete all of our Passover preparations by Friday. The hope was that following the very early meal on Shabbos morning, everyone would be able to rest most of the day and come to the Passover Seder refreshed and ready to undertake freedom.

Everything proceeded as planned. I climbed into bed early Shabbos afternoon, satisfied that I had a difficult situation under control. The house was immaculate: every nook and cranny overhauled, the four freezers and three refrigerators filled with holiday necessities and delights (products of 100 pounds of onions, 200 pounds of potatoes, and 20 cases of eggs). The out-of-town guests were all satisfactorily situated. The tables were set in royal splendor. I could now relax and get some well-earned sleep.

"The best laid schemes o' mice and men..." the poet wrote. No sooner did I close my eyes than the weather turned violent. Strong winds raged. The house shook almost as though it was at risk of blowing away. I went downstairs to find our family and other members of the community huddled together discussing the situation.

It seemed that the winds had blown over a transformer and most of the families in the community were without electricity. Our non-Jewish neighbor informed us that the electric company had been inundated with calls and was thereby only addressing life-threatening inquiries.

How long could the food last without refrigeration? Surely that evening everything would still be fine, but what about the next day? What about the second Seder on Sunday night?

I have to admit that I had visions of refrigerators stuffed full of spoiled food, leaving us to eat only matzah by candlelight. The endless hours of toil passed before my eyes. Then, a calm settled over me. This must be a reality check, I concluded.

I may have put in a lot of hours planning, organizing, and much hard work, thinking I had everything under control. The Almighty was reminding me that although we may put forth our best effort, ultimately He is in charge. It is He Who has to crown our endeavors with success. At some point, we must allow Him to decide what is best for us.

As it happened, that evening, as the community, led by my husband the rabbi, entered a darkened synagogue to usher in the Passover holiday, the power source was restored and the lights came on.

·····················A SPIRITUAL METAPHOR

All of us are dependent on the virtual sea of technology that surrounds us: refrigerators, ovens, freezers, air conditioners, etc. These are wonderful inventions, invaluable conveniences to modern living. But, they only work if they are connected to the source. A tiny crack in a transformer, a small break in the flow of current, renders thousands of appliances, and even life-giving machines, useless.

This fact of our modern life serves as a useful spiritual metaphor. We too cannot function spiritually unless we are connected to our Source: G-d.

A woman named Shirley called me recently at the request of her daughter Amy, who had taken an unusual course in life following her graduation from college.

Shirley had fully expected that, like her friends, Amy would find a job upon graduation, thereby validating all of her parents' investments in her throughout these years.

Amy however, chose to take a year to study Torah in Israel. Shirley was having a hard time dealing with the sad and sympathetic looks of her contemporaries, who like herself, could not relate to this spiritual quest her daughter was undertaking in order to get in touch with her Jewish roots, her Torah legacy.

I shared with Shirley the understanding that, "man does not live by bread alone." It's true that a livelihood, financial resources, etc., are of tremendous value, but they must be considered in the context of being connected to the Source.

Why eat? Why work? Indeed, why live? I assured her that based on my previous experience, Amy will reconnect her transformer, forming her own unique connection to the Source of all endeavors, and in that context everything will, G-d willing, fall into place.

A SOURCE OF STRENGTH ·····························

A story is told about Rabbi Meir of Premishlan, a Jew of saintly stature. Even in his elderly years, he would awaken in the predawn hours to prepare for his prayers and studies. He would make his way up steep hills to a small brook that served as his mikveh where he would immerse in his ritual of spiritual purification.

There were a number of young troublemakers in town who, in an attempt to harm the Jewish community, targeted this elderly, revered figure as their victim. They observed his comings and goings and decided that they would follow him up the deserted mountain in the wee hours of the morning where they would tackle him and give him a good beating.

They rose early and according to plan began trailing the rabbi. But to their amazement and frustration, they found themselves stumbling, tripping, and finding it increasingly difficult to keep up with him. Bruised and bloodied, they aborted their plans and waited for the rabbi to return.

As he descended, they confessed their intentions to him and asked in total awe, how is it that they who were young and strong were falling and tripping, while he, an elderly man, demonstrated such unbelievable agility. The rabbi smiled with the wisdom of years and responded, "If one is connected up Above, one does not stumble and fall down here below."

Identity
and Roles

Identity and Roles
Self-Esteem

I sometimes struggle with the issue of trying to accept myself for who I am versus trying to change myself for the better. What is the happy medium? This often occurs after being criticized or when I feel like I should be better in some way.

I know that good self-esteem is a prerequisite to being able to be happy and perhaps to grow. How do I keep my self-esteem strong when I feel criticized or sense within myself something left to be desired?

I would greatly appreciate your thoughts on this matter.

Your quest for balance speaks to all of us. Self-condemnation is never a good stance to adopt. Neither, however, is unqualified self-commendation. Accepting who we are is positive ground only if it consists of a clear assessment of both our strengths and our weaknesses.

For starters, we need to understand that the unique characteristics that make up our person are not arbitrary, but are deliberately conferred upon us by the Author of our being. They are thereby geared to the task that each of us individually needs to fulfill in our lifetime.

The blend of both positive and negative traits can be, if we are aware and sensitive to them, the substance of both the challenge and the achievements of our life. It is thus not at all paradoxical that accepting oneself and trying to change for the better are not contradictory or mutually exclusive paths.

Recognition of a shortcoming may be seen as a summons to discipline and perfect oneself. Being in touch with one's higher G-dly soul provides a reservoir of strength to help one combat his lesser self.

Consider the following scenario:

Debby, a lovely woman in her 40's, sat in my office teary eyed, as she recounted the heartwrenching story of abandonment by her husband from whom she was subsequently divorced, followed by the trials and tribulations of trying to adjust to life with her current husband and their blended family.

After much painful soul-searching, Debby concluded that her strong personality, outspokenness, and firm opinions were not always an asset to achieving marital bliss. She realized that if she were to succeed this time around, she would have to work at tempering her tough demeanor with gentleness and tolerance.

Most significantly, she was convinced that while the Almighty had indeed blessed her with formidable intelligence and competence, He had orchestrated the events of her life to draw her attention to the internal work that she still had to do. She felt very strongly that she was being urged and encouraged from Above to access her thus far undeveloped traits of humility and patience.

First and foremost, we need to assume ownership of the vast potential that is legitimately ours. The warts, blemishes, and demons that need to be dealt with do not diminish or negate the great power of the soul to reach for the stars.

It is important that we distinguish between recognition and resignation. Resignation discounts that potential and denies the exalted human capacity for growth.

Recognition serves as a point of departure, a reality check, an accurate picture of where we are at this given moment and where we would like to be down the road.

Every human being comes into this world imperfect and deficient, and it is our life's task to repair the void — the lack in our person — and thereby move on to "sheleimus," a state of wholeness.

This existential state of imperfection, of a deep sense that something within us is not whole, should never lead to self-deprecation and feelings of inadequacy. Our self-esteem should enable us to acknowledge that we are incomplete and we should stand up with all the dignity inherent in our being proclaiming, "I assume responsibility to fill this void and to deal with the shortcomings in my character, by drawing on the majestic endowment given to me by my Creator."

Our sages point out that the name "Adam," assigned to the first human being, shares a root with "adamah," which means "earth" in Hebrew. According to Rabbi Samson Raphael Hirsch, the inherent message is that just like the earth, with the care and investment of time and energy, yields products that are both nourishing and pleasing to the eye, so too does "Adam," the human soul, the psyche of man, respond to dedicated input and efforts toward growth.

The hallmark of "Adam" is the capacity to grow and to become, to look back at yesterday and see that bit by bit, we have progressed. We didn't become angry as easily today; we were able to withstand an opportunity to gossip; we ate in a more disciplined fashion; we put a smile on our face for no special reason; we didn't become undone in stressful situations; we interacted cordially with people who are not necessarily our favorites.

These may appear to be small steps, perhaps, and few and far between, but they nevertheless represent positive movement up the mountain of self-growth.

Confronting our flaws is an exercise in humility that should not be confused with unworthiness and self-derogation. Humility is positive, constructive, affirmative, and honest. Humility is a product of comparing ourselves exclusively with what we are capable of bringing into our lives. In stark contrast to the despair of self-deprecation, it fills us with joy at the prospect that every moment affords us the opportunity to access a better self.

Concurrently, every step toward realizing the potential that waits to be tapped builds our self-esteem. The journey that leads to lasting self-respect must, of necessity, be a dynamic one, of doing, moving, growing, and becoming.

We need to look at the people whom we admire and seek to emulate their behavior. We need to observe how they conduct themselves, i.e., how they interact with their Creator, their families and their friends. Our Sages exhort that every person should ask himself or herself daily, "When will my deeds approach those of my ancestors?" It is noteworthy that they do not suggest that we demand of ourselves to be equal to our ancestors, but rather to do as they did. To be is static. To do is dynamic.

If my goal is to be a scholar, a righteous person, a sage, an accomplished person in any field, I set myself up for ongoing frustration and disappointment. Because every moment that I fall short of that static goal, I am a failure.

But if I wish to do what a scholar does, to learn, or do what a righteous person does, good and meritorious deeds, then every act of emulation identifies me as a success. Success breeds success and builds self-esteem.

In a tribute dinner to my husband many years ago, our then 9-year-old son, Yanke, stood up and shared what he thought was the most powerful lesson his father had taught him. Yanke related that he would often come home downhearted, complaining that someone had criticized him. His father's counsel would always be, "If the criticism is true, then do something about it, and if it's not, then ignore it."

The wisdom of that advice applies to you, my dear reader, as well. If the criticism of others is on target, then let it be a call to action. Do something about it. Change does not require an overhaul of one's life. Change is evolutionary, not revolutionary. A small step in the right direction will boost your self-esteem like nothing else.

It will make you feel alive and healthy. It will confirm the fact that you are choosing your G-d-given strength to fill your particular "void" and every acquisition, however modest, will bring you closer to your wholeness.

In the final analysis, just as physically our cells are constantly shedding and regenerating, so too, should we be changing and growing in the spiritual realm. Our character and our knowledge base should ever be increasing. The human condition was never meant to be a fixed status quo.

Human beings are referred to in Jewish sources as "holchim," walking and dynamic, in contrast even to the Heavenly angels who are referred to as "omdim," beings that "stand" at a fixed level from the moment of their creation, unable to ascend beyond their station.

Pursuant to this thought, when going on a journey, the proper blessing to the traveler is go "l'shalom," toward peace, and not "b'shalom," in peace. The message conveyed is that as long as we live and breathe we are moving toward peace, wholeness, and fulfillment. "In peace," a state of having arrived with no work left to be done, is a departing statement reserved only for the final departure of a deceased person.

For all of us, change, movement, and growth are the marching orders for our lives. And if we are imperfect and limited today, as we all are in one way or another, our self-esteem will come from the fact that we have identified the behavior that we value and are moving, step-by-step, to integrate and incorporate it into our lives.

And for those who criticize the fact that we are not there yet and who think that we are not what we should be, we need to remember the words of Eleanor Roosevelt who said, "Nobody can make me feel inferior without my permission." Indeed, if one is on a productive and constructive path, one's self-esteem will not be threatened.

Quite the contrary, the response that will resonate within your innermost being will be, "I am moving toward wholeness." And that is the best anyone can do.

Identity and Roles
Mother Sara and Mrs. Cash

At our Shabbos table, quite often we have Mrs. Cash (that is really her name) as a guest. She is a 94-year-old woman who comes to shul dressed like a queen; she is always regal, exuding a special light, as she smiles at everyone she encounters.

Mrs. Cash never had children and has no extended family in close proximity, but the moment she enters, all the children in shul surround her to wish her a "Shabbat Shalom."

If you visit her home on a Friday afternoon, it is spotless, and you are greeted by the delightful aroma of Shabbos food cooking. The table is set for one and the candlesticks are ready to be lit.

Over and over again, she will tell you that her mother taught her to honor the day. "My mother would say to me: 'My darling daughter, no matter how heavy your heart may be, do not shame the holy Shabbos. Remember your holy ancestors at all times and behave accordingly.' I never forgot that."

It is too difficult for her to go out on Friday night, so she sits with the pictures and memories of her loved ones and eats her meal alone. Shabbos morning, she once confessed to me, it takes her three hours to get dressed to go to shul.

But she is determined that as long as there is a Shabbos, and so long as G-d gives her life, she will be in shul.

She is frail and fragile and has gone through many painful trials and tribulations in life, but she has a wonderful matriarchal aura about her.

I asked her from where her strength derived and she answered without a moment's hesitation, "G-d is always at my side, I am never alone."

In fact, G-d to Mrs. Cash is not a theoretical concept or a distant removed Being. He is her personal G-d, her Companion in life.

IN THE FOOTSTEPS OF SARAH ··················

Mrs. Cash is one of the many women who, each in their own unique way, follow in the footsteps of our Matriarch, Sarah.

A fascinating midrash teaches that in Sarah's tent the lights never went out, they stayed lit from one Shabbos to the next. In addition, there was blessing in her dough, and a cloud of Divine glory constantly hovered over her abode.

Here is the way this midrash speaks to me:

Sarah's tent had a wonderful light, an upbeat energy, a warmth. She created an environment of optimism and of joy.

Although she did not bear a child until very late in her life, she did not allow her barrenness — what others might consider a major deprivation and an obstacle to happiness — to keep her down. She infused life and brightness into every day.

This is because Sarah saw life as light, an opportunity and a gift from G-d. She was the ideal partner to her husband Abraham, and she worked together with him in G-d's vineyard, bringing light to so many people.

The blessing in her dough symbolizes her ability to be content with what she had; she wasn't driven to acquire things. She was satisfied with the dough that was her portion in life. And that too reinforced the light.

The cloud of glory represents the presence of G-d. Sarah made the Creator feel welcome, cherished, and valued in her home.

A MODEL FOR ALL WOMEN ··················

Creating an atmosphere of light, contentment, and joy — regardless of the circumstances of one's life — is perhaps the greatest gift a woman can give those entrusted into her care. Bringing positive energy into an environment can be the most powerful force and motivator imaginable.

Our Matriarch Sarah understood this and because of her, all of us have those very same resources within us.

Like her ancestor Sarah, Mrs. Cash's material needs are very modest; there is a blessing in her dough and it satisfies and satiates her. Yet, when it comes to charity, her frugality disappears.

She, as so many other women in our community and elsewhere, brings life with her wherever she goes. She inspires and teaches by example. Mrs. Cash does indeed have a veritable cloud of glory constantly hovering over her abode.

By integrating the blessings of "the light, the dough, and the cloud of glory" into their lives, moment by moment, women such as Mrs. Cash are illuminating the path of spiritual growth for their families, their communities, and the Jewish people.

Identity and Roles
Footwork vs. G-d's Work

My fiancee has had a very difficult past, filled with anger, mistreatment, and betrayal. Understandably, she wants to delay our getting married until we both finish dealing with these issues. I am working as hard as I can on these things, and she is trying too.

How much work is "enough"?

Should we wait until "everything" humanly possible has already been done? How much can we rely on G-d's help? Where is the line between our work and leaving it up to and trusting G-d?

~~~

There are two confluent concepts in Jewish thought: self-sufficiency and wholeness.

The first describes the essence of the Almighty as "G-d is powerful in His aloneness" (Psalms). Additional confirmation of the value of "aloneness" is found in the Torah narrative describing the Patriarch Jacob's victorious battle with the Heavenly representative of the evil force of Esau. This was the epic struggle that earns him and his progeny the exalted name "Israel." The introductory verse informing the context of that triumph reads "and Jacob remained alone" (Genesis 32:25).

G-d manifests Himself in our world through His many attributes. These attributes serve as models of behavior for us, who are created in His image, to emulate. Hence, if the verse places "aloneness" as a predicate for God's strength (so to speak), we need to ask what that means for us. What lesson are we to learn from the state of "aloneness" that set the stage for Jacob's definitive encounter, an encounter that transformed him and the totality of Jewish history?

Jewish sources point out the need for a person to be first and foremost sufficient to himself or herself as an integrated and differentiated entity (Medrash Rabbah, 77:1, Daas Chachmah U'Mussar). One must have the capacity to stand on one's own two feet, adequately grounded with the ability to engage the inevitable battles of life.

Fortified with individual strength, it is only then that one can move on to embrace the second concept articulated by G-d's pronouncement: "It is not good for man to be alone" (Genesis 2:18).

The conjugation of this verse, in contrast to the previous references to "aloneness," suggests an existential loneliness. It speaks to a void, the absence of another, of a missing piece, indeed of a mate with whom to share one's life. In this stage, a person may be sufficient onto himself or herself, but they are as yet not complete and fulfilled.

Wholeness that comes through finding a suitable mate is best achieved after one's own self-sufficiency as an independent human being has been established. A person unable to stand alone is not a promising candidate for marriage. The capacity for independence and being alone must precede the antidote for existential loneliness: that of sharing one's life with another.

It is true that we all come into this world with our idiosyncrasies, our flaws, and blemishes. Surmounting our deficiencies must necessarily be part and parcel of the "human becomings," the continuous lifetime process of consistent growth that takes place as we move forward day by day, laboriously, toward ever greater excellence. Growth, overcoming our faults and actualizing our strengths, is a lifelong challenge for any person who is serious about life and achieving the purpose for which we are placed on this earth.

There is, however, psychological baggage that is not within the realm of "normal" issues. These can run very deep and can have a profound crippling affect on the human psyche.

Marriage is a partnership, a union of two people committed to giving to each other. An individual desperately struggling with issues of this magnitude may not be capable, thus far, to give to another human being. His/her energy is totally tied up and consumed in dealing with the pain of their his/her unresolved issues.

In this compromised state they are insufficient to themselves. They don't yet possess the healthy state of independence and "aloneness" that would enable them to see the completion and wholesomeness that comes from the interdependence fostered in a giving marriage relationship.

Marriage, even under the most normal of circumstances, requires major adjustments. There are gender differences — the "men are from Mars and women are from Venus" issues. Additional compounding factors are dissimilar families of origin, who may have totally conflicting styles of responding and coping. Some families are demonstrative while others are reserved. Some fight; others invoke the flight and avoidance approach to conflict. There are those who come into marriage expecting the fastidious surroundings of their mother's home, to find that their partner has a laid- back nature vis-a-vis housekeeping, etc.

There has to be the basic energy available to confront and engage the "normal" adjustments that marriage inevitably requires. I would recommend that you, my dear reader, consult with the therapists involved and elicit their educated opinions and counsel as to whether you and your fiancee have the requisite emotional resources, at this point in time, to move forward into marriage.

You inquire as to how much is "enough"? There are no generic answers since each situation differs. The variables include the severity of the issues, the work already done, and the effort that still remains to be put forth.

It is not a matter of "everything" humanly possible being done. Total health requires, undoubtedly, a lifelong, continuous process of healing and thus a steadily increasing wholeness. Nevertheless, in order to successfully negotiate a marriage relationship, there does have to be that basic, initial repository of emotional well-being.

"G-d helps those who helps themselves" is a Jewish concept articulated as "the path that a person seeks to travel, Heaven makes accessible to him." Reliance on Heaven alone is inappropriate as G-d respects the choices of man to indicate the direction he wishes to take. However, when a person initiates the process and puts forth his best effort, Heavenly input and assistance is assured.

Identity and Roles
The Single's Dilemma

Many people despair that it simply cannot be true that "there is someone out there for everyone." It is simply a problem of supply and demand: there are more worthy and quality females out there than the available male counterpart population.

So assuming that we all are put into the situation that we are able to deal with and need at any given point, and in recognition that singles perforce endure a great deal with diminishing returns, can it be said that such folks one day, probably in the Next World, will be on a higher level than those "reverse mirror images" who by the grace of G-d had nary a problem in getting married?

Isn't it easier to be a Jew in New York than in Milwaukee, in Jerusalem than in San Diego? Everything is relative. The easier things come, the less appreciation there is of the true cost.

And this concept can apply to any situation of greater vs. lesser fortune — one who rises above a handicap is on a greater level than someone not as challenged, although we believe that the reward in this world is but incidental.

Looking forward to hearing your thoughts on this matter.

*T*he reader very aptly articulates the plight of single women everywhere.

While perhaps one needs to be "in it" to fully understand — as our Sages comment, "There is no one wiser than a person challenged" — some points might be appropriate and relevant even if they do come from the "outside" looking in. Looking in, I might add, with constant heartfelt prayers that the Almighty bring joy to gladden the lives of those who suffer.

I don't think it is within the scope of human beings to calculate the extent of another person's pain or to be the judge of who suffers the most and hence has earned more mileage in eternity. G-d alone "knows the innermost recesses of the heart." The circumstances of one's life, as important as they are, are only one piece of the total picture. What about an individual's inner resources based on their coping abilities and their mental health? What about events of the past, influences of their upbringing that often shape their attitudes and perspectives in a limiting and negative way? There are many factors that constitute a person's life, most of them not accessible to the casual observer.

Recently, in the span of a few hours, two women who came to see me poignantly captured the irony of the human condition. Eileen is married with a houseful of children. Her marital relationship is conflicted, and her children, in part because of the lack of a harmonious family structure, are difficult and demanding. She shared with me that more and more frequently she entertains the fantasy of leaving her overwhelming and burdened life and joining the ranks of carefree singles who get more immediate gratification and positive feedback in the work world, and who have nobody to worry about but themselves.

Within moments, literally, of Eileen's departure, Sherry walked in and proceeded to describe the familiar landscape of the single's life, the loneliness, the passing of her childbearing years, the empty void born of not having achieved the expected purpose of a woman's life, a purpose so clearly part and parcel of the fabric of Jewish existence, etc. At a superficial glance, what for Eileen was an albatross, weighty and oppressive, was the substance of Sherry's fondest dreams. As ironic as this seems, they are not exceptional cases. "The grass is always greener on the other side" mentality is ubiquitous and has been with us since the beginning of the human race.

Consider the Torah narrative dealing with the life of Jacob. He was "a wholesome man," pure and trusting, whose aspiration was simply to sit immersed in the quiet life of Torah study. Clearly G-d had other plans for him. He was thrust into a life of turmoil, mandated to expand his horizons in all directions. He was besieged by the enmity of his twin brother, a father-in-law who was the master of deceit and tried to forestall his marriage to Rachel. His life included periods of total poverty and a desire for nothing more than "bread to eat and clothing to wear" and ultimately, challenging him with serious wealth. The simple life he sought, the peace and tranquility he yearned for, was transformed into a series of painful tests and challenges: the death of his beloved wife Rachel, the violation of his daughter Dinah, the sale of his treasured son Joseph into slavery by his own brothers, his exile into Egypt, etc. Consider also that Rachel was barren and craved children without which she saw herself, as she put it, "as dead." Conversely, Leah, her sister, who had many children, desired only to find favor in Jacob's eyes. In sum, the Almighty's orchestration of events remains for us mortals totally inscrutable.

I have not yet met anyone who has everything. And it does appear that more than appreciating what we do have, we are desirous of that which eludes us.

Having said that, it must be emphatically stated that we are enjoined to pray arduously and continually for what in our estimation is missing in our life and for what we perceive as necessary for our well-being and fulfillment. The caveat is that we have to reserve a space of deference in our yearning and supplication, an acknowledgment that the Master of the Universe is the ultimate "Knower" of what's best for us.

Ultimately, Rachel was blessed with children and Leah was vindicated and buried with Jacob, and Jacob's life, replete with challenges though it was, produced the Twelve Tribes that founded the Jewish nation. We have to trust that it is G-d's script that will bring us to our ultimate destiny. Moreover, it is only His script that can take into account, in addition to everything else, the mystical concept of reincarnation, of previous lives that inform our present existence. As for us, until all the puzzle pieces fall into place and clarity replaces our finite vision, our efforts need to be directed at changing our "why" questions to "what" questions. Given G-d's script at this moment, what is the most productive and constructive course to chart? Our lives, upon self-evaluation, need to be meaningful and justifiable day to day, moment to moment, given who we are and what we have. Squandering the precious gift of life in bitterness and torment over what is not yet ours is adding insult to injury and is the ultimate betrayal of what is in our own best interest.

The bottom line is that joy in life is not the product of "a set of circumstances, but a set of attitudes." I believe that a working positive attitude can be forged only by a balance between putting forth our best efforts — in study, deed, and prayer — and then stepping back and letting the Almighty run the show. This posture is not only liberating, but also grants its bearer a demeanor and disposition that has a magnetic force to which others and all good things are drawn.

My blessing is that the Master of the Universe grant all of us that which is best for our ultimate well-being.

Identity and Roles
Goals and Contributions

I'm blessed with a loving family, teachers, and friends and I have much to be thankful for. As a senior in high school, I wonder how I'm going to be an asset to the Jewish people and to the world around me. I don't want to be a taker; I want to be a giver. I want to utilize the potential and the talents that G-d gave me.

As I look back on my high school years, I only have good memories. Yet, I realized that a lot of my activities were limited by stage fright, even though I don't give the "shy girl" impression. Many times I have the opportunity to speak in public and I convince someone else to speak instead of me. My shyness puzzles my family, friends, and teachers because in class, home, and among my friends I am not at all shy.

As I stand at the threshold of my life about to enter the real world, I am consistently plagued with the question of what is my goal, my purpose in this world. I know I want to help people but I'm not sure how. More importantly, how will I accomplish what I have to do, with my shyness and fear of public speaking? G-d has blessed me with so much and I realize that everyone is judged not only for what they have done but also for what they have failed to do. I'm fearful and confused.

One basic human need that we all have is to matter, to make a difference. At an intuitive, gut level we know that each of us has our very own unique contribution to make in life.

However, what may strike us as a significant and appropriate contribution might not be as impressive to the Almighty. Our evaluation of deeds and accomplishments is often based on the values of our society. Our culture applauds achievements of a public nature, those that are out there for all to see. The private deeds done in a modest manner, hidden from public view, are not appreciated in our strident world. G-d values inwardness, "penimius," more than outwardness, "chitzonius," and in determining what our contribution to life might be, we need to shift from that which appears as significant in a world of illusion to what realistically, by G-d's definition, is noteworthy.

Our Sages tell us of three instances where great people misjudged and underestimated deeds they had performed.

1. Reuven, the oldest brother of the Twelve Tribes of Israel, convinced his brothers not to kill their brother Joseph, but rather to throw him into a pit. As a result, the Torah records for all of history, "and Reuven heard and he saved him from their hands" (Genesis 36:21). Had Reuven been able to anticipate G-d's positive evaluation of his deed, the midrash says that Reuven would have carried Joseph on his shoulders and returned him to his father.

2. Had Aaron, the brother of Moses, known that the verse would testify, "And Aaron, your brother, will see you and he will be happy in his heart" (Exodus 4:14), he would have greeted Moses, his younger brother, the newly appointed leader and redeemer of the Jewish people, with drums and dancing to convey his total wholehearted support and enthusiasm. But, he did not anticipate how treasured the attribute of joy and delight in his brother's good fortune would be to G-d.

3. Boaz (Ruth 2:14) extended himself to provide sustenance for Ruth the Moabite convert. He is acknowledged in the Book of Ruth

for his generous act of hospitality. Had he known, our Sages tell us once again, that this would be so meaningful and so major a contribution it would merit to be recorded for all time, he would have served Ruth the most expensive, mouth-watering delicacies!

Our Sages are telling us that it is difficult, given our flawed perspective based on what feels or appears worthwhile, to assess what will impact on our lives and the lives of those around us in a real way. Only G-d truly knows.

How, then, are we to make those really important decisions in our lives and to chart a reasonable course?

A twofold program is mapped out for us:

1. Pay careful attention to the specific negative attributes that challenge our character and person. Some of us struggle with envy; others with anger, pride, etc. These are not arbitrary. They specifically address the unique challenges that we need to overcome in order to achieve the purpose for which we were created.

2. On the positive side, G-d has endowed each of us with unique talents and abilities. These are not arbitrary either. They are rooted in the depth and uniqueness of our singular soul. If people are blessed with creative dispositions toward writing, art, music, etc., they need to seek outlets for these expressions that will benefit themselves, their families, and others. Whatever our gifts, we are intended to develop and utilize them within the appropriate context of Torah living.

From a Jewish perspective the bestowal of abilities and talents mandate responsibility, that is, to serve and thereby enhance G-d's world.

The first commandment to Adam and Eve in the Garden of Eden was "be fruitful and multiply" (Genesis 1:28). The Zohar, the great Kabbalistic work, contends that the behest to be a "creator" applies not only to offspring, but to bringing to fruition the innate resources with which G-d has blessed us.

You, dear reader, understand the need to serve, but are concerned that your fear of public speaking will circumscribe and limit your efforts. There are many avenues toward making an impact. Public speaking is by no means the only way. While it is true that public speaking can be a great asset, a tool for providing guidance and inspiration, one-on-one communication is decidedly a more effective mode of fostering meaningful relationships and ultimately impacting on another's life. Certainly, the inability to speak publicly does not consign one to a meaningless life or one of lesser contribution. We all must find our own style, mode, and manner of expression that best fits our intended message.

Having said that, it is also true that there are times when fears — of public speaking or whatever else it might be — can be overcome. It requires the willingness to be vulnerable, to perhaps fail and then try again. It is a skill like any other; with perseverance and the willingness to work hard these types of fears can also be mastered.

True courage is acting in spite of your fears with the comforting knowledge that everyone experiences some anxiety and nervousness, and that with practice it gets easier and better. You might also avail yourself of the many available books written on the subject of public speaking.

Keep in mind that with time and effort you might come to terms with the issue of public speaking. When it comes to what your contribution ought to be, you should ideally pursue roles that will enable you first and foremost to engage the private arena, the inner sanctum where the strength of the soul is exercised through caring, loving, nurturing, sensitivity, enabling, and ennobling.

My father, of blessed memory, was the best public speaker and orator I have ever heard. His interaction with an audience, be it 10 or 10,000, was totally magical. He at once enlightened with his impressive erudition and keen insights, delighted with his humor, warmed with his sensitivity, evoked tears with his poignancy, and inspired with his great passion. He had a powerful public persona and an electric presence. When he walked in, it was as if the band played and the room lit up. I recall myself as a little girl holding this magnificent person's hand and looking from side to side to make sure that everyone noticed that this man was my daddy.

Despite the glory and the great pride of being the celebrity's daughter, what warms me most in the truly dark moments of my life are the gifts he gave me in the privacy of our personal relationship: the times I came home to New York from Milwaukee to find him looking out the window to catch the first possible glimpse of me; the occasion of my own speaking engagements when I faced his loving inspection to see if I looked good enough before I left the house; his remembering every birthday and occasion of note even though I remembered none; his pockets full of lollipops that accompanied his interaction with every grandchild; his unparalleled dedication to every member of his family, immediate and extended. Despite his colossal public achievements he was happiest when he was surrounded by all of us in the privacy of his home. His heart belonged to us.

In sifting through the maze of many options, you should apply the litmus test of what will really counts when the dust settles. Who matters to you and why? Is it someone who made it into the halls of fame and fortune, someone who made a big splash in the public arena? Or is it someone who reached out to you in a caring way and who, because of what was said or done, gave you the confidence and sense of worth to walk taller and to grow and become all that you could be?

In my humble opinion, based on extensive experience, the heroes and heroines worthy of emulation are those who, day to day, moment to moment, enrich our lives. These are the mothers, bubbies, aunts, father, zaides, teachers, and dear friends — sacred cherished members who perform on our inner stage of life. In the world of illusion they may not appear terribly glamorous, but their contribution, their imprint upon our lives is enduring and indelible.

Identity and Roles
The Legacy of Mrs. Cash

Some of you may remember a previous essay[1] in which I described a venerable 94-year-old woman, Mrs. Ceil Cash, whose superb character and faith served as an illustration for a point I had wished to make.

Sadly, since that time, Mrs. Cash has passed away. She had prayed that she might go peacefully in her sleep and her petition was blessedly granted. Having no biological children of her own, she was, nonetheless, fortunate to have left this world surrounded by her adopted children — members of our community who, over time, had come to love and respect her for the special matriarchal presence she provided.

The funeral procession stopped at the yeshivah school she had generously supported, where the children whom she loved so dearly stood outside in a blistering cold wind to bid her farewell. It was obvious that the children were genuinely saddened and grief stricken.

My husband was asked to deliver the eulogy and had to stop frequently during his tribute to compose himself. He spoke of the mandate by which Mrs. Cash had lived her life. He cited her mother's oft-repeated exhortation, "Remember, my darling daughter, that your deeds should never bring shame on your holy ancestors in Heaven." Her mother's words did indeed chart Mrs. Cash's course in life.

---

1. "Mother Sara and Mrs. Cash," pp. 251-253

Interestingly, there were some people who were surprised at my husband's display of emotion at the funeral. She had, after all, been 94 years old and not a blood relative.

Upon hearing of this, my husband addressed the issue on the following Shabbos during his sermon. He observed that the astonishment itself spoke to a lamentable diminishment of feeling and emotion in our times, and how we seem unable to form attachments to anything that may ultimately be cause for grieving. He then went on to explain what was really at the heart of his deep sense of loss.

SHE APPRECIATED EVERYTHING · · · · · · · · · · · · · · · ·

Each week, he related, Mrs. Cash would dine at our Shabbos table. She loved the ambience, the words of Torah, the songs, and especially relished the inspiring stories of the chassidic masters that my husband would tell during the "tish" (the Shabbos repast).

My husband stated that Mrs. Cash's uniqueness had been her capacity to express appreciation and gratitude for things that others take for granted.

"That was such an inspiring story," she would say, "that was such a heartwarming song ... you create such a spiritual environment." Her warm eyes sparkled and her bright smile confirmed her words. She took advantage of every opportunity to compliment, affirm, and validate others. Everyone mattered in her eyes.

A young friend, who on one occasion had spent a weekend with her, told me of the following incident:

Mrs. Cash had started to carry a bag of garbage to the alley. Her young friend protested insisting that she be allowed to do it instead. Mrs. Cash refused, and, since neither would relent, they decided to take it out together. Just then the garbage truck appeared and one of the men took the bag from Mrs. Cash's hands. She looked up at him and said, "Thank you very much, sir." To which he replied, "I am not a sir, I am just a garbage man."

She looked at him and stated most emphatically, "You work hard, you make an honest living, you are definitely a sir." My friend remarked that she saw the garbage man straighten up proudly and virtually grow a few inches right before her eyes.

One of the most important lessons that Mrs. Cash's life confirmed is that all of us need a good word. All of us could use a pat on the back, an acknowledgment of our worth, and an affirmation that we make a difference. All of us benefit from a smile, a ray of sunshine in our lives to brighten our down days and our dreary moments.

· IT DOESN'T TAKE MUCH

Mrs. Cash provided that for us and that's why her absence is so painful. She leaves us an incredibly rich legacy of wisdom and love. She taught us that this much-needed recognition can and should be given and that it doesn't take all that much.

We just need to remember that those next to us are much the same as ourselves. They too have feelings and needs and are, as we are at times, very vulnerable. We should demand of ourselves to do as she did, to think what we can do or say to somehow make others more equal to life and its challenges.

Indeed, we grieve over the loss of someone who let us know we mattered. And for that reason, Mrs. Cash will forever matter to us.

Identity and Roles
A Jewish Mother's Highs and Lows

I am having a very difficult time right now. I feel almost as if I have hit some sort of spiritual plateau. I am an observant Jew who didn't grow up in a religious home. I spent a year learning at a seminary in Israel, came home, and married. And now I am the lucky mother of two. While I love my children more than anything, I can't help but wonder about my new role in life. I feel like I just don't know who I am anymore, or what I am supposed to do. I used to enjoy praying; now I struggle every morning just to recite the morning blessings. I feel very discouraged, and I feel like I am failing as a Jew. And I don't feel like I am all that successful at being a mother either. I do not understand how a busy mother can still have a close relationship with God. I know the woman has a special role in Judaism... but right now I am struggling greatly in understanding it. Please help.

One of the occupational hazards of the "seminary experience" or any extensive and intense learning endeavor is that it is often difficult to translate it into day-to-day living. It is wonderful to study and expand the horizons of one's mind, but ultimately it comprises only a small piece of the resources required to cope with life situations effectively. Intellectual pursuits, of the exclusively theoretical kind, can often create the illusion of being an end-all and when the opportunity to pursue it further isn't there any longer, disenchantment and low feelings result.

There is a season for everything in life. Your years at school, the privilege of an accelerated education, certainly contributed substance to the person that you have become. The Mishnah teaches, "An ignorant person cannot strive for an exalted status." At the same time, the Sages warn us, "It is not the learning that is the main goal; the primary objective is the doing." Learning and studying are valuable only to the extent that they inform our life's experience. Life on this earth is referred to as "the world of deeds." Hence, information that cannot impact on our day-to-day behavior is of limited value.

The transition from the halls of study, from the enchantment of dreams and aspirations, to the reality of never-ending mundane tasks and responsibilities is, as you describe it, a very rude awakening. It is a most daunting challenge to find coherence, congruence and cohesiveness between the lofty halls of spiritual learning and the pragmatic, less-than-inspired existence that a young mother finds herself struggling with daily.

I cannot offer you a panacea, but I can tell you that what has to drive everything we do in life must respond to the simple question, "What does the Almighty want of me?" Much of what we struggle with masquerades as frustrated and lofty aspirations, when in reality they are no more than whisperings from the lesser part of ourselves, our ego.

Transitioning into the nurturing role of wife and mother, creating a home where the focus is on the thriving of others, requires a total shift from the focus of "me" to "them." The adjustment can be quite traumatic and might feel as though she is losing herself and her identity in the process. Compared to the productive pre-family days, our mundane-oriented days may feel like a waste of time and, as some women report, like a softening of their brain power. Indeed, the legitimate question is, "What did our glorious education prepare us for? Diapers? Dishes? Vacuuming? Sitting home as our men walk off into their daily spiritual horizons and leave us behind?"

Establishing a happy home is the hardest job. It is a counterculture move in a narcissistic society. A contemporary thinker put it this way, "How do we access the nature of essential obligation in a society that stresses only personal freedom?" Focusing on home and family requires a focus shift from the ideal to the practical, from the talk to the walk. It requires mobilizing all of the inner strength and resources available to consciously and deliberately, with unflinching determination, make every day a good day. When we succeed (and nobody is successful all of the time), in spite of the resistance of both the culture's alien values and the treachery of our inner ego, we will feel the exhilaration and the true joy that can only come of being in the right place and doing the right thing.

I suggest, my dear reader, that you consider the following:

1. "Grow where you are planted." Recognize that the life you have is not arbitrary, but orchestrated from Above and hence is, at this moment, the context to which you must bring your finest efforts. Conversely, we must recognize that there are others who don't find themselves blessed in a similar way, who need to find their own unique contribution in the specific contours of their circumstances.

2. Make a list of the blessings in your life and post them where you can see them. They will help you gain perspective in your low moments.

3. Think in your mind's eye of how you would attend to your given role if you loved it and try to behave that way. Invoke the never-failing principle that "internal feelings are shaped by external behavior."

4. Join a study group consisting of women like yourself and continue to learn. It will energize and invigorate you and provide the balance that we all need.

5. Lengthy prayer sessions may not be in the offing for this season of your life but you can fill your abbreviated encounters with feelings and concentration. Be assured that all the Torah authori-

ties unequivocally state that the mother of young children fulfills her formal prayer obligation with the recitation of the morning blessings. Carrying on your own extemporaneous dialogue with the Almighty throughout the day is a wonderful means of connection. "Know Him in all your ways" has been rendered to mean, "connect every step along the way: while diapering the baby, baking a cake, vacuuming the living room, shopping for clothes, food marketing, etc." Any and every moment is an opportunity to connect.

6. Take care of yourself physically. Eat well and set aside time for some form of exercise, a walk around the block, etc. Breathe fresh air. Align yourself with the beautiful world of nature around you. There is indisputably a mind, body, and spirit connection. If the body is tended to and healthy, the mind and spirit function is enhanced as well.

7. Credit yourself for all the victories, big and small. "The task of building eternity in the medium of fluid transience" is a mega-huge challenge. In order to maintain our perseverance, given all the stresses along the way, we must give ourselves credit for the daily victories even if they appear miniscule in our sight. Keep a list of all the times you are able to get a momentary clear glimpse of what will ultimately matter despite all the factors that work overtime to cloud your vision.

8. Take it from someone who has been around the block a few times; enjoy and make the most of these wonderful years. They go by so fast. Before you know it, you'll be revisiting this stage, these young formative years in your family's life, solely in picture albums. Your heart will ache with nostalgia for the "good old days," days where you can be everything to your children, the smartest, the best, the most beautiful, etc.— times when "my mother says so" makes you an authority on everything. As you know, we can never turn the clock or the calendar back. Despite the demanding intensity of your present household, do your best to relish the moment. Keep a notebook handy to record the cute and often insightful remarks of your

children. Share them with your husband, and delight together.

9. I guarantee you that, with God's help, there will be seasons in the future that will allow you to do all that which attending to your first priority does not allow for now. Be careful not to squander the "now" of your life. It can never be replaced.

In conclusion, I'd like to leave you with two thoughts. A noted authority remarked that situational depression is a product of when "time is passing and the journey is not progressing, the soul feels the cold hand of death. Depression is no less than a minor experience of death itself. That's why it is so painful." Recognizing that you are making the right choices and engaging in the appropriate journey is the only effective antidote.

The Zohar, the classic Kabbalistic work, offers the following guiding insight. Commenting on the verse, "and He called the light day," (Genesis 1:5), he suggests that all of us can choose to transform even darkness to "day" by the light with which we infuse it. The challenge for all of us is to bring the light of joy and positive effect into whatever season of life we find ourselves. Let us try our utmost not to give darkness any claim to the precious moments of our life.

Transitions

Transitions
Coming to Terms

I need guidance in my journey to become more observant. I was raised in a very Reform community in the South. For my family, being Jewish means having Jewish friends, going to shul for the High Holy Days and marrying someone Jewish. I have always wanted more. I have consistently been involved on a leadership level with Jewish causes throughout my life, so I feel that it was only a matter of time before the Almighty brought me back to a more traditional form of Judaism. I have always felt so connected and never knew why.

I have started learning and am working my way toward being Sabbath observant and keeping kosher. I have found such amazing joy, fulfillment, peace, strength, and excitement in learning Torah. I am now the happiest I have ever been in my life.

However, my family is very upset. My mother tells me she is "puzzled" as to why I keep Shabbos and asked me why I am doing something so extreme. I don't need them to change; I just want them to be happy for me and currently they cannot.

I have spiritual needs and I need to listen to them. I am ready to move forward and learn full-time. I am a third year attorney and I plan to take time from my job and move to Israel to learn for at least a year. This is something I have wanted to do my whole life. I can't keep putting it off and waiting. I am 28 and I am ready. But I am meeting opposition not only from my parents, but from my siblings as well.

At first, they tried to be supportive. But last night they ambushed me by inviting me to dinner and then both started crying about how they are scared that I am brainwashed. They think that I will move to Israel and never come back, that I am abandoning my family, that other people are influencing me. They have three friends who became religious in college and moved to Israel and are now married with children and rarely visit the U.S. They are scared this will happen to me. I tried to explain to them that the opportunities to learn are not available where we live. That I feel I need to focus for a while on learning to be able to provide my future children with the life I want them to have and to be able to live my life in a way I feel is right for me.

They said if I leave they will not be able to handle it, that I am abandoning my family and that I will never come back. I feel helpless. I am so sad that I am making my whole family cry; my sister said she has been having recurring nightmares about me moving. It is so hard that they are not happy for me also. I don't want to run away to Israel, I want to be free to go with their blessing, but right now I know I cannot get that. HELP!

The Torah, the timeless wisdom and counsel of the ages, outlines for us the necessary steps in the journey toward Jewish identity and self-discovery.

Abraham, our first Patriarch, earned his designation as "Ivri," Hebrew, because he was willing to stand alone against the entire world and the spirit of the times. The words in the verse of that defining commandment from the Almighty to Abraham were, "Go alone for yourself from your country, from your birthplace, and from the house of your father to the land that I will show you" (Genesis 12:1).

Rabbi S. R. Hirsch, a foremost commentator, renders this: Go for yourself, go your own way, go the way that will isolate you from your land, from your birthplace, from your father's house — from all previous connections. The land, the birthplace, and the home are the soil from which the human personality emerges. Such conduct, he asserts, demands courage and firm belief in the truth of one's inner convictions and one's awareness of G-d. It demands Jewish awareness, Jewish "stubbornness."

This was the first challenge thrust upon Abraham, the father of the Jewish people. He continues, "This was the attribute demanded of Abraham at the starting point of his own mission and that of the nation that was to descend from him. True, strong ties bind a person to his homeland and to his family. Nevertheless, the bond that attaches us to G-d must be stronger. How could we have survived, how could we continue to survive, had we not inherited from our Patriarch, Abraham, the courage to be a minority?"

My dear reader, moving into a new lifestyle mode, changing your milieu, and leaving family behind can be daunting under the best of circumstances. It is a passage and by definition every passage is strewn with emotional land mines. What you are experiencing, however, goes far beyond the "necessary losses" of leaving familiar territory, that of your home, friends, and, most significantly, your family. The fact that you don't have the support of your family at this critical juncture in your life is sad and unfortunate. But don't let these emotional roadblocks blindside you. Good things often come with great difficulty. "Commensurate with the pain is the reward," is the reassurance of our sages.

You articulated very clearly your longstanding and continuing quest for knowledge and exposure to your roots. Your journey is not, as your family would like you to believe, a departure. It is, in fact, a homecoming. You are returning to who you really are — to your legitimate birthright as a Jew — to your exalted heritage. Your soul yearns for its rightful place of belonging and you have no choice but to respond by exploring your horizons.

The pain and disappointment you are experiencing because of your family's emotionally charged adversarial position will pale in comparison to the resentment and anger you would feel, down the road, if your journey to your true self is aborted or thwarted.

Assure your family that you are merely changing "containers" (the place you will occupy), but that your love and attachment to them will remain constant and consistent. Emphasize that nobody will ever replace them. Promise them that you will maintain continuous contact (not like the three families they know whose experience gives them cause for apprehension). You will call, e-mail, write, and visit.

Tell them that their blessings will give wind to your sails and that their encouragement will give you the boost you need in order to better succeed. Include them in your journey; try to make them a part of your dreams. Remind them that you are you because they shaped you by who they are and that you are grateful for it and always will be.

And remember: your character and humanity have to grow commensurately with the more observant you become. Don't posture. Don't adopt a "holier than thou" attitude. Don't behave condescendingly to anyone, least of all your family. Always try to find the beauty and the positive in every person. Don't ever to stoop to negatively stereotyping people regardless of where they find themselves on the spectrum of spiritual growth.

Finally, the likelihood is that if you take the above-outlined counsel seriously, your family who, by your description seem to be people of merit, will come around when they see you thrive and will take joy in your achievements.

May G-d bless you and your journey.

Transitions
One Step at a Time

Sometime ago we decided to eat only kosher food. Now I ask myself every day if this is a good thing, considering that we do not observe Shabbos and other religious commitments. I'm wondering if the fact we keep kosher now makes us "good Jews" even though we don't observe anything else. Is it useful to keep kosher when we do not abide by any other commitments?

Keeping kosher is one of the mitzvos (commandments) in the Torah. By definition, in doing a mitzvah we connect to the "Mitzaveh," the Commander, the Master of the Universe. Moreover, the Aramaic root word of "mitzvah" is "tzavso," companion. This suggests that in doing a mitzvah, we invite the Almighty to become a companion in our lives. Any act we do in response to G-d's will invokes a relationship with the Supreme Being. By eating kosher food, we have, so to speak, made Him welcome at our table. This is no small achievement. The more precincts in our life into which we invite the Almighty, the more spiritually enriched we become.

My husband used to visit his elderly mother every morning. Arguably, from any humanitarian standpoint, we might contend that visiting an elderly parent is no more than the right and decent thing to do. Nonetheless, he would pause at the threshold of her home and recite a short prayer, dedicating this gesture of according honor to his mother to the will of G-d Who declared it a mitzvah. As such, he removed the act from the limited, nonreligious "do good" parameter and sublimated it to a mitzvah whereby it became an act connecting him to the infinite Eternal Being.

One might argue that the act is the same, regardless of intent. However, that which is rooted in human understanding and definition becomes negotiable and eventually part of a morality by consensus, a product of rapidly changing values and attitudes of our society. A mitzvah, by contrast, is rooted in the timeless, unchanging wisdom of G-d. It is stable, reliable, and steadfast. It was, is, and always will be the same. Those deeds in our lives that we designate as mitzvos will have everlasting perpetuity and uncompromised foreverness, as does their "Mitzaveh," their Commander.

Any mitzvah we do, regardless of what we are not yet doing, changes us and changes the world around us. The person I am before the mitzvah and the person I am after having invited the Almighty into my life is totally different. The prism through which I view life, given the change in my inner world, is commensurately modified and altered. And concurrently, I have introduced positive, G-dly energy into the cosmos, the world outside of me. Positive deeds enhance the world I occupy. Misdeeds, flaunting the will of the Almighty, in contrast, introduce negative, compromising energy both into my inner person and into the external world that I inhabit.

The nature of growth, generally, and spiritual growth, specifically, is that it is achieved in small increments. We take on a mitzvah, like one of eating kosher food, and we integrate it into our lives. The mitzvah will speak to us. It will connect us to Jews everywhere in the world, and to Jews across time and across generations, and to a tradition of almost four thousand years. And, by virtue of this nascent connection and enhanced perspective, we may perhaps be inspired to acquaint ourselves with additional dimensions of the rich practices of our tradition.

My husband has on many occasions taught that a ramp, rather than steps, provided access to the Altar in the ancient Temple in Jerusalem. According to Jewish law, this ramp is to be negotiated by placing one foot in front of the other, toe to heel. So too, spiritual growth is not achieved by big steps but by small integrated movements toward holiness.

Neil Armstrong put it well: "One small step for man and one giant step for mankind." Similarly, there are no small steps in spirituality because inevitably they mark the beginning of a journey.

The inevitability of the journey can be a frightening thought. Hence, it might explain the reader's reluctance to assign importance or "usefulness" to eating kosher. Consider the following humorous but insightful anecdote.

Five-year-old Yossi, stubbornly refused to repeat "aleph," the first Hebrew letter, in response to his rebbi's instruction. Frustrated and exasperated after many attempts, the rebbi's stormed out of the room. Yossi's classmates confronted him angrily, and demanded an explanation as to why, perfectly capable as he was, did he obstinately refuse to say "aleph." Yossi matter-of-factly explained that if he conceded and identified the "aleph," predictably, the rebbi would soon demand of him to read the next letter "beis." He was stopping right now, at the beginning, and not getting sucked into the resulting learning process.

I commend the reader for the decision to eat kosher. I don't know the particulars, but generally speaking, it takes courage to venture out into new uncharted territory. While the judgment of who is "a good Jew" can be made only by G-d, Who has total knowledge of our lives and circumstances, I would venture that your commitment flows from your "Yiddishe neshamah," your Jewish soul. Giving life and expression to your G-dly spiritual investiture can only be good.

Parenthetically, I would caution the reader about voices out there or internal ones that question the "usefulness" of her decision. Inevitably, she will encounter accusations of "hypocrisy", i.e. ,if you don't keep Shabbos and all other mitzvos, the inconsistency of observing merely one mitzvah makes you a hypocrite. Be advised that in fact these statements are not only not "useful," they are completely erroneous and undermine our resolve. First, human beings can never be totally consistent. Even those who pride themselves in being observant have lapses in guarding their tongues, tempers, etc., which in no way invalidates the mitzvos they do observe. Second, the journey up the mountain begins with a single step. And last, every positive deed is precious in the sight of G-d.

I would encourage the reader to keep eating kosher and to continue learning, to expose herself to the wealth and beauty of our rich legacy, whose mitzvos and practices have hallowed and continue to hallow the lives of our people.

Transitions
Help! My Spouse Is Becoming More Religious Than I!

My husband and I have been married for eight months. My husband has changed his outlook on a number of religious issues since we met and we have recently been experiencing some conflict over differences in religious observances. I wish that my husband could accept who I am and not try to change me. I feel that if I change certain things to please my husband, I will resent this. When is it appropriate to do what one's spouse would prefer and when is it appropriate to ask one's spouse for acceptance?

his young wife's letter has touched on some very critical issues because at the core lies the question: "Do I have to give up me to be loved by you?"

Her dilemma is indicative of a no-win situation. If she doesn't do as her husband would like, she risks his disappointment at the very least, or a diminution in his regard for her and perhaps further repercussions. If, despite her aversion, she does defer and comply, her perception in all likelihood is that she is not being true to herself and that her husband is trying to change her.

I don't think it is ever appropriate in a spousal relationship to impose one's opinion or will on the partner. Controlling and determining a mode of behavior or response should be limited to one's self. Marriage does not confer that right. As someone aptly put it, "marriage is not a rehab center." At the very least, this type of controlling approach does not work. At the worst, it is destructive and counterproductive. Invariably, it will give rise to resentment and ultimately anger. Everyone is entitled to make his or her own decision and the refusal to extend that right is demeaning to the spouse.

Torah philosophy sees the human being created in the image of G-d. We understand this to mean that the Almighty has invested us with His likeness, His attributes. The Master of the Universe is the only wholly and totally independent Being. He answers to no one. While we are mere mortals and certainly cannot be totally independent of others and certainly not of G-d, being created in His image does posit within us a natural resistance to being controlled, manipulated, and being told what to do. Deference, while often necessary, is a learned response, not a natural one.

Perhaps that is why, when babies becomes aware of their separateness from their mothers, one of the first words they learn is "No."

The basis of a marriage must be mutual respect, appreciation and even a celebration of differences.

At the same time, one of the manifestations of an intact relationship is an openness, a nonthreatened posture that allows for one to consider possibilities previously unexplored.

This can only happen if there is no fear that the spouse has hidden agendas or ulterior motives. Such relational issues can muddy the waters of the marriage. They need to be addressed, clarified, and dealt with.

· ·**TORAH VIEWPOINT**

"Her paths are those of pleasantness" is the description of Torah and observance of its value. The Torah views the spousal relationship as pivotal to Jewish life and the mitzvos are intended to enhance rather than to thwart this objective.

The writer points to the fact that her husband has "changed" since they were married. In other words, the conditions of the contract were changed. I would point out for her consideration that while it is true some change has taken place along the way, we know that human beings are not meant to be stagnant. We should ever be learning and growing. Today should be different than yesterday, and tomorrow we should hopefully have insights and understanding that we don't have today. In the professional, material, and physical arenas we would not be satisfied to remain in a status quo state.

There is always the necessity of continuing education and upgrading our standard of living. Certainly in the world of the soul that impacts on eternity, we need to aspire to loftier goals.

I would advise the writer to pursue further learning and exposure to Jewish experiences on her own initiative. It is only when we are informed that we have choices. Perhaps she can then more objectively, without the distortion of a bruised ego or control issues, make her own decision of where she wants to be religiously at this moment with the understanding that tomorrow is another day with its endless possibilities mandated by continuous learning and growing.

Additionally, I do need to point out that deference does have its place in a healthy marriage. Each partner should be respected in his or her particular domain, his or her area of expertise. The suggestion has been made that we ask ourselves on a scale from 1 to 10 how much does this issue mean to me or, as one put it, "is this the hill I want to die on?" This kind of self-examination may help determine whether we stand our ground or defer.

There is a humorous anecdote about a husband who says that he makes all the important decision in his marriage, such as whether to go to war with China or whether the Federal Reserve Bank should lower interest rates. He leaves the smaller decisions to his wife, where to live, what schools their children should go to, etc.

Acknowledgment and appreciation for a decision that necessitates negotiation and is not mutually arrived at is critical to a marriage. Gratitude and continuous positive feedback are extremely important dimensions in all relationships and certainly most critical in the marriage relationship.

Transitions
Bridging the Gap

I appreciate your column with its practical suggestions and helpful advice.

I am a ba'alas teshuvah, someone who became religious later in life. I have young children of my own. At times I feel immense resentment toward my nonreligious parents who, although they have largely compromised on personal religious issues with both myself and my husband, still comment on matters that govern our lives. For example, they resent the fact that we have a large family. They informed us that they and my husband's parents don't want us to have any more children! To keep "shalom" we listen, but afterward feelings of resentment and hurt build up inside me and I can't seem to release them.

How is it possible to keep one's perspective on this issue of resentment when parents/in-laws are not observant?

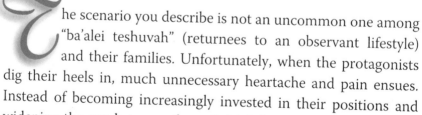

he scenario you describe is not an uncommon one among "ba'alei teshuvah" (returnees to an observant lifestyle) and their families. Unfortunately, when the protagonists dig their heels in, much unnecessary heartache and pain ensues. Instead of becoming increasingly invested in their positions and widening the gap between them, I think both sides would do well to consider the following points.

You inform me that your parents have made compromises on your behalf and that only the issue of a large family remains a source of conflict and overwhelming pain. I hope that I am assuming correctly that you understand and fully appreciate the major adjustments a lifestyle change such as yours imposes on your family. The accommodations they have made for you must be recognized and interpreted as generous expressions of love and caring. You must not take them for granted and moreover you must be sure to express your gratitude every step along the way.

Aside from the practical adjustments and compromises, parents find themselves at a loss to intellectually grasp and comprehend the necessity for this change in course and the major upheaval that it brings in its wake. At a deeper emotional level, it may feel to them as a condemnation, a negative judgment and assessment of the quality of life they had heretofore provided in the upbringing of their children. It threatens the core of their being because it computes in their mind as a rejection of what they deemed as their best efforts.

The only antidote to their feelings of being left out in the cold as you march off to the beat of your own drummer is to be inclusive rather than exclusive.

You need to rewind to your formative years in your parents' home and identify what it was that gave you the spirit of inquiry, the seeds of your metaphysical quest for search and meaning. What gave you the courage to strike out and the ability to search for truth? Invariably you will find that parents, while not committed to the specific behaviors of the lifestyle you have embraced, nonetheless instilled in you the potential, the wherewithal to return to your roots. Undoubtedly, they created an environment of love, affection, common decency, and openness, etc., and other components of a positive nature that encouraged you along the way.

It is important that you recognize that in large measure you stand on their shoulders. The choices you have made do not emerge out of a vacuum. Hence, you are beholden to them and must give credit where credit is due. Let your parents know that your journey was made possible by them and the many years they invested in you and that you are eternally grateful. Inclusive not exclusive.

Having said that, I would advise you to sit down with your parents and have an open, heart-to-heart talk with them. Don't be defensive. Don't try to explain the many reasons for a large family; they have heard them before. Just allow yourself to be vulnerable. Let them know that you understand their concern for you. All parents want to see their child "happy" and comfortable. In their minds and to their way of thinking, increasing the pressures of life by assuming more and more responsibility with each additional child does not configure or fit in with the picture of a good and easy life.

The following incident may prove instructive. Emily, a young attorney with a brilliant future, made the decision to embrace an observant Torah life. Initially, her parents dismissed it as a fad, a passing phase, reminiscent of her "hippie" days given to unconventional and antiestablishment behavior. But the test of time proved otherwise, and they watched in horror as their accomplished daughter began to produce baby after baby.

On one occasion, her mother blurted out in exasperation, "When is it going to be your turn? You will never be able to afford the good things in life: vacations, Las Vegas, cruises, etc., and all other earthly delights and pleasures. You will be paying tuitions for the rest of your life!"

Emily realized that at the core of her parents' outrage and disapproval was a genuine concern for her. They wanted their beloved "baby" to have a "good life." Emily assured them that her chosen path, though inscrutable to them, was best for her and having children was her greatest source of joy. She had "been there and done that." She had as a youngster already experienced affluence and had known the "good life." She found that though her current life was not easy and raising many children did exact a tremendous toll, ultimately the opportunity to bring decent human beings into the world was the most meaningful and rewarding calling.

At the conclusion, with a gleam in her eye, Emily pointed to her delightful crew and asked, "By the way, which one of these precious gems would you like me to send back?"

I think it is important for you, my dear reader, to openly enlist your parents' assistance. You need to share with them the pain that their disapproval causes you. You should also share the fact that under the best of circumstances, even as committed as you are to the way of life you have chosen, it is not an easy road to navigate. Even the most healthy and delightful children demand enormous physical, emotional, and psychic energy, and that you find it hard to do it alone, without their support and involvement.

Let them know that while your way of life is not negotiable, you desperately need their support and approval. You need to see them take delight in their grandchildren. Tell them it will warm your heart and give you the necessary strength to go on. Additionally, assure them that you are acting responsibly, that there are Torah criteria and authorities to consult if mitigating issues concerning having more children should arise, and that you will avail yourselves of these resources when necessary.

In Emily's case it took a number of years. She bided her time. She continued to interact lovingly and respectfully with her parents. They exchanged visits a number of times a year. Anxiety and trepidation seized Emily every time she would inform her parents that a new baby was on the way.

At the Bar Mitzvah of her oldest child, when her father beheld the beautiful and accomplished young man, he conceded with tears in his eyes. He admitted that he had been misguided in his intransigence and that she had in fact been on the right track. Nothing in the world, he admitted, could give him more nachas and joy than his wonderful grandchildren, every one of them.

Admittedly, not every situation is as happily resolved. But you must put forth your best effort to celebrate every expression of progress and every move in the right direction. I would advise you to do the following:

Surround yourself and network with people of like values and if possible similar challenges.

Try to maintain the high moral road of respect and love to parents even when the situation is tough and you would desperately want to see a more accepting and approving stance from them.

Remind them that you are their child, who bears the imprint of the values they have impressed upon you even if they do manifest themselves differently in the life of your choosing. Inform them that though your horizons may now encompass "a road less traveled," you are and will always be their beloved offspring who needs their love, approval, and support.

Pray and beseech the "Ultimate Parent" to give you strength and wisdom and to bless your wonderful endeavors with success as only He can.

Moments and Reflections

Moments and Reflections
Anchor in the Stormy Sea

The nature and extent of our personal reactions to the tragic events of 9/11 have forged a new social reality. Those personal reactions are based on where we come from, how we have been shaped by our past experiences, and who we have become as a result.

My initial reaction, perhaps not unlike many others, was one of horror, disbelief, and outrage. It was a totally emotional response. Attempts at reason were to no avail. I cried incessantly, realizing this tragedy invoked memories of long ago. I realized that it wasn't only dealing with myself in the present, but also the little 6-year-old child of some 50 years ago who is still such an integral and indivisible part of who I am.

I was born in a small town in Romania during World War II. My father, of blessed memory, had been deported to a labor camp; our home had been taken away from us, and my mother, of blessed memory, and my 18-month-old sibling were in hiding in a cellar. I was born a breach baby and my mother's life was at great risk since no doctor was allowed to assist a Jewish woman in labor. The woman hiding my mother endangered her life and offered a doctor anything she owned to help my mother. May G-d bless this righteous women's soul.

LIBERTY WITH OPEN ARMS······················

My father was one of the fortunate men who returned home to Falticeni, Romania at the war's end. He immediately began extensive efforts to leave Europe and find a safe haven somewhere. Our odyssey as the proverbial wandering Jews began. Predictably, our hearts yearned to go to Israel, then known as Palestine. My family finally gained access to a boat that was leaving and we were on our way to the Promised Land.

After a long and arduous journey, we finally arrived at the shores of Haifa. I was very young, but I still remember the amazing blue hue of the Mediterranean. Relatives in little rowboats came out to greet our ship and threw oranges up to us.

But alas, the British did not want us. They had enough Jews. They had more than enough of us to meet their quota. We were not even permitted to get off the boat. The authorities turned our ship around without so much as a thought on their part as to where else we could go.

We journeyed on. Many disembarked in Cypress. My family went to a refugee camp in Italy where we waited for over a year to be sponsored for American immigration.

I will never forget the two horrendous weeks aboard the ship en route to America. We were all violently seasick. My poor mother spent the entire trip caring for us sacrificially, trying to ease our immense discomfort and endless heaving, without regard for her own poor condition. To this day, I respond incredulously to my friends' enthusiasm for their next cruise vacation. "Are you serious?" I always ask in disbelief. "Are you, of your own free will, voluntarily about to place yourself on a boat?"

As our journey neared its conclusion, I was struck with my first ever glimpse of the Statue of Liberty. My memory records her unlike she appears in reality — arms wide open, welcoming and embracing me, my family, and all the tired, rejected, homeless, and those nobody else wanted or cared about.

The terrorist acts so near to this site rekindled my memories and reminded me of the precious safe haven this wonderful country had provided for us.

ONE SHIP, ONE ANCHOR·······················

The Talmud relates a parable of a ship traveling along on the seas that comes across what appears to be a grassy island. With great excitement, the travelers disembark and make the island their home. They begin building houses, eager to finally leave the confines of the ship. They light a fire to warm themselves, and to their dismay the island flipped over, revealing its true identity as a huge unfriendly fish. The Talmud concludes that the stunned voyagers were evermore grateful to see their old, faithful ship, still standing and available to save them.

The impact of the events of September 11 on the world's opinion of Israel and its relationship with the United States is yet unclear. Jews have dwelled among many civilizations and cultures that have come and gone. Many have been hospitable to Jews for at least a limited period of time. When does the heat become too much for even the friendliest, kindliest, and most free of nations? History has shown us that we were never prepared for the fish to turn, for the island of security to disappear.

I am a patriot. In my heart, I truly love America. But my head tells me that while I am grateful, I must also be wary. We have only one ship; the Almighty is the only reliable Anchor in our stormy history, and it is to Him that we must address our prayers and fervent hopes for the long-awaited millennium of peace for all mankind.

Moments and Reflections
Tears in Heaven

Ten months after the tragic bus accident in Israel that left our dear son-in-law in a coma, on the ninth day of Kislev, Rabbi Eliezer Geldzahler passed away. Notwithstanding the unprecedented volume of vigils, prayers, supplications, importuning, and acts of charity, kindness, and piety worldwide dedicated to his recovery, the response of the Master of the universe, our Heavenly Parent, was "No."

From the depth of our collective pain, comes the inevitable question, "Are we to understand that our prayers were in vain? That the never-ceasing recitals of Psalms of our devoted friends everywhere were for naught?"

One of Reb Eliezer's students related a parable of two fathers who enter a clothing store to purchase garments for their family. One is very specific about the requirements, i.e., style, size, etc. The other moves through the store quickly, choosing one suit after another. When asked for an explanation about their different approaches, it came to light that the former had only one child to clothe and wished to make sure that the suit was perfect for him. But the latter had a house full of children and figured that if a garment wasn't quite right for one, it would undoubtedly fit another one of his children.

Similarly, the Almighty has many beloved children. For some unfathomable reason that only He knows, our prayers could not fit or work for Reb Eliezer in the way that we had hoped. But without a doubt, the massive, positive, spiritual energy released by our supplications will work for the many others who need them. And hopefully, they will also provide strength for his wife, our daughter Baila, and their 13 beautiful children.

Most certainly these prayers will accompany Reb Eliezer to his eternal abode and be a merit for his soul. Our friends everywhere, who invested heart and soul in their prayers on our behalf, please be assured that we will always be grateful, and that your efforts were not wasted. They are a good fit for someone, somewhere and certainly we and our world are better because of them.

The mind-boggling impact of the far-too-brief 46 years of Reb Eliezer's life on so many is impossible to distill in words. Thousands came to the four different funeral sites, hearts heavy with personal grief, to pay tribute to a great man. The mother of one of his students spoke of her son's love for him, remarking that her son had convinced her that he had been Reb Eliezer's favorite student, until she later met scores of other mothers who had the same experience. They added that for these young men, the loss of a biological father could not have evoked a greater sense of loss. Reb Eliezer had molded and shaped them into "menschen," with positive self-esteem and self-worth.

The capacity to bring out the best in others and make them feel special was not limited to his hundreds of students; it extended to every person who crossed his path. The wailing and sobbing and oceans of tears shed on the day of the funeral by young and old, men, women, and children alike, testified to the dark, empty void left in the heart of so many to whom he is irreplaceable.

Reb Eliezer was an imposing figure in his broad 6'2" frame. He had the physical stature of a leader. Impressive as that was, most notable however was the light that accompanied his presence. A "bren," a fire, a light of joy and aliveness. The earth literally danced beneath his feet. He was thrilled to be alive.

Life to him was always beautiful, exciting, and full of opportunities. Nothing ever dampened his spirit. "Gevaldig — awesome!" was his ever-ready response when asked how he was and how things were going. When his 16-year-old son, Mordechai Dov, who is very much his father's son, was in the hospital undergoing his many surgeries to restore his legs injured in the bus accident, the nurses used to greet him with, "Come on, Mordekai, let's hear the G word." "Gevaldig" became part of the vocabulary of the hospital staff.

His passion for life extended first and foremost to the study of Torah and to the recitation of prayers. He was a first-rate Torah scholar. Anyone who knew him can easily conjure up the image of Reb Eliezer baby-sitting, a child in his lap, one on each shoulder, and another climbing over his head — and all the while he is unfazed, fully concentrating on the tome of the Talmud open before him, yet, at the same time exuding his overwhelming love for his children.

His sense of privilege and fiery excitement for learning created an effervescence, a breath of fresh air in a school system that generally promoted learning as a heavy-duty responsibility that smacked of burden and pressure. His magical spirit created an environment where his boys engaged in all of their daily activities with fervor. They played, they ate, they sang, and they danced with passion and zeal. Paradoxically this continual enthusiasm, which one might have thought would detract from their learning and praying, liberated an energy that produced greater volume and depth of study than in any other parallel institution.

His keen understanding of youth (perhaps because he never ceased to be young at heart) literally revolutionized the yeshivah system. One summer we visited with him in his yeshivah in their summer campus in the mountains. He set a goal of 500 "blatt" (folios) of Talmud for his students' summer study — an enormous amount. Though it was a formidable undertaking, they forged ahead in their inimitable style, working tirelessly to achieve their objective. At the successful conclusion of the summer session, they celebrated with a "siyum," a celebration upon accomplishing their goals in learning where the boys each presented gleanings from their impressive achievement. This was followed by singing and dancing. And at 2 a.m., Reb Eliezer announced that since the boys had done so well, the evening (or morning) will conclude with a swimming jaunt. It was pitch dark outside, but that did not deter him. The Rosh Yeshivah, or "Rosh" as he was lovingly referred to, drove his car down the steep hill to the pool and provided illumination for the boys with its headlights. Initially I shuddered with my conservative sensibilities on edge, but I had to admit that it sure worked wonders for the boys.

His care and concern for each student was legendary. Long after they left his yeshivah, they drew on his counsel and guidance. He would come to our community in Milwaukee with his family for the holidays and was constantly on the phone, sought out by his students, his alumni, and people in general from every corner of the globe. He lovingly gave of his wisdom and direction.

A Rosh Yeshivah is generally assumed to be an aloof, removed, distant figure to be revered from afar. Reb Eliezer defied that definition. One mother at the "shivah" tearfully shared that contrary to the truism that "familiarity breeds contempt," the closer the boys drew to him and the better they got to know him, the greater was not only their love for him, but also their respect and awe. Perhaps most remarkable of all, she added, was that his accessibility and love for his students bonded all of them together, creating an atmosphere where each student took delight in the other's accomplishments and achievements, unlike the conventional competitive environment that can permeate institutions of learning.

The weeks leading to Reb Eliezer's passing could easily be categorized as a "season in hell." We were suspended somewhere between heaven and earth. There were momentary flashes of hope, quickly dashed by reality. It is important to note, that while only G-d Himself determines the outcomes of painful situations such as ours, people and their behavior do create the context. It makes a world of difference to a suffering family that a nurse is caring and sensitive or that a doctor carefully chooses his words in pronouncing inalterable facts. It makes a world of difference to be surrounded by a community of people, organized or individual, who dedicate their lives to alleviate the enormous burden of suffering families, by attending to the many details — the meals, the rides to and from the hospital, night shifts, day shifts, etc. What a blessing these people are! How often I was struck by the fact that these were virtual bright stars on a very dark horizon. The Almighty has ample reason to be proud of His people.

Our daughter, Baila, Reb Eliezer's wife, is a truly amazing person. These last ten months she assumed responsibility for his care. She left no stone unturned in considering every possibility regardless of personal cost to her well-being. Against the advice of most of us, she took advantage of her training as a registered nurse to transfer him to her own care at the summer location of his yeshivah, where he could be surrounded by the life he loved and cherished — his family, his students, and the sound of Torah learning, fervent praying, Sabbath celebrations, and spirited singing. She was always dreaming and eagerly awaiting the moment when he would regain consciousness and he would tell her what parts of it had reached him.

She did all of this in the late months of pregnancy. Two and a half months ago, Refael Aryeh Leibish was born. The bris was preformed on his unconscious father's lap. Suffice it to say that it was a bittersweet time.

Then a massive recurring infection set in and Reb Eliezer was readmitted to the hospital. After a number of weeks, he underwent surgery to place a shunt to drain the fluid in his brain. Three days later, he suffered a massive brain hemorrhage. Baila sat at his bedside, day and night, for the next 12 days, up to his passing — talking to him, stroking him, and crying oceans of tears.

Maggie, Reb Eliezer's nurse, teary eyed, commented that in all of her experience, she had never seen such devotion, so much praying, and so many people who cared about one another.

After the funeral in Boro Park, it began to drizzle. Someone remarked to 7-year-old Naftoli Tzvi, Reb Eliezer's son, that even the heavens were crying. He vehemently protested and said, "No. When my tatty was born, the heavens must have cried because they had to part with him. But now, these must be tears of joy because they have him back with them."

To hear the voices of the little children as they belt out the "Kaddish" (memorial prayer) is nothing short of heart wrenching. The little ones do it with real gusto, especially since one of their teachers told them that when their father who is now in Heaven hears their voices, he joins hands with the angels and dances. The image of their father dancing is a very real one to them. The only question they had was whether the angels know how to dance.

In his eulogy, Rabbi Eliyahu Yehoshua Geldzahler, Reb Eliezer's father, commented on the verse recited at the time of loss, "G-d has given and G-d has taken." He confessed that at this moment his tears were spent, so he preferred to concentrate on the great gift of the 46 years of Reb Eliezer's life: the pure nachas, the daily highs he received from his every phone conversation, his humor, his infectious joy, and his great accomplishments.

As for myself, Baila's mother, presumptuous as it might be, I ask the Almighty to remember His promise to be the "Advocate of widows and the Father of orphans." Only He can step in and give Baila the requisite strength to raise her children, to nurture the great potential within each one of them, and bring to fruition Reb Eliezer's legacy encased in their very genes.

And for all of us collectively, may G-d finally usher in the long-awaited millennium, when there will be an end to all suffering and wherein "He will wipe the tears from every face."

Moments and Reflections
An Embrace From Eternity

achel, a recently orphaned woman in her 30's, listens intently during my class and, no matter the topic, she finds a way to raise her ever-consuming question ..."Does G-d provide that our lives should continue to be intertwined and connected with the lives of our loved ones, who are no longer with us?"

Recently, I was a presenter at an international conference. My first session was offered to "women only" and was one of many concurrent sessions. A male participant approached me and asked if I objected to his attending my session. I responded that he would have to get permission from the organizers. He was advised not to and didn't. Shortly thereafter, a second gentleman approached me with a similar request and I gave the same answer. Though he, too, was discouraged from attending, he felt somehow driven to hear my presentation. I proceeded with my talk, in the midst of which I mentioned my father, the Faltichener Rav, of blessed memory, and his tremendous love of Jews, regardless of background or orientation. I spoke about how powerfully his legacy had influenced my life and the work I do.

At the conclusion of the class, the man approached me, visibly shaken, and with tear-filled eyes, began to tell his story. Several decades earlier, as a talented but restless teenager, he attended the funeral of one of the luminaries of the time. The eulogy was delivered by my father, who was a world-class orator, and the young man was visibly moved. He had never heard anything of such powerful substance and delivery. The impact was so great that he felt compelled to push his way into the room where they had whisked my father, insisting that he needed a moment with the Rabbi. Yielding to his insistence, he had an opportunity to tell my father how overwhelmed he was and that he had never heard a message of such force and inspiration. Warming to the compliment, my father asked him to repeat what he had heard. The young man demurred, but was urged on by my father's exhortation to "make a special effort."

Encouraged, the teenager proceeded to repeat the speech verbatim with every nuance and intonation. As he did so, he recounted, tears were streaming down my father's face. Clearly, my father was moved by the faithful rendition of his words. At the conclusion, impressed by the young man's recall and presentation, my father asked him what his aspirations in life were; what did he want "to be" when he grew up. The teenager hesitated, certain that his response would be severely condemned and denounced as unbecoming of a "yeshivah bachur." Nevertheless, he found the courage and said, "My dream is to be an entertainer." My father asked him what about that career so appealed to him. The youth shared that he loved, in particular, the singing of the great cantors and the dramatic works of various Jewish writers. To his great shock, not only was my father familiar with the names mentioned, but asked him for a sample of that which appealed to him so greatly. Hesitant at first, he was again advised to "make an effort," which he did, and with great poise, drama, and emotion, proceeded to present one of his favorite literary pieces, a tragic, heart-wrenching and gripping story. Again the flow of tears attested to how moved my father was by his presentation. As he finished, my father took his hand, held it tightly and with great emotion said, "My dearest child, indeed you should be an entertainer, but work hard and exert yourself to become an entertainer in the theater of G-d."

That was the defining moment for the now fifty-year-old man standing in front of me. He had received his marching orders from a chassidic rebbe who, instead of excoriating him for desiring that which was less than becoming of a yeshivah bachur, understood his needs and validated his impressive talent, thereby opening his heart and mind to the wise counsel that followed. The man concluded his story by saying that he had since become a fund-raiser of distinction, using his talents to engage substantial donors to establish some of the major Jewish institutions of our day. He had, indeed, become an entertainer in the theater of G-d, facilitating the journey of so many of the Almighty's children back to their roots.

Unexpectedly, my father's legacy had surfaced and warmed me. I felt his nod, his presence, and his embrace.

That very same weekend, upon my return home, I received the news that my grandson, Shea, the eldest son of my daughter in Manchester, England, was soon to become betrothed to a wonderful young lady, the daughter of his Rosh Yeshivah. It was this particular grandson's birth that I had missed twenty years earlier. This had been no small matter since my daughter had come all the way from Israel to Milwaukee to have the support of her parents at the birth of her first child. Everything would have worked out had my father not unexpectedly insisted that I travel on that very day, her due date, at that exact time, to Florida to inform my mother of the unfortunate death of her brother. He felt that the news would be less traumatic coming from me than from him. No sooner did I arrive in Florida than I was informed that my daughter had gone to the hospital. Despite my haste to return on the first possible plane, I returned to Milwaukee to find my daughter had already given birth to her first baby, her "bechor," without the maternal support for which she had hoped. Difficult as it had been, there was, however, an immediate reward, a silver lining in that cloud. My father called her from Florida and, with great excitement and emotion, blessed her and said that in deferring her own needs, she had made it possible for me to honor my mother and consequently, he assured her, this child would grow up to be extra special. And extra special, indeed, he is! When my daughter called from London, from "Shea's" engagement celebration, amid the excitement and good wishes, she noted how remarkable it was that the festivities coincided with Zaida's (my father's) birthday. Coincidence? I doubt it. Here he was again with a nod and a tangible embrace.

It got even better. My daughter reminded me that twenty years ago, when this very Shea was born, she had decided to name him for one of my husband's ancestors. She had already apprised those who needed to know of her decision. On the morning of the "bris," when the name was actually to be given, my father called from Florida requesting that she name her son for one of my forebears instead, since this day marked and coincided with the "yahrtzeit" of this illustrious ancestor. She later confessed that she was quite perturbed at the time by this last-minute change, but her zaida had spoken and she felt she could not deny his request. Now, my daughter remarked, twenty years later, came the stunning realization that the original name that she had wanted to give to this baby turned out to be the very name of her "mechutin," her son's future father-in-law. The significance of this is that in our circles, it would have invalidated this "shidduch" (match). There is a strongly held custom among many, that a son-in-law and father-in-law not share the same first name. Thus, twenty years later Zaida's intervention had been vindicated.

Again, my father was here, his presence and invaluable participation clearly felt and his loving embrace as strong as ever.

I am certain that the readers have many similar experiences of their own, where loved ones in eternity connect with them in many different ways. Our loved ones in Heaven do, in fact, escort us, ever present in our hearts and minds, with their perspective, their lessons, their words, their likes and dislikes, their favorite comments, predictable sayings, individual styles, and, yes, even their quirks. Unquestionably, in a very real and tangible way, at critical moments, both expected and unexpected, they reach out to us from eternity and, with a wink and a hug, make sure that we sense their presence.

Moments and Reflections
The Season of Lilacs

Lilacs are in bloom. The fragrance of these magnificent flowers goes far beyond the aromatic pleasure and delight that they provide. For me, lilacs immediately takes me back in time to a place where life was richer in emotional quality and texture. During the weeks between Passover and Shavuos my parents, of blessed memory, would make one of their semi-annual visits to Milwaukee. Seasonally, it always coincided with the emergence of the luxurious blossoms on the lilac tree in our backyard. Lilacs were my mother's favorite flower. I can close my eyes and, in an instant, I can see the look of special pleasure that suffused her beautiful face as she took a deep breath and inhaled their sweet fragrance. Freshly picked bouquets adorned every room of the house and even the little children understood that lilacs surfacing everywhere in the house heralded Zaide and Bubbie's imminent and much-anticipated arrival.

Our Sages teach that while other human faculties of man diminished considerably after the fateful act of eating of the Tree of Knowledge, it was the sense of smell alone that remained unchanged and did not suffer diminution. The far-reaching significance of this lies in the fact that the olfactory sense is inextricably associated with the "neshamah," the soul, as the verse describes the creation of man, "and He (G-d) blew into his nostrils the soul of life and man became a living being" (Genesis 2:7).

The essential distinctive feature of the human being, namely his soul, was conferred upon him by the Master of the Universe through his nostrils, the very apertures used for the sense of smell.

Additional confirmation of the connection between the soul and the olfactory faculty is the tradition of smelling spices during the Havdalah service at the conclusion of the holy day of Sabbath. The Sabbath day, the holiest day of the week, brings with it a conferral of a "neshamah yeseirah," an additional dimension of soul, an extra dose of spiritual energy. Commensurate with this gift is the sense of loss at its departure. At the conclusion of the Sabbath we are left with an emptiness, a spiritual void, a sense of depletion. Hence, we smell aromatic spices to revive ourselves and to compensate for the departure of the additional Sabbatical spirit that elevated our being for the duration of the Sabbath day.

Smell and soul are thus closely intertwined. In a mystical way, it appears as though the Almighty channeled our essence, the uniqueness that animates us and makes us who we are, through the medium of our nostrils, our very sense of smell.

Perhaps this is why lilacs in bloom carry such powerful sway over me. A whiff of their fragrance connects me not only with my mother's presence and her preference or choice of flowers, but more significantly with her essence — who she was at a soul level. The fragrance of her person was so unique that I find it totally appropriate, symbolically, that since her passing, my lilac tree in the backyard has ceased to produce its blossoms.

My mother's life was replete with twists, turns, and challenges that no one could have foreseen at the outset. She was born the eldest daughter of an aristocratic chassidic dynasty. Illustrious luminaries of the past century were familiar figures in her life as they came and went, interacting daily with my saintly grandfather who was a leading scholar in his day.

My father, of blessed memory, came from less-celebrated lineage, and achieved a magnitude of personal excellence that qualified him for the hand of "a princess" — my mother. He became the Rabbi of Falticeni, Romania and life started out looking good. Then Hitler (may his name be obliterated) came and the shattering of lives and dreams ensued.

My father, together with all of the men of his town, was sent off to labor camps. My mother and her 18-month-old son were banished from their home. Alone and expecting another child, she sought refuge in the cellar of a kindly woman. Shortly thereafter, I was born — and because of complications during my birth — my mother nearly died because gentile doctors, on the penalty of death, were forbidden to help Jews.

Fortunately, my father was among the few who survived the labor camp, and upon his return immediately sought to flee and resettle with his family. The boatload of refugees that we joined were denied entrance to the Land of Israel. The British in command had more Jews than they wanted and they sent our boat away. Our odyssey as wandering Jews, and all that entailed had begun: Cyprus, Italy, and finally the long-awaited papers to America.

My parents, among many others, crossed the ocean, their five children in tow, with nothing more than the clothing on their backs — but we were a family.

An apocryphal anecdote is told of a 5-year-old child, part of a refugee family (it could easily have been me), who was approached by an observer, who, with great pity in her voice, remarked, "You poor darling, wandering from place to place with no space to call home." The child looked up and with great pride countered, "You are mistaken. I do have a home and I have always had a home. I just don't have a house to put it in."

In the formative years of my childhood, fraught with challenges as they were —wanderings, new countries, new languages, poverty, losses — we always had a home. A home is not defined by mortar and bricks, draperies or furniture. A home is an environment of love, caring, and affirmation. My parents, always, even under the most difficult of circumstances, provided us with a home. And my mother was the stalwart spirit who kept everything together.

I was 6 years old on the ship coming from Italy to America and the memory of two weeks of constant motion sickness and nausea is still with me more than 50 years later — especially if someone suggests a cruise or a boat ride. None of us, the entire family of seven, could lift our heads off the pillow without heaving. And it was my blessed dear mother, herself as sick as we all were, who attended to us nonstop for two weeks straight. The image of my mother, pale, drawn, and exhausted, sitting at our bedside, setting herself aside for her loved ones, captures the selfless dedication and devotion that defined her existence.

Rabbi Dessler writes, "We see life not as it is but as we are." We all have lenses through which we perceive the world. If the lenses are transparent, we get a clear view of reality. But if they are clouded over, our view of things become myopic and distorted. The most common clouding agent that obstructs our clear vision is self-interest and ego. We can all attest to the fact that "me-ism" can delude us and cause us to rationalize the most twisted of postures, easily convincing ourselves that skewed convictions are valid and, at times, even exalted.

My mother's lenses, the prism through which she interfaced with life, were crystal clear and she achieved what is most elusive for the majority of us in our time: the ability to be in touch with true reality.

Indeed, the rare fragrance that my mother's life exuded was one of self-effacement and singular devotion to husband and family. Not, I must add, in the negative spirit of the suffering martyr, but one that emanated from a sense of privilege and joy. Wealth and material objects meant nothing to my mother. Power and prestige didn't make it onto her radar screen. Her solid values never wavered regardless of her surroundings and the constantly changing world in which she found herself.

Her weltanschauung was simple and clear. She was not tormented by the tentativeness and conflict that punctuates contemporary life. The fragrance of her soul, manifested in her values, aspirations, and her mission, was pure, straightforward, and unadulterated.

There are times when I dream that my mother's legacy, her fragrance and essence — her remarkable ability to transcend self and her unobstructed vision — will rub off on me. And I am certain that when that happens, my lilac tree will once again bloom and blossom.